Praise for Being Geek

"Michael Lopp is that rare beast: the completely honest manager who uses plain language. You want to know how to cultivate a thriving career in this industry? Listen to Lopp."

John Gruber, Daring Fireball

"I've seen too many people who were technically brilliant but who you didn't want to let out of a locked room, because you knew they'd get eaten alive in the real world. Being Geek gives them a fighting chance to adapt to corporate life and manage the 'messy parts' of real life."

Thomas "Duffbert" Duff

"Being Geek is a must-read for geeks and the people who need geeks to achieve the impossible."

Gina Bianchini, Founder of Ning.com

"The geek shall inherit the earth. Michael Lopp uncovers the soul of a generation that is usually quite happy to keep to themselves."

Jim Coudal, Coudal Partners

Michael Lopp has an audacious message that geeks everywhere need to hear: Unpredictability is our friend, not our enemy. And his book Being Geek is the essential resource for anyone who wants to learn how to harness the power of unpredictable career moments—so we can fail faster, learn more, challenge our own expectations, and ultimately achieve something epic.

Jane McGonigal, Director of Games Research and Development at the Institute for the Future

Being Geek

The Software Developer's Career Handbook

Michael Lopp

O'REILLY®

Beijing · Cambridge · Farnham · Köln · Sebastopol · Taipei · Tokyo

Being Geek
by Michael Lopp

Published by O'Reilly Media, Inc., 1005 Gravenstein Highway North, Sebastopol, CA 95472.

O'Reilly books may be purchased for educational, business, or sales promotional use. Online editions are also available for most titles (safari.oreilly.com). For more information, contact our corporate/institutional sales department: (800) 998-9938 or corporate@oreilly.com.

Editor: Mary Treseler

Production Editor: Kristen Borg

Copyeditor: Genevieve d'Entremont

Proofreader: Kristen Borg

Indexer: Denise Getz

Cover Designer: Mark Paglietti

Cover Image: © Mark Weiss/Corbis

Interior Designers: Ron Bilodeau and Edie Freedman

Illustrator: Robert Romano

Printing History:

July 2010:

First Edition

RepKover. This book uses Repkover,™ a durable and flexible lay-flat binding.

ISBN: 9780596155407

[CS]

[8/10]

To Spencer and Claire.

My daily reminders of the value of caring

about someone deeply.

Contents

Preface. xi

SECTION 1: A CAREER PLAYBOOK

Chapter 1
How to Win 3

Chapter 2
A List of Three 9

Chapter 3
The Itch 17

Chapter 4
The Sanity Check 25

Chapter 5
The Nerves 31

Chapter 6
The Button 37

Chapter 7
The Business 45

SECTION 2: DECONSTRUCTING MANAGEMENT

Chapter 8
The Culture Chart. 57

Chapter 9
Managing Managers. 63

Chapter 10
The Issue with the Doof 73

Chapter 11
The Leaper 81

Chapter 12
The Enemy 87

Chapter 13
The Impossible 93

Chapter 14
Knee Jerks 99

Chapter 15
A Deep Breath. 107

Chapter 16
Gaming the System 113

Chapter 17
Managing Werewolves 121

Chapter 18
BAB. 127

Chapter 19
Your People. 133

Chapter 20
Wanted 139

Chapter 21
The Toxic Paradox. 147

Chapter 22
The Pond 155

SECTION 3: YOUR DAILY TOOLKIT

Chapter 23
The Nerd Handbook 165

Chapter 24
The Taste of the Day 173

Chapter 25
The Trickle List 181

Chapter 26
The Crisis and the Creative 189

Chapter 27
The Foamy Rules for Rabid Tools 195

Chapter 28
Up to Nothing 203

Chapter 29
How to Not Throw Up 209

Chapter 30
Out Loud 215

Chapter 31
Bits, Features, and Truth 223

Chapter 32
The Reveal 233

SECTION 4: YOUR NEXT GIG

Chapter 33
The Screw-Me Scenario 245

Chapter 34
No Surprises 251

Chapter 35
A Deliberate Career 257

Chapter 36
The Curse of the Silicon Valley 265

Chapter 37
A Disclosure 271

Chapter 38
Mind the Gap 279

Chapter 39
The Exodus 287

Chapter 40
Bad News About Your Bright Future 295

Epilogue
Hurry 301

Appendix
The Rules of Back Alley Bridge 305

Index 311

Preface

I'm a geek, and I might be a nerd, but I'm not a dork.

I've been at these definitions long enough to see them transformed from cruel words of judgment to badges of honor and labels of praise, but even with dramatically better PR and social standing, we're still a demographic saddled with debilitating social skills, strange control issues, and an insatiable appetite for information.

...and we don't even have a good definition for the labels we've given ourselves.

Some of the content for this book was first seen in the Rands in Repose weblog, and many years ago I made a snap decision about whether to embrace the word *nerd* or *geek* to describe my demographic. I was writing a lightweight article regarding attention deficiency disorder and I needed an acronym, because nothing dresses up an idea like a clever acronym.

The choices were Nerd Attention Deficiency Disorder (N.A.D.D.) or Geek Attention Deficiency Disorder (G.A.D.D.). While neither rolls of the tongue, N.A.D.D. struck me as slightly less terrible. This brief decision had lasting impact because, moving forward, I exclusively used *nerd* in my articles.

It is a defining characteristic of the nerd or geek to seek definition. This makes my off-the-cuff nerd naming choice an ongoing source of annoyance for me. What is the actual definition of the nerd? And the geek? And what about those dorks?

This annoyance became a full-blown inconvenience as I worked with my editor on this book that is now in your hands. As titles we debated, she came up with the elegant and precise *Being Geek*. Right. Right. Dammit. That's perfect. Problem is, I've never written about geeks. I'm a nerd. Or am I?

The origins of the word don't help. Geek originally described a circus performer who bit the heads off live animals. Nerd has a more honorable origin in its first documented appearance in Dr. Seuss's 1950 book *If I Ran the Zoo*, where the narrator claims he would collect "A Nerkle, a Nerd, and a Seersucker too."

Since then, the words have blended. There are clever Venn diagrams that describe the respective traits of nerds versus geeks. Some suggest the geeks are more obsessive than the nerds. Others call out the social ineptitude of the nerds, but for every definition you find, another can be found to contradict the previous definition.

So, it's a toss up.

The good news is the lack of a clear delineation between nerd and geek doesn't prevent us from tackling dork.

Dork is derogatory, there's no doubt about it, but it does have a place amongst the geek and nerd definition. The term geek can be added to any number of fields, many of which have little to do with technology. Movie geek, music geek—this describes a deep appreciation of a thing. My belief is that the term *dork* is used by geeks to position their geekery above another's geek field. For example, I'm a computer geek, but those movie geeks are dorks.

Make sense?

The point being, depending on where you're standing, we're all dorks.

As becoming comfortable with ambiguity is one of the goals of this book, perhaps it's a good opening to understand there really isn't a clear distinction between geek and nerd. While this book is called *Being Geek*, I'm likely to throw a few nerds in there for good measure.

A couple of other conventions to be aware of before we begin:

For much of this book, my prototypical geek is a he as a convenience. There are plenty of she geeks out there for which the observations of this book equally apply.

The narrator throughout this book is Rands. This is a pseudonym I've been using for over a decade. The comfortable anonymity of Rands provides a professional distance from the topics I cover. Similarly, just about every proper name and situation described in this book is fake. They've been deliberately constructed in order to tell a tale.

And that tale starts now.

How to Contact Us

Please address comments and questions concerning this book to the publisher:

> O'Reilly Media, Inc.
> 1005 Gravenstein Highway North
> Sebastopol, CA 95472
> 800-998-9938 (in the United States or Canada)
> 707-829-0515 (international or local)
> 707-829-0104 (fax)

We have a web page for this book, where we list errata, examples, and any additional information. You can access this page at:

> *http://oreilly.com/catalog/9780596155407*

To comment or ask technical questions about this book, send email to:

> *bookquestions@oreilly.com*

For more information about our books, conferences, Resource Centers, and the O'Reilly Network, see our website at:

http://oreilly.com

Safari® Books Online

 Safari Books Online is an on-demand digital library that lets you easily search over 7,500 technology and creative reference books and videos to find the answers you need quickly.

With a subscription, you can read any page and watch any video from our library online. Read books on your cell phone and mobile devices. Access new titles before they are available for print, and get exclusive access to manuscripts in development and post feedback for the authors. Copy and paste code samples, organize your favorites, download chapters, bookmark key sections, create notes, print out pages, and benefit from tons of other time-saving features.

O'Reilly Media has uploaded this book to the Safari Books Online service. To have full digital access to this book and others on similar topics from O'Reilly and other publishers, sign up for free at *http://my.safaribooksonline.com*.

Acknowledgments

I would like to acknowledge and thank:

Angela, David, Gregor, Ryan, and Tony. Time will only teach me that you represent one of the finest management teams I've ever had.

Melle Baker. Your understanding of my which/that impairment and my love of the word "primal" are one of the many continued contributions you continue to make to my writing.

Mary Treseler. You discovered the name of this book, you asked the hard questions, and you made this a better book.

The readers of Rands in Repose. Your comments, your interest, and your mails keep me writing.

42. You remain the answer to life, the universe, and everything.

SECTION 1:

A CAREER PLAYBOOK

For each new job I've considered, I can remember the moment I decided to make the leap. The consideration that went into each of these decisions was epic. There were Pro and Con lists, there were spreadsheets that did financial modeling, and there were endless conversations with trusted people that started with support and, weeks later, finished with, "Enough talking. When are you going to decide?"

This first section of *Being Geek* walks you through the endless list of decisions and tasks you can perform as you consider and engage in the search for your next gig. From early warning signs in the current gig to figuring out how to constructively stalk your future employer, these chapters document the various plays you can make as you consider the next move in your career.

These chapters leave the hardest part to you—making the decision.

CHAPTER 1

How to Win

You've had a small number of career-defining moments.

Small decisions cross your desk, your inbox, all day, but this isn't a small decision. It's massive, and once you've made this decision, there is absolutely no going back. It is in this moment you make a painful discovery—shit, I'm a geek.

You don't have an MBA. You know there are HR people in the building somewhere, but you've no idea what to do with them. You want to hide in the comforting structure of code, but you know that in this moment, this decision is going to significantly affect your career…if only you knew how.

Can I argue for more money after I received an offer? OK, how? What do I do when my boss lies to me? What do I need to do to resign? What's a program manager? Should I apply for a management gig? They make more money doing less, right? Can I get a promotion without talking to a single human being? There isn't a class in college that teaches any of this. Wikipedia can give you definitions, but it can't help a social introvert who sees much of the world through a keyboard.

This is the hand you've been dealt. Let's embrace the geek.

A System Thinker

We're different, and understanding these differences is a good place to start. At our core, I believe geeks are system thinkers. A simpler way to think about this is that in the mind of a geek, the world is like a computer—discernible, knowable, and finite. After years of successfully using the computer as a means of interacting with the world, we've come to follow a certain credo:

We seek *definition* to understand

the *system* so that we can discern

the *rules* so that we

know what to do next so that

we *win*.

Definition, system, and rules. It all goes back to our ever-favorite tool, the computer. Our success with the computer has tweaked out perspective of the planet. We believe that given enough time and effort, you can totally understand the system. *A hard drive has these attributes and make this type of operation faster. More memory will improve these types of operations. When my boss tells me I'm passive-aggressive, I should....*

Wait, what? Passive what?

A crisis occurs when a situation appears that doesn't follow the rules, doesn't fit in the system, and is inherently indefinable. We go into high alert when we see a flaw in the system because the system is what we tell ourselves to get through the day. Unfortunately, this structure is a comfortable illusion and full of certain flaws that I like to call people.

People Are Messy

People screw things up. They are the sources of bugs. They ask odd questions, and their logic is flawed. In the pleasant mental flow-chart we have in our geek heads, it's a single person who causes us to frustratingly ask, "Who are these people and why the hell don't they follow the rules? Can't they see the system? DON'T THEY WANT TO WIN?"

Yes, they do.

No one wants a reminder that life is a crapshoot. That we're all making it up as we go based on reacting to whatever random strangeness occurs in our corner of the world. The lack of control is especially discomforting to the geek, which is why we construct imaginary structured versions of our world to make the chaos a bit more palatable and predictable.

I'm a geek, and while I'm just as ambiguous and emotionally slippery as that comic book dork in the cube next door, I've been staring at geeks struggling with messy parts of high tech for over a decade. I believe I can improve the chances that we can win, even with all these people stumbling around and touching our stuff.

The advice and this book begin with a contradiction: prepare for the unpredictable.

The unpredictable shows up on your doorstep in two forms: simple unpredictability, which you can assess and act on immediately, and world-changing unpredictability that rocks your world and requires serious work on your part. In *Being Geek*, my hope is to first equip you with a system of improvisation that will help you act on the simple unpredictability and, second, to encourage you to develop a blueprint for your career to prepare for when the sky really falls.

A System of Improvisation

In my head, a handbook is a book with curled pages, a beaten cover, and folded pages that is never far away. It's achieved this state by being repeatedly and tactically useful. *Being Geek*'s chapters are structured around a single job. From the initial job search, the interview, the offer negotiations, and learning about your company and your coworkers, to finally deciding it's time to search for a new gig. The idea is not the arc; the idea is that as you're going through a small bit of unpredictability, you can flip to Chapter 34 and read about how to interpret your yearly review so you can make a decision: *am I or am I not going to get fussy about this poorly written review?*

The chapters of *Being Geek* are standalone, meaning there are minimal threads tying one chapter to the next. This is partially a function of where some of the chapters originated—my weblog, Rands in Repose—but also a function of the geek attention span, which can be…limited. My hope is these fully contained, easily consumable chapters are useful when small decisions show up, in that they help you take apart your decisions. They aren't prescriptive, because whatever decisions you have on your plate are yours to make, and the best I can offer is to tell you the story of when I found that decision, what I thought, and how I moved forward.

It's satisfying: the completion of a task, the making of a decision, getting a thing done. These small bits of motion you apply to your day make up the majority of the decisions you make in your life, and they happen with little pomp and circumstance. Making these decisions and seeing what happens make up the bulk of your experience and how you continue your endless search for rules that define your system. The better you get at them, hopefully, the more success you have and the quicker you make them the next time they show up.

Still, these are the small bits of unpredictability, and you also need to know what to do when the massive unpredictability appears.

A Career Blueprint

You read a book. From beginning to end. While the chapters of *Being Geek* can stand alone, this book is written around a single hypothetical job and is intended to tell a long story. The time it takes to read this book will, hopefully, give you distance from the day to day work of your job and remind you that you're working toward something bigger. Your job is not just what you're doing; it should be preparing you for what you want to do.

As you read this book, you need to keep three classes of questions in your head:

- What am I doing?
- What do I do?
- What matters to me? What do I care about?

Your work day is deviously designed around focusing you on the first question. Think about your state of mind when you get in the car to drive home, when you're sitting on the subway, when you're barely pulling yourself out of the sea of things to do. You're not dreaming about your next gig, you're not thinking strategically about your career; you are recovering from a day of tactical tasks. That's what you're doing, but is that what you do?

Maybe you're lucky. You're the software architect. You're the director of design. You're the guy who cares more about databases than anything else on the planet Earth. You've discovered a larger theme to what you're doing and that's what you do. It's your career, and a career is much bigger than a job.

Perhaps you don't know. It's your first gig, and while all this coding is delicious, there sure seem to be a lot of people running around talking about career growth. That's what HR is going to do for me, right? My boss has that covered, right?

Wrong.

As an avid watcher of management in the Silicon Valley for coming up on two decades, I can safely say that the good intentions of HR and partial attention of your boss does not a career make.

Whether you know what you do or you don't, the act of reading this book from cover to cover is a few hours of your time when you get to ask, "What matters to me? What do I care about?" Does this management gig float my boat? Am I a developer for life? Is the fact I spend the entire subway trip home cursing my gig a bad sign? It's professionally fashionable to bitch about your company and your inept manager, but when you start bitching about your career, I call bullshit. The idea that anyone besides you is responsible for your career is flawed. Your boss is only your boss while he's your boss. Your career is yours forever.

You choose your career and the choice makes life easy when massive unpredictability arrives. Think about it like this: how much easier would it be to make that big decision if you knew exactly what you wanted to do? Is it easier or harder to argue for that new project at work when you know it's perfect for your career goals? How would the review conversation go with your boss when you're completely sure that you want to get into management?

All decisions are easier when you're clear where you're headed.

A Collection of Moments

Your career is a collection of moments when you make a decision. PC or Mac? Answering that recruiting email or not? Confront or retreat? Even with this book in hand, you're going to screw up as many decisions as you make correctly, which is a troubling thought for the system-searching geek who is simply trying to win, but there are still rules to discern.

With time and experience, you'll learn there is a finite set of personalities walking the halls. Yes, they have their individual nuances, but these personalities and their motivations can be understood. Your boss and his motivation will vary from company to company, but it's a knowable set of motivations varying somewhere from "hiding until I retire" to "driving everyone absolutely crazy as I attempt to conquer the world." You can make most meetings useful. You can dig yourself out from underneath the endless list of things to do. It's OK to quit a job with people you like because there are a lot of people to like out there.

Being Geek is a distillation of 15 years in the Silicon Valley working at companies both large and small. I've had equal parts of calm and chaos, and I've been keeping notes during the entire time because I believe I'm always one rule away from figuring it all out, and that's how you win.

CHAPTER 2

A List of Three

The number three has been mystically bouncing around my life for years. First, there was the VP of Marketing who was obsessed with it. "Triangles, Rands, I see them everywhere. There's power in there." She kept three pieces of polished obsidian on her desk in a triangle formation at all times. Then was the Director of Engineering. All of his advice was dispensed in digestible lists of three. It was a handy, lightweight way of distributing bright ideas.

As means of simplifying the infinite, I see no reason why three can't help. Three is everywhere. Yes, no, maybe. Socialism, communism, capitalism. Memory, understanding, will. Of the people, by the people, for the people. I'm a fan.

This is why it comes as no surprise that I can pack both a career development and management philosophy into a list of three items:

1. Technical direction
2. Growth
3. Delivery

Conveniently, the list applies to both managers and individuals, but let's talk about it from the individual career perspective. Let's turn the list into questions:

1. Are you actively defining the technical direction for your product?

2. Do you understand what you need to do in order to grow?

3. Are you hitting your dates? Are you meeting your commitments? Are you doing what you say you're going to do?

That's it. That's all. There are shelves full of management and career development books that are going to explain in excruciating detail the 27 aspects of a good manager or 42 habits of effective developers, and I'm certain there are gems in those books. It is the nature of experts to dive deep, to explain in detail, and God bless 'em, but I've got work to do, so let's keep it brief.

Technical Direction

Whether you're a manger or an individual, in software development, you own code and that code is in—wait for it—one of three states: you're writing it, you're fixing it, or your maintaining it. When you're writing the code for the first time, technical direction as a goal isn't hard to keep in the front of your mind. What am I building? What tools am I using? Is it going to perform? I don't know what you're building, I don't know what company you work for or your development culture, but I do know that for the code that you own, you set the technical direction, not your manager.

A manager's job is to forget. That's what they do. They get promoted and begin the long processes of forgetting everything that got them promoted in the first place. I'm not joking. Manager amnesia will be the source of much professional consternation throughout your career.

Now, in defense of my brethren managers, we don't forget everything, and during all that forgetting, we're learning other useful things like organization politics, meeting etiquette, and the art of talking for 10 minutes without saying a thing. The things that we do remember are the painful scars of being an engineer. The scars of experience pop up as random inspiration and make it look like we're keeping track of it all, but we aren't. We don't. This is why my management strategy is to assume those closest to the problem can make the best decisions. That's how I scale.

There are those managers who are desperately trying not to forget. They believe that given enough time and effort they have the same degree of visibility they had when they owned the code. These people are called micromanagers, and they are going to fail because they're not learning how to forget.

It's not just micromanagers driving their teams up the wall with their weekly status reports, 1:1 code reviews, and a complete disregard for the management structure. It's their quest to know it all that is destroying trust on their team. *Why did you hire these people?* To get more done. They're not extensions of you; they're entirely themselves. Deal with it. Again, those who are closest to the code are imminently qualified to set the technical direction of the work.

Rands, he's not a micromanager. He fashions himself a visionary and he won't shut up about Scala. How the hell can I get things done when I'm being Scala-beaten?

That's the beauty of my list of three. Your manager, micromanager or not, has the same goal. It's his job to set technical direction— just like you. So, yeah, he's going to do research at the technical edges, he's going to think about radical re-architecting. Hopefully, he's competent and has the ability to do so, but that's not the technical direction you care about.

It's easy to forget with micromanagers and visionaries cluttering your day with their agenda, but as the owner of the code, it's your job to care—daily. Whether it's during the joy of writing the code, the annoying days of bug fixing, or the seemingly endless maintenance tasks, it's your call where the code is going to go next. Are we spending too much time on maintenance? Is it time to throw it away and start over? Sure, it's not necessarily your decision to make, but it's absolutely your responsibility to raise the issue, to have an opinion, and to affect the plan.

This code is crap. We need to start over.

Growth

Early in my career at Borland, I was baffled by the stock. What is it? Who sets it? What's an option? How do I spend it? Borland was in its heyday, so during all of the stock confusion, the price just went up...for two years. My thought was, "That's what stocks do. They grow." Then we missed our number. The earnings we had predicted were missed and the stock took a beating.

More confusion.

Everything in the building looked exactly the same. Everyone was working hard, but we were suddenly worth 25% less? This was my first lesson in perception being reality. The market sees growth as a leading indicator, and the panicky mob that is the stock market equates a lack of a growth with death.

And they're right.

As the second item in my career philosophy, growth represents the strategy by which you are learning, doing more, getting promoted, getting the shit kicked out of you, and garnering more responsibility. There's a simple rule designed to grab your attention: "If you're not growing, you're dying."

Let's see if you're dying. Ask yourself the following:

- Have you failed recently?
- Is there someone within throwing distance who challenges you daily?
- Can you tell me the story of something significant you learned in the last week?

Any answer of "No" is a troubling sign. You're coasting. Sure, it's comfortable, but while you're sitting there in your mediocrity, your industry is aggressively attempting to make you irrelevant. It's not personal; it's a function of all of those other bright people who aren't scared of failure, who have surrounded themselves with catalytic personalities, and who thrive on understanding.

Rands, isn't it my manager's job to grow me?

There are two parties responsible for your growth. You and your manager. Now, this isn't actually true, but early in your career, it's a convenient illusion. It is your manager's responsibility to care more about your growth than you. They do have more experience and are able to identify and assign opportunity suitable for that growth. *She's ready to be a tech lead. I can feel it.*

Unfortunately, you're always second in line when it comes to growth with your manager. I pessimistically believe that your manager will consider his interests before he considers yours. It sounds devious, but the same rule that applies to you applies to your manager: grow or die.

Perhaps a healthier way to think of it is that your manager is responsible for your job, but you're the manager of your career. The primary goal of both jobs is to identify and act on opportunity inside of the company that is going to challenge you, force you to learn, and push you to the edge of discomfort. These opportunities are going to confuse you because it's unfamiliar territory and you don't have a map...which is the point. A good manager creates opportunity, but it's your responsibility to take it.

However, your boss is not going to discover opportunity outside of the company. They're likely never going to say, "Yeah, we're doomed. Get the hell out." There is no one more qualified and informed to make decisions regarding your larger future than you.

I am ready for more.

Delivery

It's an unfortunate necessity that in our industry, the shit hits the fan. Just under two decades of experience in the Silicon Valley working at big companies, and I can confirm that random disasters are a constant.

Let's assume that you're a responsible person in the next disaster. Let's assume it's of a deeply technical nature, and let's assume you're not capable of handling this disaster. Who do you call?

Got a name? I bet you do. It's the guy who can do anything. He's probably got an office in a company where only managers have offices. He probably wears very strange T-shirts and has odd eating habits, but what's important about this guy is he delivers—like a machine. There's nothing that you can't ask this fellow to do that he doesn't leap on, can't explain, or can't argue about.

My guess is this guy is deeply technical—maybe an architect, perhaps a free electron—but going back to the question, why'd you call him to help with the disaster?

He delivers. It's not even a question. You don't consider for a moment that he won't be able to help. Even if the technical expertise you require has absolutely zero intersection with his experience, you know that he'll be able to help.

It's a skill, yes, but it's not the skill that everyone admires; it's the reputation. It's the expression you'll see on your boss's face when you tell him, "Yeah, I know it's a disaster, but Ryan's helping." *Oh good, it's handled.*

If technical direction is your ability, and growth is the refinement and shaping of that ability, then delivery is the reputation you construct around that ability, and the rule is also simple: "Do what you say you're going to do."

Quips, quotes, tweets, and clever names are littered all over my writing, but don't let their simplicity imply they are easy to apply. Doing what you say you're going to do is hard. Let's do the math.

- How many requests were made of you today? Let's call that X.

- How many of those requests have you completed or plan to complete to the satisfaction of the requestor? Let's call that Y.

If X is ever larger than Y, then your reputation is suffering. Any task, big or small, that has landed on your plate and you failed to complete is eroding your reputation. Here's why:

It wasn't a big deal. They didn't even notice. Yeah, they did. Maybe they didn't follow up and maybe it wasn't that big of a deal, but there was a brief moment when they internally measured you: *Didn't follow up. Didn't complete. Doesn't care.* That's what they remembered.

I couldn't say no. It was my boss. When you accept a task from your boss, whether you're able to complete it or not, the assumption is that you'll do it. Saying no to the person who signs the checks is tricky, but again, think about your reputation. Are you going to lose more points for saying no to a task or for failing at that task?

But I want to be a team player. Yeah, good teams don't fail.

The Quakers have a tenet that reads, "Speak truth to power." When the boss is signing you up for failure, your move isn't laying down the no; your move is to tell the truth. *Hey, I have no idea how to be successful here. I care about being successful, and so should you. Help.*

You need to be maniacal about your reputation. Yes, a single failure to deliver isn't a disaster. Mistakes happen. X is sometimes bigger than Y, but some misses are vastly bigger than you expect. That one off-handed request from your VP that sounded like it wasn't a big deal? Well, by itself it wasn't a big deal, but the three tasks after that were a big deal and when she reverse-engineers where the failure originated, she's not going to remember that the request was off-handed. She'll think, "Right. Unreliable."

A reputation is a community-based opinion that you don't control. It takes years of work to develop and a single missed key responsibility to destroy.

Simplifying the Infinite

I use the word "rule" a lot in this chapter, but I'm not a rule guy— I'm a direction guy. If you're looking for the definitive 38 ways to effectively manage your career, I'm sure there's a book for that. The "List of Three" is intended to give a semblance of structure and a sense of direction.

For me, technical direction is a reminder to care daily about my work. Growth is actively watching my career and making sure that today is not a dull repetition of yesterday. Finally, delivery is my daily investment in my reputation. Keeping this list in my head keeps me asking questions and, more importantly, keeps me growing.

To me, the fundamental unit of growth is knowledge. Knowledge isn't facts, and knowledge isn't data. It's your consumption of facts, data, situations, and personalities, and the consumption yields a discovery. It's when you mentally build something new. This knowledge may not be novel, but what makes it unique is that you built it for yourself.

The act of creation makes knowledge yours. It grows your mental arsenal—giving you a new experience to reflect upon forever.

CHAPTER 3

The Itch

My expiration date for a gig has, historically, been three years. Strangely, this mirrors what I believe is the development cycle to get a product right—three releases before it's real. One release per year, the product is done...and so am I.

I say this like there's a plan, like I know that after three years it's time to move on, but this is not a science. This is historic observation. As I look at my resumé, it's obvious. In fact, I often start leaving before I even notice I'm leaving.

Leaving starts with an itch.

Are You Answering the Phone?

I rarely answer my phone at work. There are really only two types of people who call: lawyers and recruiters. The lawyers are calling for good reason. They know that anything that passes through the keyboard is forever, and since their jobs hinge on conversations that we might not want to be forever, they use the phone.

Recruiters, on the other hand, are just cold calling. They've got a name and the main number of your company and they're dialing. They don't care who you are—you're just 10% of your first year's salary. And they're the main reason I never pick up my phone.

The phone rings maybe 3–5 times a day. The ringer is low, and 99% of the time I just ignore it, except when I don't. In the moment of considering the ring, an instant mental analysis occurs that sounds like this: *Recruiter. Meh. But I wonder if it's something interesting? More interesting than what I'm doing right now? More potential? A raise? I could use a raise....*

I'm making it sound like this inner dialog is complex and drawn out, but it's not. It's a gut check. *Am I happy in my job?* Yes? OK, ignore the phone. No? Well, let's see what they have to say.

As I reach over to pick up the phone, a silent alarm goes off in my head because it's likely I haven't admitted to myself that there's a chance I'd consider another gig, but here I am reaching for the phone, picking up, and seeing what the world has to offer.

I've never actually ended up in a gig that started with a cold call, but I have ended up in a new gig because a cold call knocked me out of professional lethargy and created a professional itch I needed to scratch.

The Pissed Itch

Before we figure out whether you're ready for a new gig, let's first figure out your mindset because it's going to dictate whether or not we proceed. Are you pissed off at your boss? Did you just get a really bad review? Did you just learn you weren't included in the next fancy project? Are you seething?

Right, stop reading.

The rest of the chapter assumes you're in control of your temper and your current gig. You are driving. If you're pissed, you're not in the mindset to make solid strategic decisions about your next gig. You're motivated by a single thought: I. Am. Out of here. There's a litany of good reasons to be angry with your boss, your company, or your team, but you don't want to start a job change being pissed off. Nothing taints common sense more than being pissed off.

Early Warning Signs of Doom

Choosing to subject yourself to a recruiting cold call is just one sign that cracks are forming in your job satisfaction. There are others...

Engagement

How engaged are you in your work? I know you love working on that new feature in the product—you'll always love doing new things—but how about the busy work? How engaged are you in the work that is necessary but tedious? Remember when you joined the company and everyone was bright and you had no clue the boring work was, well, boring? Now that it's boring, are you able to crank through it, or are you finding excuses to not do it? I'm not talking about a lull of interest; I'm talking about a complete lack of interest in the inane but essential work that moves the company forward.

It's a warning sign when the onerous busy work drops off my plate. I'm not doing it, because I've got a new gig in mind, though I'm months away from that realization. It's an early sign that the core satisfaction in my job has begun to erode when I'm unable to charge through the work I hate.

Wanderlust

How much are you thinking about your job when you're not working? When you go to sleep? My question is: how much are you thinking about your job when you don't have to?

There's a larger job satisfaction analysis going on inside of wanderlust. In hi-tech, 9 to 5 jobs are dead. I'm a fervent supporter of maintaining a work-life balance that allows you to explore as much of the planet Earth as possible, but I'm also the guy who thinks if you're going to do this job, you should be absolutely fucking crazy about it. This doesn't mean that you're obsessively working 24 hours a day on the product, but it does mean that the work you are doing is part of you.

If your work isn't finding you in the car or on the bus, if you're not thinking about the things you build when your mind is wandering, it might be a sign that you're going through the motions with your work.

Software development is puzzle solving. *Given this esoteric set of problems, people, and code, how am I going to build the best possible thing I can?* You don't always solve these problems sitting at your desk. You solve them in the bar, in the shower, in the places you let your mind wander.

If my mind isn't always passively chewing on the things I need to build, again, it's a sign that I might not care about what I'm doing.

Whether your engagement is fading or you are lost in wanderlust, both mental states are hurting your current gig more than you think. When your engagement fades, you stop doing busy work. When you are mentally wandering outside of your gig, again, you're decreasing your daily investment in your gig.

It's not all bad news. Your big projects are getting attention. The people that stand in your door yelling, they get your cycles, but the quiet work isn't being touched. A decent percent of the day is busy work, and when you choose to not do that work one day, no one notices, because it's not high-priority work. When you don't do that work for three weeks, the busy work becomes an untended garden where the low-priority work slowly grows into reputation-affecting mistakes.

You can go months giving the boring work half of your attention, but it's just a matter of time before you ignore a task that really matters. Now you're the person who's looking for a gig not only because you're bored, but also because you're screwing up.

You need to consider your new gig from a place of confidence. You don't want to be running from a mistake, but walking toward a new opportunity.

The Contradiction List

Before you pick up the phone, before you answer that tempting recruiting email, there are a couple of questions I want you to ask yourself, and then, with these answers in hand, I'll explain why you should ignore them.

Who are you leaving behind?

I have a Rolodex. It's not actually a Rolodex, it's a list, and on that list is every single person whom I'll call when I do the start-up thing. In each company I've worked at, I've had the Rolodex moment when I realize that someone I'm working with belongs on this list. It's a rare, wonderful moment.

There's a risk when you leave a gig that you're leaving people behind who you're going to need at a later date, who aren't going to survive the transition to your new gig. There's also a chance that you've missed an obvious Rolodex candidate.

The reality is: Inclusion on the Rolodex is defined by the ability to survive job changes, although, paradoxically, you won't actually know that for sure until you leave. Part of my inclusion criteria is that I see my relationship with this person as something larger than the current gig. If they're on the Rolodex, it means I believe our relationship is no longer defined by the current job, and there's no better way to test this hypothesis than switching gigs.

Are you done?

In your current gig, are you close to a state where all of your major commitments are either complete or won't come crumbling down if you leave? I'm not saying every single task has been crossed off; I'm saying that the work that you can uniquely do can either be completed or handed off to a competent person. My real question here is: what's the story that will be told about you when you leave? Will it be, "He's the guy who bailed when it got tough" or "He left us at a tough time, but left us in good shape"?

The reality is: You're never done. There's never a good time to go. If you're a key player in the organization, everyone will likely freak out when they hear you're leaving, meetings will be held to brainstorm backup plans, you'll leave, and things will pretty much proceed as they did when you were there.

Nature abhors a vacuum, and while your absence will be visually obvious, culturally, one or more people will start jockeying for your gig the moment the departure rumor starts wandering the hallways.

What itch are you trying to scratch?

This is the last question, but it should be first. You're still reading, so your motivation isn't "I hate this company." What is your motivation? You want a raise? That's great, that's a place to start, but you know you can get a raise just doing a good job where you're sitting right now, with people you know, in familiar surroundings. Switching gigs strikes me as a pretty radical change given all you want is more money.

Is your motivation bigger than that? Dumping all your current responsibilities and everyone you professionally know is a shock to the system. You're in for months of confusion sitting in a place you don't know with people who speak in strange acronyms. Your motivation around looking for a new gig should be commensurate with the confidence beating you're about to take.

The reality is: Take the beating. Every job is a fascinating new collection of people and responsibilities. You need to pay careful attention to whether you'll fit in to this potential new gig, but even with that due diligence, it's a crapshoot. You'll never know exactly what you'll learn, but I guarantee in the chaotic flurry of new, there is invaluable experience to discover.

Bright and Shiny

Once you have telemetry on the potential new gig, my last question is: "Is it just new or is it unique? And is it progress?"

A new job is not like a new car. The morning after you bought the car, you walk into the garage and think, "Holy shit, a new car. I can't believe…all the New." Then, you get in the car and start your drive to work swimming in the new car scent, and halfway to work you realize, hey…it's just a car.

In analyzing a potential new gig, you need to separate the new from the unique. "What is genuinely unique about this new job?" For me, answers have varied: it's a start-up, it's shrink-wrap, it's not another fucking database product, or it's a step back, but it's a company I've wanted to work at since I was a kid.

Once you've defined what's unique about the potential gig, you've got a bigger question: "Is it what you what to do?" This is the career question. This is when you figure out whether or not you know what you want to be when you grow up.

It's OK to not have a solid answer to that question. I'm still working on it, but just because you don't have an answer to a very hard question doesn't mean you shouldn't ask it. Does this new gig fit into whatever hazy goals you have for yourself? If you want to be standing in front of a thousand people talking about changing the world, does this gig feel like a step in that direction?

The place to start thinking about a new job, about figuring out what itch you need to scratch, isn't whether or not you want the job; it's considering *do I know what I want to do?*

CHAPTER 4

The Sanity Check

The amount of infrastructure sitting between you and your next gig is impressive.

Ironically, this infrastructure was purchased and configured to get you as close to this job as quickly as possible, but it doesn't. Corporate job sites are usually outsourced affairs, because HR departments traditionally have neither the budgets nor the expertise to build the system they'd actually use. They shouldn't; it's not the core competency.

With half-baked solutions manned by contract recruiters, it's almost a miracle when your phone rings or an email shows up with a recruiter wanting to set up a phone screen. Someone, somewhere in the organization has successfully mapped you to an open position. This is a really big deal because, in my experience, the chance that you'll get this job has improved logarithmically. It's not 50/50, but it's vastly better than when you were a random resumé sitting on a desk.

There's a sense of relief when you have an actual conversation with a human being, and as soon as you hang up the phone with the recruiter, you're going to call your best friend and say, "Hey, I got an interview with The Company!"

No, you didn't. You got a phone screen, and a phone screen has little to do with an interview. While your situation isn't as tenuous as the 30 seconds you have to make an impression with your resumé, you're still not in the building, and nothing real is happening until you're in the building.

Here's the precise mental process I use as I walk through the phone screen, but before I do that, you've got homework.

Stalk Your Future Job

Before you even talk to me, you're on a fact-finding mission. You've got a job description, and after the phone screen has been set up, you've got my name. You might also have an idea of the product or technology associated with this gig or you might not, but even without a product name, you've got plenty of information to start with.

Do your research. Google me. Find out anything you can about what I do and what I care about. This isn't stalking, this is your career, and if I happen to be an engineering manager who writes a weblog, well, you can start to learn how I think. Maybe I don't have a weblog, but I post to mailing lists. That's data, too.

How is this going to help you during the phone screen? Well, I don't know what you're going to find, but anything you can gather is going to start to build context around this job that you know nothing about. This helps with phone screen nerves as well. See, I have your resumé, and you have nothing. Aren't you going to feel better about talking with a total stranger when you figure out from staring at my Flickr pages that I absolutely love Weimaraners? Isn't it going to be reassuring to know I swear in my Twitters? A bit of research into who you are talking to is going to level the information playing field.

Similarly, if you have a product name or technology, repeat the same process. What is the product? Is it selling well? What do other people think about it? I'm not talking about a weekend of research here. I'm talking about an hour or so of background research so that you can do one thing when the phone screen shows up: ask great questions.

That's right. In your research, you want to find a couple of compelling questions, because at some point during the phone screen I'm going to ask you, "Do you have any questions for me?" And that is the most important question I'm going to ask.

Initial Tuning

Before I ask you the most important question, I need to figure out a couple of things early in our chat. What I need to learn is:

Can We Communicate?

I'm going to lead off with something simple and disarming. It's either going to be the weather or something I picked up from your extracurricular activities. "Do you really surf? So do I! Where do you surf?" These pleasantries appear trivial, but they're a big deal to me because I want to see if we can communicate. It's nowhere near a deal killer if the pacing of our conversation is awkward—I'll adjust, but how off is it? Are we five minutes in and we still haven't said anything? OK, maybe we have a problem.

One More Softball

My follow-up questions will now start to focus on whatever questions your resumé left me with. I've no idea what I'm going to ask because it varies with every single resumé, so my thought is that you should have your resumé sitting in front of you because it's sitting in front of me as well. It's my only source material.

Whatever these follow-up questions are, I'm still figuring out how we communicate. This means you need to focus on answering the questions. It sounds stupid, but if it's not absolutely clear to you what I'm asking, it's better to get early clarification rather than letting me jump in five minutes into your answer to say, "Uh, that's not what I was asking."

See, you and I are still tuning to each other. It's been 10 minutes now, and if we're still not adjusted to each other's different communication styles, I'm going to start mentally waving my internal yellow flag. It doesn't need to be eloquent communication, but we should be making progress.

No More Softballs

We're past the softball phase of the interview, and now I'm going to ask a hard question. This isn't a brainteaser or a technical question; this is a question that is designed to give you the chance to tell me a story. I want to see how you explain a complex idea over the phone to someone you don't know and can't see.

Again, who knows what the actual question will be, but you need to be prepared for when I ask the question that is clearly, painfully open-ended. I'm not looking for the quick, clean answer; I'm looking for a story that shows me more about how you communicate and how you think. Being an amazing communicator is not a part of most engineering jobs, I know this. I'm not expecting Shakespeare, but I am expecting that you can confidently talk about this question because I found this question in your resumé and that is the only piece of data we currently have in common. If we can't have an intelligent discussion about that, I'm going to start wondering about the other ways we aren't going to be able to communicate.

Your Turn

We're 20 minutes into the phone screen, and now I'm going to turn it over to you when I ask, "Do you have any questions for me?"

When I tell friends that this is my favorite question, the usual response is, "So, you're lazy, right? You can't think of anything else to ask, so you go for the path of least resistance." It's true. It's an easy question for me to ask, but it is essential, because I don't hire people who aren't engaged in what they're doing. And if you don't have a list of questions lined up for me, all I hear is: YOU DON'T WANT THIS JOB.

A well thought out question shows me that you've been thinking about this job. It shows me you're already working for it by thinking about the job outside of this 30-minute conversation. Yeah, you can probably wing it and ask something interesting based on the last 20 minutes, but the impression you're going to make with me by asking a question based on research outside of this phone screen will make up for a bevy of yellow flags. It shows initiative and it shows interest.

The Close

And we're done. It went by pretty quick, but the question is, "How'd it go?" Here's a mental checklist to see how you did.

Long, Awkward Pauses

Were we struggling to keep things moving? Were there long silences? Well, we didn't tune appropriately. Again, not a deal killer, but definitely a negative.

Adversarial Interactions

What happened when we had different opinions? Did we talk through it, or did we start butting heads? This happens more than I expect on phone screens, and it's not always a bad thing. I'm not interested in you telling me what I want to hear, but if we are on opposite sides of the fence, how do we handle it? If a candidate is willing to pick a fight and dig in their heels in a 30-minute phone screen, I'm wondering how often they're going to fight once they're in the building.

How'd It Feel?

This is the hardest to quantify, but also the most important. Did we click? Now, I haven't done a technical interview in years. Others with more recent experience are going to drill down there if we bring you in the building. There's a risk that if you get past the phone screen and you don't have the technical ability, we're going to waste a half-day of my team's time interviewing someone who can't do the job, but I'm vetting a more important aspect of you.

You are not a cog. The story we tell ourselves when someone we like chooses to leave the group or the company is, "Everyone is replaceable." This is true, but this is a rationalization designed to lessen the blow that, crap, someone we really like is leaving. We are losing part of the team. Professional damage is done when a team member leaves, and while they are eventually replaceable, productivity and morale take a hit.

All of my softballs and questions are designed to answer the question, "Are you a person who we'd miss if you left?" As the leader of my group, I am hopefully representative of my team, so if after 30 minutes you and I haven't figured out how to communicate, there's a good chance you won't click with part of the team as well.

Specific Next Steps

How did I leave it? Did I give you a song and dance about how "we're still interviewing candidates and we'll be in touch within the next week"? Well, that's OK, but what you're really looking for is a specific next step like "I'm going to bring you in" or "Let's have you talk with more of the team." An immediate and actionable next step is the best sign of success with a phone screen. If I don't give you this as part of the close, ask for it. If I stall, there's a problem.

A phone screen is not an interview; it's a sanity check. I already know you meet the requirements for the job by looking at your resumé. The phone screen is going to tell me whether you meet the requirements of the culture of my team.

Unlike your resumé, where you send your hope to an anonymous recruiting address, the phone screen gives you leverage. The phone screen is the first time you get to represent yourself as a person. It's still a glimpse, but it's the first time you can actively participate in your next job.

CHAPTER 5

The Nerves

There's a collection of emotions competing in your head before an interview, and no matter how many interviews you go through, some version of them will always show up. I think they can be collectively viewed as the Nerves.

The Nerves are the jumble of every single emotion and question bouncing around your head trying to get out. Questions like:

- Who am I going to meet?

- Are they going to ask me to code?

- Can I accurately communicate how cool the stuff is that I build?

- Is my love of this potential new job going to come off as desperation?

My opinion is that the biggest source of the Nerves is judgment. In the next six hours, your career is literally on trial. You are about to be cross-examined by a handful of strangers regarding your education and your experience. The result of this cross-examination will be a decision regarding your future livelihood.

An interview is a crucible where everything you've learned and everything you've done is being measured and understood in a day, and it's your responsibility to elegantly and eloquently describe this experience to a bunch of strangers.

I understand why you are nervous.

In this chapter, I'm going to give you a simple strategy for handling the hardest part of the interview: answering questions.

Question Types

First, let's understand the questions that are going to show up. There are three classes of questions you're going to encounter.

Specific

These questions are focused. *How'd you end up at that company? Why'd you leave?* While the answers to these questions might make them feel open-ended, these are warm-up feeler questions intended to giver the interview context. They're exploring you and your resumé, but they haven't really asked a hard question. Answers to the questions are short, specific, and don't require much strategy.

Problem solving

These questions are intended to qualify and demonstrate ability. *How many times a day do a clock's hands overlap?* These are the dreaded coding or brain-teasing questions that, while hated, give the interviewer an idea of how you think. You go into these questions intentionally not knowing the answer, because they want to see how (and if) you arrive at an answer. These are "show your work" questions intended to shine light on your thought process.

Open-ended

These are like problem-solving questions, except they're for the other side of your brain. *Explain your design philosophy. Tell me about your biggest failure.* Even though we all dread the problem-solving and coding questions, I believe open-ended questions are where we screw up the most, and I blame the Nerves.

While I think the strategy listed next helps with any of these question types, I think it's best suited to tackling ambiguously slippery open-ended questions.

The Answer Process

First, understand the question.

Tell me what you learned at your prior gig.

It's a big, ambiguous, open-ended question, and because you have the Nerves, you're going to want to just start talking, but before you say a thing, before you even think of an answer, you need to make sure you understand the question.

Sure, I learned all about design in my last gig and....

Stop, no. You're answering and you still don't understand the question. It's not what you learned, it's what did you learn that this specific person is going to care about? Who is this person, and why is he asking the question? If it's an engineer, it's the engineering version of the answer. If it's a program manager, go for the program manager version.

You're spinning these folks by altering your answer. They asked a big, huge, vague question and you, hopefully, learned a ton at your prior gig and are using some of that knowledge to give the interviewer an answer that will be relevant to him.

OK, can I start talking now?

No.

Before you do that, you need to have an answer.

You understand who is asking and what he's asking, but do you have an answer? You don't open your mouth until you can feel the answer. My biggest interview pet peeve is when I ask a question and the candidate wastes three minutes of our time talking and never answering the question.

The flawed reasoning here is that you need to say something immediately. But since you don't immediately have an answer, you're going to open your mouth and, hopefully, verbally wander toward one. This strategy can work, but when it fails, when you're two minutes into a rambling answer that has nothing to do with what I asked, we're both going to know it. Two minutes have passed and all I've learned is that you're mentally messy.

Wait until you have an answer. Wait until you can feel it, and don't start talking until you do. If a couple of seconds have passed and the silence is becoming palpable, it's one of two situations:

a) You really don't understand the question, or

b) You really don't have an answer.

Here are three moves:

1. If you don't understand the question, clarify. *Are you asking what I learned that I cared about or what I learned relative to design?* The clarification demonstrates active participation in the interview and I love it. I love that someone is past the Nerves and is engaged in the interview and actually listening.

2. If you don't have an answer, if you've clarified, maybe twice, and you're still drawing a blank, I have a cheap trick that is going to give you another 10 seconds: repeat the question.

   Yeah, repeat it. Word for word. It's lame, but you've got a mental logjam in your head. Maybe it's the Nerves. Maybe you really don't have an answer, but the simple act of sounding out the question can sometimes fire the right neuron.

   Don't look at the interviewer; the Nerves are going to tell you that they're wondering why you're stalling. Look at the ceiling, look at the window, and repeat the question.

3. You've clarified twice, repeated, and you're 10 seconds into another round of silence. Still nothing. The Nerves are screaming, but I want you to ignore them. The Nerves see silence as a weakness, but I believe silence demonstrates composure and thoughtfulness, and you're going to need that composure because your next move is to look them straight in the eye and say, "I don't know."

It feels like interview suicide, the admission of ignorance, but look at the alternatives: rambling, praying, and hoping that inspiration strikes.

Both problem-solving and open-ended questions are designed to show me how you think. Even though I'm giving you space for being nervous, when your answers come out as a rambly mess, I'm wondering how much control you have over your facilities. Where's your head going to be when we're three months into a shipping death march? Are you going to be rambly then? How about when you're demoing to the executives?

I understand the courage it takes to acknowledge ignorance during a time when you're pitching yourself as a worthy hire, and it's that courage that will make an impression.

The Confidence of Knowing a Thing

Understand the question and have an answer. As interview advice goes, it's pretty simple, but you've got to keep it simple because of the Nerves. Think of your last interview when you totally blew the question and went so off-topic that neither you nor the interviewer knew where the hell you were going. Tell me about the Nerves after that disaster of an answer.

By keeping your answer strategy simple, but making sure you understand what is being asked and being certain you have something to say, you're providing comfortable mental structure around your interview; you're making it a bit more predictable.

The mental state I want you in is the one after you nailed that open-ended question. They vaguely asked you about your design philosophy, you clarified, you considered, and then you spoke for three whole uninterrupted minutes about your philosophy, and as you watched the interviewer, you saw him getting it.

Your job in an interview is to lose the Nerves and show them who you are. With each successful answer to a question, you provide a more complete picture of who you are and gain confidence, and confidence kills the Nerves.

CHAPTER 6

The Button

Getting your head on straight and intelligently answering questions is only half of the game. An interview is an exchange of information, and the first and best way to screw that up is to forget that it's as important for you to gather information as it is to give it.

You may really need this job, and this might give you the impression that the steady flow of people who are grilling you are calling the shots. And yes, if you let them, they will be, but while they need to learn about you, you need to learn about them. You need to figure out their Button.

Creatures and Structure

Before you start pushing buttons, you need some context in the form of the interview list. Some employers don't want to share this until you're in the building, but even in that case, you can spend a few minutes figuring out your day.

Who do they have talking with you? Is it just your peer group? OK, then this is round #1 and, if things go well, there will be another round. Is it the entire org chart? Well, looks like you're interviewing at a start-up and will be exposed to the entire business. Awesome.

The next thing you want to discern is whether the interview schedule is structured or unstructured. This is likely not going to be obvious until the interviews have begun.

In a structured interview, each person interviewing you has a specific topic area: people skills, technical skills, etc. This means that each interview has a specific purpose, and no two interviews that day are going to be alike. Someone has put in effort to make sure the different interviewers don't step on each other's toes.

The unstructured interview is a free-for-all. There's an interview list, but no one has been given guidance about what to ask, so they wing it. With each person who walks in the door, an unstructured interview is a study in personality identification. More on this in a moment when I explain about interview creatures.

In general, the participants in structured interviews come prepared. There is a process, which occurred before you showed up. This might have involved a pre-interview meeting. They've read your resumé, and each person is likely capable of carrying the interview.

Unstructured interviewers waste the first 10 minutes of the interview doing the homework they should've done before you arrived. It's annoying, but, as you'll see, it's a great way to figure out what they are about.

As an aside, my preferred use of interview time is a structured/ unstructured hybrid. While I don't give interviewers specific topics to cover, I've chosen specific people because I know they gravitate toward certain professional areas, such as technical aptitude or cultural fit. This structural ambiguity means interviewers can creatively adapt their questions to each person while also assuring that I get a complete professional picture of the candidate.

Understanding who you are talking with and the structure of the interview process gives you some of your first insight into the organization, but the information doesn't start to flow until you stare at and understand your potential future coworkers.

Interview Creatures

Structured or unstructured, each person who walks into the interview will bring a different agenda. The sooner you know what their agenda is, the sooner you're prepared to handle your only job during this interview. You need to get them talking.

That's right. Your goal is exactly the same as their goal, which is to learn by getting them to talk. It might strike you as a bad strategy because if they're talking, they're not learning anything about you, but that is not your problem. In fact, if I get through a round of interviews and the interviewers have done most of the talking, I'm wondering if I want to work in a group where they haven't figured out how to vet candidates.

Like meetings, there are different personalities that are going to walk into the interview, and each person has a Button. When you press this button, they're going to be compelled to talk. This is not interview chitchat. This is essential telemetry regarding their thoughts about their job and the company.

Some personalities hide their buttons better than others, but most people have at least one.

Here's a list of some common interview creatures organized by increasing difficulty of button discovery as well as their likely influence on the interview.

Pissed-Off Pete

Pete's agenda is obvious 30 seconds into the interview because he's pissed off. This isn't an interview; this is an opportunity for Pete to rant to a captive audience. He's going to go through the motions by bringing in your resumé and feigning interest, but all he really wants to do is gripe about "the situation."

The Button: Ask anything. Doesn't matter, Pete is going to twist the answer so that he can ramble some more about how screwed up "the situation" is.

Perhaps your best tactic with Pete is to spend as much time as possible understanding "the situation." If it's so bad that he's going to ignore the opportunity of learning about you, a potential coworker, maybe "the situation" is something you should understand before you consider joining the company. Even better, asking about "the situation" is a great button exploration technique in later interviews.

Influence: Low. These interviews are normally a waste of time, and there are two red flags to consider. First, who thought it was a good idea for Pete to interview you? Don't they know he's a one-trick rant pony? Second, why is Pete so pissed off? What kind of organization lets Pete get this tense?

Chatty Patty

Patty loves to talk, and the moment you ask anything, she'll start and it'll be hard to get her to stop.

The Button: Ask any question.

Influence: Like Pete, I have concerns about an organization that puts Patty on the interview schedule. Similar to Pete, Patty can be a huge source of information, so use the time well. She'll answer any question: "Why do you love your job?" "Who's a jerk?" "Why's Pete so pissed off?"

Given that Patty is going to do most of the talking, her report on you is going to be vanilla and dull. Don't sweat her.

The Poet

This is an advanced, artful combination of Pete and Patty. Like them, The Poet really has something he wants to tell you about, but unlike them, he's not going to give it up unless you specifically ask him about it. He's aware of what his job is, and that's to ask you questions.

The Button: The Poet is sneaky, but he's still going to reveal his button via his questions. What is he asking about? Where is he repeating himself? "He's an engineer, but he keeps asking interaction design questions. I wonder what happens if I ask him a question about interaction design?"

WHAM.

Pure poetry. Listen hard, because what's coming out of The Poet's mouth is important, and he's not going to talk for long because, unlike Patty's chattiness and Pete's pissed-off-ed-ness, he's not dedicated to his poetry. He's going to turn it around quickly because he really wants to hear about your poetry.

Influence: Medium. The Poet is articulate and artful, and this will not only color his opinion of you. The distinctiveness of his report will travel further in the organization than the useless vanilla crap captured by Patty and Pete.

Gotcha Greg

Halfway through the interview day, Greg is going to walk in the room and say nothing. He's going to size you up for 10 seconds, and then he's going to ask, "How…would you…test a soda machine…in the dark…submerged in strawberry Jell-O?"

What?

Greg is on a power trip. He believes his job is to confuse you with the dazzling brainteaser. His belief is that catching you off-guard with this left field question is going to demonstrate whether or not you're mentally nimble, but my belief is that Greg mostly just likes to see people squirm.

The Button: You're going to need to first get past Greg's question, and my advice is to relax and have fun with it. These types of brainteasers are usually designed to demonstrate your thinking process, so think out loud and when you're done, go on a button hunt.

This can be tricky since Greg clearly likes to be on the offensive, but I've found that interviewers who lead with random, huge, bizarre questions are compensating for the fact that they don't really like having a normal conversation. So. Have one.

Influence: Low to medium. Greg believes his value is high, but it's likely the rest of his team know what you figured out with his first question. He's a mental bully.

Slick Steve

Now we're getting into some tricky personalities. Slick Steve is probably not a part of the engineering organization. He's the product manager or some other Marketing denizen. This means that he doesn't natively speak engineering, but as part of the strategic portion of the organization, he routinely talks to a lot of people, so he can wing it. He's read this chapter, and he knows that you're trying to gather information. He's a tough nut to crack.

The Button: Steve is going to completely ignore your attempts to find his button. "So Steve, what do you think the biggest challenges are for product marketing?" His response, "What do you think they are?"

Dammit.

You've got to fake Steve out a bit to find his button, and that means getting a little tricky. Try this: hit Steve with an esoteric engineering question you're sure he won't know. Remember, Steve is slick, which means he wants to maintain the calm, controlled elegance of his interview, so being unable to answer a question might trip him up. This is why you follow up with a question you're sure he'll be able to answer. Ask him that lame marketing challenges question again. He'll answer it this time because he's presently feeling ignorant and flustered, and needs to get back his feeling of control.

Like The Poet, Steve isn't giving up his button easily, but once you've got him talking, you have a chance to listen and see if you can find it.

Influence: Medium? Steve's here and he's not an engineer, which means the organization values him. He's here to vet something. The question is: what?

Silent Bob

Bob is a button problem. Bob will sit down, ask his first question, his second question, his third, and you will learn nothing about him except that he's silent. He's not going to engage in witty repartee; he's literally going to ignore your button exploration questions, and this is going to annoy you. Yeah, Bob is the guy who is going to have you code at the whiteboard until you break. We'll talk about that in another chapter.

The Button: Don't get rattled. In my experience, Bob is the senior technical guy on the team, and his social skills just aren't that good. He's there to vet your technical chops and that's it. He has no button. He's not qualified to assess team fit or cultural fit, and he knows this, so show him what you've got.

Influence: Very High. If you're interviewing for a technical gig, this is the interview. This is the one you were losing sleep over. This is why you bought *Dive into Python* and read it over the weekend. No one, other than the CEO, is going to trump Bob. Good luck.

The CEO

Interviewing with The CEO is not necessarily an interview with the actual CEO; it's the interview with the highest-level manager during your interview process. This is likely the hiring manager's manager.

Where's the Button? Simply put, you need to be prepared for some serious Jedi Mind Shit with The CEO. The feint'n'jab you used on Slick Steve isn't going to work here. In fact, the CEO may start the whole interview with, "What questions do you have for me?"

Oh good. This is going to be easy.

Yeah, it's not.

The Button: As you'll see, the influence of The CEO is extraordinarily high, and like Silent Bob, I want you to ignore your button acquisition activities with this guy. I want you to talk. I want you to sell yourself and tell great stories about your successes. Gather your organizational intelligence in other interviews; this is your opportunity to sell yourself to one of the major influencers in the organization.

Influence: Very High. The CEO is going to say that he isn't the decision-maker. He'll say that the hiring manager is, but if you do poorly with the CEO, it's unlikely that the hiring manager will contradict his boss.

A Fresh Perspective

Interviews are exhausting. Baring your professional soul for multiple rounds of interviews with a bunch of strangers will wear you out and, when you're done, you'll be wondering, "What did they learn about me? Did I nail it? Am I a fit? Did I get the gig?" All good questions, but you should also be asking, "Do I want this job? Do I like these people? Is it a healthy organization?"

By the end of a few rounds of interviews, you're going to know more about the health of the group you interviewed with than a lot of the people who interviewed you do. Freaky, isn't it? Fact: all the different creatures you interview with are lost in the day to day of their respective jobs. The fresh perspective that you have after many hours of interviewing is unique and informative, and while you still need Ninety Days to figure out what is really going on, you still have a lot of data.

...if you pushed a lot of buttons.

CHAPTER 7

The Business

You've had a small number of career-defining moments. These are the select few moments in time when the trajectory of your career changed instantly and drastically. I have two buckets of these: ones I expected and ones that completely blindsided me. While the surprise and subsequent scrambling involved in being blindsided are chock full of delicious adrenaline, I highly recommend the moments you can predict.

One such predictable moment is the first glimpse of the offer letter for your new gig. This is the culmination of hours of resumé tweakage,* a series of phone screen gymnastics (see Chapter 4, *The Sanity Check*), and two grueling days of in-person interviews (Chapter 6, *The Button*). This is a rare moment where you can answer the question, "How much does the world think I'm worth?"

Fact is, you should already know. You're the business.

---

* See "A Glimpse and a Hook," *http://www.randsinrepose.com/archives/2007/02/25/a_ glimpse_and_a_hook.html.*

You Are the Business

Before I break down the offer and offer negotiation process, I want to reset your head. I've no clue how badly you need your next job, and the degree of your need will affect your negotiating position, but here's some reality. You are the business. If you get an offer and take the gig, I think you should pour your heart into it, but I want you to remember that you're going to have another five to ten other jobs in your lifetime just like this next one. This means that for each moment you spend being pumped about the new gig, you'll have an equal and opposite moment at the end of the gig where you can't wait to get the hell out.

Amongst these five to ten jobs that you'll have there is one constant: you. You're the one who has to pay rent, ride the subway, buy a condo, get married, have some kids, and build your dream house. Your welfare is not your employer's first priority. It takes one layoff to figure that out.

You are the business, and the one consistent metric business is measured by is growth. A new gig represents one of the few moments in your career when you can directly and drastically change the trajectory of that growth.

Pre-Game

The offer negotiation process starts earlier than you think. Think back to that first phone screen. The recruiter was asking you warm-up feeler questions like, "Why do you want to leave your current gig?" and "What's your ideal job?", when they slide in a casual, "So, what are you making now?"

You stop. You sense that this seemingly off-the-cuff question is important. Your inner dialog goes something like, "I'm making 64K, buuuut, I'm going to round up to 70k because, well, I'm worth it."

Yes, you are, but it's a lie and it's not a very good lie. You also broke the number one rule in negotiation: be informed. You don't make 70K; you don't make 64K, either. You make closer to 90K.

I'll explain where this magical raise comes from as well as the other rules in a bit, but first let's understand how to answer the question "What are you making now?" Your answer: "I'm full-time and I'm making 64K. I'm getting a review in October, and my last raise was 4% plus a 2K bonus. I'd be walking away from 500 unvested options with a strike price currently 12 bucks under market, all of which are going to be totally vested in 12 months."

Expect an uncomfortable pause on the other end of the phone. That's the sound of the recruiter furiously scribbling "Candidate knows their compensation shit" on the top of your resume. What you're saying with this lengthy informed answer is complex, yet simple. You're saying, "There are many ways to be compensated. I'm aware of all of them and, when the time is right, I'm ready to negotiate."

How Am I Doing?

Whether you're expecting an offer letter imminently or not, I have an exercise for you. Let's figure out what you actually make.

Like frequent resumé updates, this career maintenance exercise is designed as a professional checkpoint that answers the simple question, "How am I doing?"

Let's start by breaking down how I calculated your hypothetical yearly compensation earlier:

- Base salary: 64K
- Benefits: 25% of 64K = 16K
- Bonus: 2K
- Stock: 6K
- Total: 88K

There are two fuzzy areas in this calculation. First, if you haven't worked for yourself, you probably haven't considered benefits as part of your compensation before. That 25% is an educated swag that most companies use to account for health and life insurance and 401k. You spend a lot of time ignoring this 25% because it involves things like retirement and health benefits and—duh— you're immortal. There will, however, be a time, probably sooner than you'd like, when you'll fully appreciate this portion of your compensation.

The other fuzzy area is stock. This example assumes you got 2,000 options when you were hired and these options vest at 25% each year. I'm making an optimistic wild-ass leap and saying that you're grossing 6K a year using the idea that you are making 12 dollars per option per year. Congrats.

Now, grab a piece of paper and use these rough calculations to figure out what you make. Don't sweat perfection. You just need to be close.

The Swag

Fast forward. You've just finished the interviews. Traditionally in high-tech, the recruiter is the last interview of the day and their job is to get inside your head and take your temperature regarding the gig. The guiding rule here is: the more they know you want the gig, the less they need to offer you.

And they haven't offered you a thing yet.

There's a time and place for negotiation, and it's not at the end of six hours of interviews on a Friday when you don't even know if you're getting an offer letter.

So you wait. You send off a set of references, sit in bed replaying interviews in your head, and send thank-you emails to the interview team. All professional karma-aligning activities, but what you really need to do is build your own offer letter. Just like you built your compensation, I want you to build your offer.

Base Salary

The business model everyone loves is a business built on recurring revenue streams. This is why you can get a good mobile phone for absolutely nothing. You're going to pay for that phone many times over with your monthly subscription of $39.95. You're still happy paying $40 a month because that feels like a deal, but carriers don't see $40; they see the $1,500 you're going to spend over that three-year contract.

Your base salary is your recurring revenue stream. It's your financial lifeblood, and we want to get it as high as possible because a 1% increase doesn't affect just this year; it affects every year after it.

For the swag, you need to figure out what you want to be paid in the new gig, and my first question is, "For someone doing exactly the same job as you, how much are they being paid?"

For a question that everyone wants to know the answer to, the Internet is surprisingly useless here. Salary survey sites litter the Web, but after several days of research, I couldn't find a job description on these sites that came remotely close to my current gig.

Go ahead and check out those salary info sites and confuse yourself a bit, but I've got two pieces of advice for your swag. First, talk to friends with similar jobs and figure out what they're making. Salaries vary greatly depending on the industry, geographic location, and specific company, but after you've talked with a few folks, you're going to have a rough feel for base salary,

Second, if you don't have a clue, take your current salary and add 10%—that's your salary swag.

Title

Titles, like salaries, vary from company to company, but what you're looking for in a new job is a sign that you are growing. Associate software engineer now? OK, drop that associate title from your business cards. Stuck as a software engineer for three years? I'd be looking for that senior prefix when I jumped ship.

Like salaries, the internal value of a title varies by company. A director at one company could easily be a vice president at another. Unfortunately, this is the type of cultural data you might not discover until you've made it into the building.

This makes your desired title more of a personal decision. Think of it like this: what title do you believe needs to be added to your resumé for this new job to demonstrate that you're actively growing in your career?

Sign-On Bonus

It's difficult to swag a sign-on bonus because this type of incentive is often used to augment weak parts of an offer, and you don't have an offer letter yet. If a recruiter knows you're keen on stock and that you'll be disappointed with a low-ball stock offer, they might dazzle you with a large sign-on bonus. Sign-on bonuses are one-time cash windfalls that may never show up again. For now, all you need to know is that they're often a band-aid, and the question will be: what are they hiding?

Stock

While representing the largest potential for unexpected financial gain, stock, stock options, and restricted stock units are also the hardest to swag. Rather than focusing on a hard number here, the question you should first ask is, "How much do I believe in this company?" If your answer is, "I like the company, but I don't see a lot of growth," then focus your negotiation energy on base salary. If your answer is, "I love this start-up; it's the next Google," then stock grants are clearly going to play a major role in your negotiation.

In terms of valuing the stock, whether we're talking about a start-up or an established public company, you're speculating. For a publicly traded company, take a look at the past five years. What's the average stock price? For the start-up, well, my rule of thumb for stock is no different than a venture capitalist's success rate. A VC's expectation is that 1 out of every 10 of their companies is going to hit it big and will cover the investment for the other nine. My expectation is that 1 out of every 10 jobs will result in a stock windfall. This should depress you.

Any value you place on stock or options is a wild-ass guess, but it's still an important piece of data. The value you put on stock is a measure of your belief in the company.

Negotiating Roles

You're done. Two phone screens, two rounds of interviews, reference checks, and a lot of waiting have paid off. Before we take a look at your offer, let's figure out who you're going to negotiate with.

In any reasonably sized organization, a strange switcheroo occurs the moment you start talking money. If you've reached the offer phase, it means you've likely professionally connected with your potential future manager. He's sending you follow-up emails and generally paving the way for a clean transition to you joining the team. The moment you start talking compensation, he'll vanish.

This far into the process, you're probably pretty close with the recruiter. You've probably had a couple of professional heart to heart conversations and might be under the impression they're representing your best interests.

Wrong.

The recruiter's role in negotiation is the bad guy and deliverer of bad news. Recruiters are measured not only by the number of hires they make, but how the compensation for those hires measures up to the rest of the company. Yes, recruiters want to make the hire, but they're also driving toward internal corporate hiring standards that may or may not be aligned with your ideal offer letter.

Your future manager's role is to make a great hire; the recruiter's job is to make that hire and negotiate it so that it's fiscally palatable to the rest of the organization.

You need to be prepared to dig in your heels and fight for what you want. This may be uncomfortable and might involve beating up the recruiter a bit, but here's the deal: once the offer is signed, you're likely never going to hear from this person again.

Offer Compromise

I've never received an initial offer that I've loved. There has always been an aspect that has disappointed me. The stock is off, the title is unexpected, or the base salary just isn't that close. I've always needed to construct a counteroffer, and I've done it using facts.

As a hiring manager who has been involved in many offer negotiations, the safest way to get me to ignore any counteroffer is to make it without data.

Recruiter: "The candidate wants a higher base."

Me: "Really? Why?"

Recruiter: "He just does."

Me: "Grrrrrrr."

Negotiation is a discussion of facts. Any counteroffer needs to be constructed with the impression that it's based on data. "I want a 10% raise because, based on my research, that represents the average salary for this gig elsewhere in the industry."

Sure, it's still a swag, but your swag demonstrates effort and research, and in an interruption-driven industry full of bright people racing around doing nothing in particular, I'm a fan of research. It demonstrates that you care about your career, and that's someone I want to work with.

As I don't know what your problem is with your particular offer, I can't advise what you need to say specifically, but here are some common frustrations and a plan of attack.

Lower base salary

If you're staying in your industry and you're staying at an established company, I can't see how a pay decrease is ever a positive sign. Yes, if you're moving to a start-up, you're going to trade salary for stock. You need to figure out if you're cool with that.

You wanted a 10% increase and they came back with 5%? Why? Sure, your 10% was a pie-in-the-sky swag, but how is the recruiter justifying this base salary? They're probably saying something about comparable salaries across the company and how you'd be making more than 90% of the people in your grade. That's a warm fuzzy, but I call bullshit: you're in the wrong grade.

But it's OK, here's a bonus

If the recruiter is pitching this bonus as a fix for your low base, I call bullshit again. A sign-on bonus, like a bonus plan, is a finicky thing that has a habit of vanishing when the sky falls. You can't count on them. There's nothing like an instant pile of money to distract you from the fact that, over the long term, you're bringing less money home.

Even better, here's a pile of stock

How do you value this stock? Sure, for the public company, you have a stock price, but you're not going to see a penny of that stock for a year. And what about that start-up? Well, did you know they have a stock price, too? They have to in order to give it some sort of value. This is how a start-up values itself when it goes to a VC. They say, "We've issued x amount of shares and we believe they're worth y per share. How much would you like?"

You can ask about this internal stock price. You can ask about how big their pool of outstanding fully diluted shares is, and that will give you some data about how much of the pie you're getting. But here's the rub: I assume start-up options have zero financial value, but this doesn't mean they have zero absolute value. Again, your measure of the stock is merely the measure of your faith.

And this is our final offer

If some part of the offer blows and there's absolutely no way to fix it, you have two options: walk away or find another way to ease the blow. If you can't walk away, have you thought about:

- Asking for additional vacation hours right out of the gate?

- Getting a start date a month later than they're asking? There's nothing like 30 days of work-free bliss to adjust your perspective.

- What their work-at-home policy is? Perhaps Fridays working at home will remove that bitter "I'm not getting a raise" taste in your mouth.

- Perhaps my favorite "This offer blows" move is to negotiate a six-month performance review. You know you rock, but they don't...yet.

Meh

My single worst gig was one where I got everything I wanted out of the offer letter, but in my exuberance for being highly valued, I totally forgot that my gut read on the gig was "meh." Ninety days later, I couldn't care less that I got a 15% raise and a sign-on bonus. I couldn't stand the mundanity of the daily work and I happily resigned a few months later, taking both a pay cut and returning my sign-on bonus for the opportunity to work at Netscape.

All of this compensation strategy ignores a simple question you need to be able to answer: "How much might I love this gig?" That's the question you need to be able to answer.

DECONSTRUCTING MANAGEMENT

The list of words that define management are revealing: direct, in charge, handle, control, and force. Looking at this list, it's not a surprise that the term "management" has a distasteful Orwellian air.

Whether you have direct reports or not, you're a manager. It might not say manager in your title, but I guarantee that on a daily basis, you are directing someone, you are handling a situation, and you are forcing your day in a certain direction.

This section of *Being Geek* is about management. Managing your manager, managing your peers, or just managing to get through the day, you are already in management.

CHAPTER 8

The Culture Chart

They played bridge every Wednesday at Netscape. In the middle of the cafeteria. Like clockwork.

The players were a collection of ex-SGI guys, and they worked for a variety of different groups at the company, but as I learned a few months later, this core group of men quietly defined the engineering culture of the company...with a bridge game.

Ninety Days

In the first 90 days of a new job, you're going to have a solid feel for the construction of your team. Who is who. Who does what. What they know. Who the freak is. Who the free electron is. In a start-up when there are only 12 of you, you're done. You know the initial people landscape because, from where you sit, you can see them all and you interact with all of them regularly. In a larger company, however, 90 days is only going to give you a brief glimpse of what you need to know about your coworkers, the company, and its culture.

Fortunately, in a large company, tools and documents have been created to help you traverse the culture and process and figure out where people fit. For example, what do you do when you get a random urgent mail from a coworker stranger? Even if the stranger takes the time to explain who they are and what they do, you still fire up the corporate directory with the simple question: "Who does this bozo work for?"

The corporate directory is the digital representation of a formerly very important document: the organization chart.

A quick glance at the org chart answers a lot of ego-based questions like:

- Which org does he work in? A cool one?

- How many direct reports does he have? More power?

- How close is he to the CEO? More influence?

As sources of information go, the org chart is essential, but it is an incomplete picture of your company, which brings us back to bridge at Netscape.

Bridge

If you looked up the four core bridge players on the org chart, you'd learn a bit. One engineering manager, another guy from some oddly named platform team, another guy who had a manager title but no direct reports, and the last guy who looked like a program manager.

My org chart assessment: Meh.

What I learned months later was that the folks sitting at that regular bridge game not only defined much of what became the Netscape browser, they also continued to define the engineering culture, or what I think of as a *culture chart*.

Unlike the org chart, you're not going to find the culture chart written down anywhere. It doesn't exist. The culture chart is an unwritten representation of the culture of your company, and understanding it answers big questions that you must know:

- What does this organization value?

- Who created this value system?

- Given this value system, who contributes high value?

- Who is most aware of how value is being created?

This is fuzzy philosophical mumbo jumbo, so let's bring it home. In your current job, right now, tell me what it's going take to get you a promotion.

"I need to work really hard."

OK, so you knew you need to work hard to get a promotion before you set foot in your current gig. My question is, what specific thing do you need to do in order to be promoted? I'd argue that for any engineer who is actively managing his career, it's essential to figure out the answer to this question as quickly as possible, and to do so you need to understand the culture.

Detecting Culture

If you are going to be promoted, you are going to succeed when you provide a certain group of people with things it thinks it needs. Now, your gut instinct is that this group of people is the management team, and that's a good org-chart-centric answer. The guy who signs the checks might be the guy who instigates promotions. The problem is it's your job to stay ahead of your manager. You're not going to get promoted by giving your manager what he wants; a promotion comes when you give him what he wants as well as what he does not expect but desperately needs.

It's unfair. This guy is tasked with your career development, and I am saying it's your job to tell him what he wants. You don't have to do this; you can take the reactive cues from your boss, but I derive intense professional satisfaction when I deliver the unexpectedly needed, and I discover the unexpected by first finding the culture.

To deduce the culture of a company, all you have to do is listen. Culture is an undercurrent of ideas that ties a group of people together. In order for it to exist, it must move from one individual to the next. This is done via the retelling of stories.

"Max was this nobody performance nerd, and three weeks before we were supposed to ship, he walked into the CEO's office with a single piece of paper with a single graph. He dropped the graph on the table, sat down, and said, 'No way we ship in three weeks. Six months. Maybe.' The CEO ignored the paper and told him, 'We lose three million dollars if we don't.' Max stood up, pointed at the chart, and said, 'We lose 10 if we do. We must not ship crap.'"

Whether this story is true or not is irrelevant. The story about how Max saved the company 10 million dollars by telling the CEO "no" is retold daily. In hallways. At the bar over beers. The story continually reinforces an important part of this company's culture.

We must not ship crap.

There isn't a corporate values statement on the planet that so brutally and beautifully defines the culture of a company.

There are other stories that you're going to hear over and over again, and inside each of these stories are the real corporate values. Each one, while designed to be entertaining, teaches a lesson about what this particular company values, and learning how to deliver that value is how you're going to get promoted.

There's a chance you're not going to find these stories. My hope is that you're in a company where engineering is valued and, as such, has an influence on the culture of your company. If it's been six months, you've been actively looking, and no one has told you a great story about how engineering shaped the fortunes of your company, there's a chance that engineering doesn't have a seat at the culture table in your company. My question is then, "How are you going to succeed, how are you going to be promoted, where engineering isn't an influential part of the culture?"

Culture Definers

After you have a healthy collection of stories, you're going to have a good idea about some of the culture, but you're still missing essential data for your culture chart. See, the folks who tell the stories about culture usually aren't the folks who created them.

Stories are told, but first they are born.

The people who are responsible for defining the culture are not deliberately doing so. They do not wake up in the morning and decide, "Today is the day I will steer the culture of the company to value quality design."

They just do it. The individuals who have the biggest impact on the culture and company aren't doing it for any other reason than they believe it is right thing to do, and if you want to grow in this particular company it's a good idea to at least know who they are and where they sit. You need to pay attention to this core group of engineers because as they do, so will the company.

Game Over

Your company is networked in more ways than you can possibly imagine. Just because you've reverse engineered the development culture in your organization doesn't mean you've got a complete map of the overall culture. There are endless connections tugging any decent-sized group of people in multiple directions at once. There's the been-here-forever network, the I-survived-the-layoff people, and the untouchable did-something-great-once crew.

Culture assessment is an information game, and it's never over. Your career depends on your ability to continually situate yourself in such as a way that, as quickly as possible, you can assess subtle changes in the culture of your company.

I wasn't concerned when Netscape started losing market share to Microsoft. I didn't sweat it when the stock price stalled. The reason I started thinking about my next gig was, months before either of these two events occurred, one of the lunchtime bridge team left.

The game stopped. The small group of four no longer spent a long lunch quietly, unknowingly defining the culture of the company, and everyone who was watching noticed.

They noticed when one of those who had humbly done the work that defined the company no longer believed enough to stay.

CHAPTER 9

Managing Managers

Everyone knew something was up. The executive staff was scarce. Meetings weren't being canceled; they were being ignored. It smelled like a re-org, but the start-up was doing OK. We'd closed another round of funding. The adjectives in the all-hands were positive, so where were the execs?

Finally. A hastily scheduled meeting with executives and senior managers.

"We're letting the VP of Engineering go."

My boss? Tony? He's, like, good. I...don't understand.

In hindsight, the disconnect between my VP and the rest of the executives was never clearly explained, but understanding boardroom shenanigans isn't the point of this chapter. The two brief lessons that have nothing to do with this chapter are: first, just because you like your boss doesn't mean he's playing nice with others, and second, expect surprises.

A solid replacement was quickly found. As new bosses go, Gimley was an easy transition. The lights were on. He soon scheduled a meeting with me and made it clear it was my meeting by letting me vent for a solid 20 minutes. "Get it out of your system, Rands, I'm here to listen."

It wasn't a meeting to resolve anything; it was a rough sketch of the playing field in the company. A high-level getting-to-know-you. Gimley didn't say much, he nodded a lot, but at the end he had his marching orders ready. There was only one, and I was initially disappointed with its simplicity.

"Rands, I want no surprises."

It was a deceptively simple request, but the more I thought about it, it was an empowering one. *Rands, I'm trusting you to know when to keep me in the loop.*

A Management Assessment

The one thing I know about your manager is that he is different than you. There's a book to be written about all of these differences, but for this chapter, I want to focus on how you're going to communicate with your manager because until you figure that out, you're not even going to know how different you are.

Whether you've just inherited a new manager or are in year three of this professional relationship, the following set of questions will give you insight into how your manager communicates, as well as his appetite for information.

Is There a 1:1?

It pains me to write this, but my first question about your boss is this: is he taking the time to talk with you in a private setting? A 1:1 is a frequent, regularly scheduled meeting between you and your boss, and if it's not happening, I, uh, don't really know where to start.

A 1:1 is a time for the person who is responsible for your professional well-being to check in and see how it's going. Yes, a 1:1 is a time for team and project status, too, but I'm certain that information is bouncing around elsewhere in the company. A 1:1 should, on a regular basis, involve a frank discussion of how you are doing professionally.

There are large and successful companies like Google that have stunningly large employee to manager ratios, which means there is no practical way for regular 1:1s to occur. My question is, "How are these employees growing?" Yes, there's a world of experience to be had writing your code, arguing with Felix the QA guy, and working 27 hours straight to hit a deadline, but there's free and hopefully painless valuable experience sitting in your boss's brain right this very second.

One of the hats your boss should wear is that of mentor. He's likely seen more than you, which means there's a high likelihood that you can bring any random question, idea, or disaster to his desk and he can comment...hopefully valuably.

The absence of a 1:1 is the absence of mentorship, and that means you need to gather your experience in the trenches. And while there is nothing to replace "real-world experience," I'm wondering what the value add of your boss is. If he's not taking the time to pass on what he's learned, isn't he just a project manager?

If you don't have a 1:1, ask for one. Maybe it's not every week, maybe it's once a month, but it's an essential time to reflect on your job and career and to plan.

Is a Staff Meeting a Casual or Structured Affair?

Your boss's appetite for information can be discerned by how he runs his staff meeting. By understanding how he constructs and runs this one meeting, you can get a good idea of how he wants his information presented. I have a spectrum that I use to assess engineers that also applies to managers. They're either *organic* or *mechanic*, and I'll describe each briefly.

An organic manager uses the word "feel." A lot. He understands the personality makeup of his team because, of course, he has 1:1s. He wants to know how you feel because he understands that the messy parts of being a human very much affect his team and his projects.

The mechanic manager understands the world through structure. Like any typical geek, his interaction with the world follows the mental flowchart of "how things work." The mechanic manager values predictability, consistency, and facts.

With that brief description, let's see how these personalities define a staff meeting:

- Is there an agenda? *Mechanic.*

- Is it followed? *Mechanic.*

- Is random debate encouraged? *Organic.*

- Can debate occur without involving the manager? *Organic.*

- Is debate limited to a specific time? *Mechanic.*

- Is the time allotted for the meeting always filled? *Mechanic.*

- Can it go over? *Organic.*

- Does it always go over? *Organic.*

- Is it a fun meeting? *Organic.*

Understanding whether your boss is organic or mechanic is directional, not definitive, data. I'm organic with mechanic tendencies. Your boss is also a mix of both, and different aspects of his personality are going to manifest depending on different scenarios. My last boss was intensely organic until senior management started to lean on him, and then he went completely mechanic.

Your job if you want to communicate with your boss is to figure out his particular mix and how he uses it.

You don't really need to worry about adapting to or shaping your communication style for a primarily organic manager, because he's willing to adapt to whoever you are and how you communicate. The organic gets people and, as such, will deftly manage the conversation towards the information they need.

Mechanics need structure. Mechanics need predictability. I had a manager who was so mechanic that if I changed the order of my 1:1 updates, he became visibly flustered. "We talk about people before products, right?" You don't wing it with mechanics. You tell them what to expect, deliver, and then confirm the delivery.

Contrasting communication styles are a hindrance to the ability to effectively communicate. Mechanics think organics are frenetic babblers. Organics think mechanics are passionless automatons. We're both wrong.

If you happen to be on the other side of the communication chasm with your boss, remember that it's just as much his job to build the bridge as it is yours.

Are There Status Reports?

Over my career, I've gone back and forth on the value of status reports. The mechanic manager in me loves the weekly structured rhythm of ascertaining and communicating your week. My organic tendencies remind me that if you're relying on a status report to understand what's going on in your organization, you're probably hiding in your office too much.

The presence of status reports is a sign of a mechanical manager, and it might not be your boss, it might be his boss, but that's not the interesting data. Let's assume it is your boss who is asking for status reports. What do you learn?

My impression is that the presence of status reports is an indication that your boss doesn't trust the flow of information in your organization. I'm not talking about paranoia; I'm talking about unfulfilled information acquisition needs. Your boss sees the status reports as a means of filling a perceived information vacuum.

The question you need to answer is: why is he seeing a vacuum? Maybe he is intensely mechanic and doesn't have the social skills to gather the data in the hallway. Maybe status reports are just the way he's always done it, or perhaps he'd prefer more data in your 1:1?

If status reports are a corporate mandate from on high or just part of the culture, you're likely stuck with them, and I say embrace it. A good status report doesn't read like a passive-aggressive, boring bulleted list. It's your chance to write what happened this week, why it matters, and what's next.

If the status report is just being requested by your boss for no valuable purpose, your job is to kill it, and you do that by determining what communication gap he's trying to fill.

- He's mechanical and doesn't like face-to-face communication. OK, how about 1:1 with a well-structured agenda sent in advance, strictly adhered to, with the meeting completed on time? Yeah, it's not really a 1:1, but it's a start, and over time, maybe he'll loosen up.

- He has too many direct reports and doesn't have time. Great, how about adapting staff meetings to have aspects of a good 1:1?

I'm heavily pushing direct human-to-human communication because while status reports might be structured and reliable, nothing compares to the understanding you gather when you look someone in the eye.

What Meetings Does He Schedule?

Another good way to assess your boss's information appetite is to look at the meetings he schedules outside of 1:1s and staff. I'm not talking about the meetings he attends, I'm talking about the ones he takes the time to schedule either on a regular basis or as one-offs. These are not the meetings he has to attend; these are the ones he *wants* to attend.

There are two classes of meetings you'll find:

Technical

> The technical deep dive. This is a meeting where your boss wants to go deep on the technology. This isn't a review of already-made technical decisions; this is where the decisions are debated and then made. Technical meetings scheduled and run by your boss are his way of reminding himself that he, too, was once an engineer.

Alignment

> Project meetings, status meetings, all-hands; the alignment meetings have a million different names, but they all serve the same purpose. They answer the question, "Are you and I on the same page?" These meetings are usually the domain of project and product managers who have their fingers on the cross-functional pulse of a project, so the question is, "Why is your boss scheduling an alignment meeting?" Who isn't on the right page?

In your scheduling assessment of your boss, you're less interested in a single meeting than in the meeting aggregate over time. You need to step back and look at two weeks of boss-scheduled meetings. Lots of technical meetings? He still thinks he's an engineer. Alignment meetings everywhere? Your boss is attempting to reconcile differing opinions somewhere in the building.

Conventional wisdom is that when you become a manager, you're going to forego the technical aspects of your career. Let those closest to the bits make the hard decisions. But I think there's a balance to be struck here. A totally technical manager won't see the larger project landscape and will stumble when tricky people-based issues get in the way, whereas a project-focused manager has likely forgotten the basic rules that motivate engineers.

In your meeting assessment of your boss, like organics and mechanics, you're looking to see where they land on the technical/alignment spectrum because you want to know what they need to hear. Are you bringing in the technical minutiae or the project details?

How Often Is His Hand in the Cookie Jar?

If everything is working, your boss can get everything he needs to know from you, his boss, or his peers. However, "everything working" is rarely the case in companies. Information moves at different speeds in the company based on a dizzying number of factors that we'll talk about in the next chapter. And there will be times that your boss will, inexplicably, put his hand in the cookie jar.

The cookie jar is a metaphoric representation of when your boss crosses an organization boundary that he shouldn't. The classic cookie jar move is when a senior manager bypasses one of his direct reports to talk to one of their direct reports. There are perfectly acceptable reasons for this manager to make this request, but there are equally many ways this can screw up team communication and morale.

I'll explain. Senior manager Frank has a manager named Bob who has a bevy of employees, one of whom is named Alex. One day Frank is frustrated that a bug hasn't been closed in Bob's group, and Bob is nowhere to be seen—virtually or otherwise. In his frustration, Frank goes straight to Alex, who owns the bug, and asks what's up. Alex happens to be all over this bug and has proven it's a user error and is happy he's able to instantly defuse Frank's frustration. Everyone's happy, right?

In isolation this is fine, this is a team of people communicating, but now Frank knows he can get instant bug gratification from Alex, and Alex knows he did a solid for the big boss. My question is: where the hell is Bob?

Maniacal rules regarding the chain of command are the domain of the military and don't belong in software development, but the organizational chart, and the manager and employee relationships, exist for a reason. These relationships define who is accountable for what. The precedent that is unintentionally set by a cookie jar violation is that it isolates people who should be in the know.

A cookie jar violation can occur in any direction on the organization chart. It is the act of deliberately circumventing individuals from the flow of information and decisions, and if your boss is a cookie jar violator, he's either not getting the information he expects or he doesn't understand how teams of people communicate.

The Essential Elements

It's going down. Third floor of headquarters. You're sitting in a cross-functional meeting where a VP stands up and says something innocuous. It's designed to be a throwaway line, but when you hear it, you see the entire game board. You see him making a move to grab one of your boss's teams and the people who work on it. Oh yeah, it's going down.

With this information in hand, my question is, "How are you going to present this essential, time sensitive, and contentious information to your boss?" Yes, I'm assuming you like your boss and want to keep him in the loop. How are you going to shape the information just right for efficient transfer? The organic manager wants the impassioned plea, "He's stealing your team!" as quickly as possible. The mechanic wants the data, delivered deliberately and constructively, at the appropriate time.

The shaping doesn't stop there. What aren't you going to say? Where are you going to add your opinion? It's an honorable instinct to want to share every piece of information with your boss, but if that's your strategy, what exactly are you doing other than moving data from Point A to Point B? I can do that with IM, Twitter, or two cans and a string.

The trick is to boil the story down to its essential elements, insert your opinion if appropriate, and deliver the message in a way appropriate to your boss's appetite. You can skip details. Trust me, he's heard this story before. Not exactly the same story, but that's why he's going to ask lots of questions. He's using his experience to figure out which version of the story you're telling.

The Loop

Gimley was a declared organic with passive-aggressive mechanic tendencies. This meant that he held regular, productive 1:1s, he worked the hallway, and he played well with a diverse set of personalities. When he was stressed, when he was cornered, or when he was pissed, he turned into a raging mechanic diving deep on every detail, volunteering to help with the code, and generally regressing back into an engineer.

He made his initial request of "No surprises" because he was aware of his personality quirks. He knew that when the sky fell, he was not on his game, so he instructed his directs, "No surprises," which implied, "You're not going to like what you get if I end up surprised."

CHAPTER 10

The Issue with the Doof

We wanted the VP fired.

The architect, the Director of Product, and I wanted him out. It was a start-up, and he was absent when we were grinding away on weekends. When he was in the building, his ideas felt reactionary and knee-jerk—he lacked vision. Most importantly, during a time when we were pouring our souls into the start-up, he did not inspire.

The three of us stood at the whiteboard in the boardroom for three nights enumerating our reasoning, documenting our experiences, and cross-checking our evidence. After constructing our arguments, we finally scheduled a meeting with the CEO.

"What's up, guys?"

Our pitch was clean. Each of us had a well-defined role in describing, relative to our jobs, how the VP was a zero. Twenty solid minutes of incontrovertible professional negligence. Solid and sold. When we finished, the air was filled with potential.

"So?" said the CEO.

So? we silently thought.

"So, what's your proposal?"

Proposal? Aren't you the boss? Don't you decide what....

"It's clear you're justifiably upset, but what are you going to do about it?"

What are we going to do about? What are you going to do about it? You're the boss.

On Experience

In order to appreciate this chapter, you need to make a leap—you need to believe that your boss's experience is valuable. You need to believe and accept that the fact he's been doing this 10 years longer than you means his opinion is more informed. His decisions are based on something more than gut feel and delusions of grandeur.

We're knowledge workers, which is an awkwardly lame way of stating that we don't actually build physical things with our hands. We build nonphysical things with our minds. We create interesting arrangements of ones and zeros in the confines of our caves, coalescing our ideas into things that are, hopefully, useful enough that someone else is willing to pay for them.

There are no sets of physical tools we need to collect and master to make our jobs easier. Our tool sheds are empty. Our skill is entirely dependent on the kung fu of our minds. Relative to your career, the only thing your boss has to give you is his experience, and sometimes you need to ask for it.

I get issues with authority. I get how power corrupts otherwise bright people and gives managers a suspicious air. I know you want to figure it out on your own, but there are times when it is simply more efficient to go your boss, lay out the problem, and let him weigh in. You're not going to get the educational satisfaction of knocking together the solution yourself, but you are going to be living the #1 rule of teamwork: together we can do more than separately. Together we scale.

The word "scale" sounds like managementese. It's an executive way to say, "I want better, more, and faster." While managerial definitions normally give me the shakes with their punchy venality, this definition of scale works for me.

Whether your gig is as an individual or manager, given any professionally tricky situation, your job is to decide what decisions you can handle and when you're going to need help from someone with more experience.

There are risks and rewards at both ends of the spectrum. If you're asking for help all the time, my question is: what value are you adding? If you're never asking for help, it statistically means you're screwing up unnecessarily by ignoring the experience of those around you who've probably already efficiently solved this particular problem.

When do you choose to manage up? Let's define that.

Up

At each level of the org chart, each manager is responsible for the folks below them. I mean it. The CEO is responsible for the care and feeding of each and every person in the organization. This doesn't mean that he's going to understand the minutiae of you; it means he's responsible for you and your well-being, and he can be fired for your screw-up.

How, in an organization of 1,000 people, does he accomplish this? Well, he has minions. He has his staff, who have their staff, and so on. This is the organization chart, and while HR is going to tell you the org is held together with reporting relationships, it's actually the flow of information that holds the org together.

The traditional view of the way information moves around an org chart is that information, decisions, and strategy are being designed by those with more experience who are further up the org chart, and that information slowly makes its way down the chart. It's called trickle down. However, an equally large and important amount of information moves up the chart, and that's what's happening when you're managing up.

An org chart only scratches the surface in describing how work gets done in a company. I guarantee your org chart is broken in some fascinating way, but figuring that out is another chapter. Your job is to figure out what information your boss needs and when—not only to keep him the loop, but also to help make your work life easier.

Partial Information

Let's start with the Issue. We're not going to be too specific regarding the Issue. All we're going to say about it is that it's stopping you in your tracks. It's unique, unfamiliar, and your first thought is, "I...don't quite know what to do with this."

Good. Figuring out the unknown is the best way to learn. The question is: are you going to pull in the boss to handle the Issue?

The simplest rule to remember about deciding whether to involve your boss is that, if you ask, he will answer. There is no half-engaging your boss when it comes to his opinion. The moment you say, "We might have an issue here," there's officially an Issue.

I'm not suggesting that your boss isn't informed and well intentioned, but he is living in a constant state of low-grade fear induced by being partially informed. This state began the moment he decided to no longer be an engineer and to jump into management. See, he believes what you believe, that the only truth is the code, but he doesn't code much anymore, so he's developed a semi-irrational fear—*what's going on out there that I don't know and is it going to screw me?*

The irony here is that while your boss is expecting you to do your job and handle all the issues in your area, he's also unreasonably expecting you to keep him in the loop on everything. You can't. You won't. You're getting paid big bucks to do exactly the opposite. Things are going smoothly when you're efficiently and independently handling the issues in your team and your boss doesn't hear a damned thing except the efficient silence of the productive.

Some issues need to be pushed up, though, and here's the checklist I walk through as I size up the Issue and determine whether I'm going to engage the boss.

Is it your Issue?

Is this Issue your responsibility to handle? Would an external, informed stranger look at this Issue and say it's yours? If it's your Issue, you must handle it. The Issue not being obviously yours isn't necessarily a reason not to handle it. Handling an issue outside of your area of expertise or responsibility can have a significant political upside, but also has equal risk. Successfully resolving an external Issue makes you a hero; failure leaves everyone asking, "What the hell was he doing there in the first place?"

Can I handle it?

What's your gut feel on the Issue? Can you handle it? Have you seen it before? Is it similar to other Issues? Do you feel like you have a chance to handle it *sans* management intervention? OK, keep reading.

What's the magnitude of the Issue?

How big a deal is this Issue? There's an important threshold that, when crossed, requires immediate boss notification. Some of the obvious ones are any issues involving HR or lawyers, sticky personnel matters, or extremely juicy gossip that might be related to your team. No matter whether or not you think you can handle the Issue, confirmed big deals need to be pushed up to your boss as soon as possible.

Is this Issue at all related to one of your manager's hot buttons?

What are the three areas your boss is always interested in? Performance, scale, and anything related to that manager he hates in that other group, right? OK, what are his high-octane pet peeves? What are the topics that when they land on his desk, he loses it? Is the issue at all associated with areas your boss is always interested in? Unless there is a compelling reason to keep him in the dark, you pull the trigger on engaging him. Failure to at least give the boss a heads up on issues related to hot-button topics is a sure way to incur his micro-managerial wrath.

What's the upside of solo success here?

What happens if you nail this Issue *sans* management intervention? Experience, trust, credibility—these are all valuable aspects of what you might get when you solo an Issue without your boss. Confirmed success can even cover for the sketchier aspects of handling the Issue. Not your direct responsibility? *Who cares, it's fixed!* Didn't give the boss a heads up on a hot-button topic? *No problem, I knew you could do it, but maybe next time you'll tell me what's going on?*

What's the downside of the solo screw-up?

Conversely, can you estimate the damage if you screw this up? Is your boss going to trust you less? Is he going to fire you? Are there additional people who get pulled in if you blow it? Is unsuccessfully resolving the Issue just going to create more Issues? If this isn't an Issue you've handled before, know that theorizing about the downside or the upside is tricky business. Can you effectively predict what is going to happen?

Will you learn?

This is one question that I can answer for you right now. If you're sitting there carefully considering the Issue, if you're walking through this list of questions and trying to decide whether to go it alone or not, I guarantee you're going to learn something. Success or failure, choosing to tackle this Issue is going to give you knowledge and experience.

While the goal is a job where you can handle all the issues without help, remember the leap—we're assuming that your boss has something to add. His experience can help you crack the issues faster because he's seen them before. This alone is a reason to occasionally lean on your boss, but there's one more reason.

Beware the Doof

Right, let's pitch the leap and admit the truth: there are useless managers. They vary by uselessness and ineptitude, but I want to describe one in particular: the Doof.

The Doof used to be healthily paranoid. He used to care about what he did not know, but he gave up. Maybe he had enough success and began to believe he could do it all in his sleep. Maybe he began to believe that he'd seen it all and lazily thought there were no more surprises. Whatever the reason, he became the Doof.

Because he believes he's figured it all out, the Doof sits back and just lets it all happen. The issues show up on his desk, and he quickly maps them into prior experience, throws down brief judgment, and hands them back to you without actually helping at all.

The frustrating thing about the Doof is that he sounds like he knows what he's talking about. When you bring him the Issue, he nods knowingly, he asks insightful questions that give you the impression he knows what to do, and you leave the meeting thinking, "Alright, I did my job. I managed up."

A week passes, you're back in your 1:1 and you bring up the Issue again, and you have precisely the same feel-good conversation you had a week ago.

Whatinthewhatwhat?

You've been doofed.

You manage up for two reasons: to communicate and to ask for help. Managing up to the Doof accomplishes neither, and having worked for a bunch of doofs in my career, I believe it's partially my fault.

Yes, a good manager knows when it's time to swoop in and help. Yes, it's your manager's job to have his finger on the pulse of the group and be thinking several steps ahead, but they miss stuff. Important stuff. The upside of getting a team of people to work together is that, collectively, we error-correct for each other. Part of your job is to catch the things your boss and your team miss, and part of your job is to ask for help with the things you miss.

The most important part of managing up isn't that you've chosen to manage up; it's that you insist on help. The Doof is created by extensive experience conjuring the illusion that the game has been won and the puzzle has been solved. When you decide to bring your boss in on the Issue, it is your responsibility to see past their management spin and seek out what I hope is their valuable experience. If you don't, if you let him allow you to believe his clever words are action, you're contributing to the creation of the Doof.

Everything

I love that I work in an industry where everyone believes they can do everything.

While I understand wanting to be in a world where you have the experience, intelligence, and chutzpah to make all the decisions yourself, you're never, ever going to get there. While experience and choosing to tackle issues is going to help you get better at making decisions, you're also going to get better at knowing when you shouldn't. Yes, the goal over your career is to make the transition from asking for help to giving it, but you're always going to need help.

Yes, the Issue was that the VP we wanted to fire was a Doof. Yes, the CEO's question, "What are you going to do about it?" is the right thing to ask a senior management team: *don't bring me a problem, bring me a plan*. The problem was, we needed specific help that only the CEO could provide.

We'd walked through all the risk assessment questions before we'd talked with the CEO. We knew we had a problem with our manager. We knew it was an issue of magnitude, and we knew there was significant upside if we could instigate a change. But we could only describe the problem; we could not execute the change.

I remember this story because I remember the disappointment when we walked out of the CEO's office feeling like we'd failed. We'd failed to define the issue, but more so, we'd failed to bring a solution into the room. Years of hindsight have altered this disappointment and turned it to frustration because I know our failure to get the CEO to act was our first step into letting him turn into the Doof.

The Leaper

On my short list of professional competitive differentiators, I would list my Inbox strategy. I have a zero-tolerance policy for unread mails. Zero. Any mail, however big or small, that lands in my Inbox is instantly read. There is an industrial-strength set of mail filters that move mailing list noise out of the way, and yes, that means I ignore a good portion of my incoming mail, but most mail addressed directly to me is consistently and expediently read.

There are other Inbox strategies I employ to figure out when and how I respond, too, but I admit the combination of these strategies is not foolproof. I read mails and never respond, despite having good intentions to do so. I passive-aggressively ignore mails I just don't want to answer, and sometimes I just forget to respond. I have a carefully constructed excuse when I'm called on these mail transgressions. It's a standard preface in all emails and phone conversations where there needs to be an acknowledgment of neglect and it's...

"Sorry, I've been swamped...."

This isn't a lie; it's an excuse.

Now, there is a bit of pride in that I have a life where I'm scrambling. Yes, I'm proud that I'm busy. I'm a happy member of the busy club because I've been to the bored club meetings and, well, they're boring.

The pride vanishes in the guilt that there was neglect. I forget to respond, I screwed up in some manner, and here I am with my standard disclaimer: "swamped." The guilt is the emotion that lingers. I just checked my Sent box of 20,483 messages and found the word swamped 712 times…in the last year. How unoriginal and pathetic.

And then I remember the worst part. It's pathetic because when I use the excuse that I'm swamped, I'm telling you absolutely nothing.

On Excuses

I had a boss—we'll call him the Leaper for reasons you'll understand in a moment. The Leaper was a bright guy, a worthy mentor, politically savvy, and generally a person who would look out for his team. The Leaper had a lot of responsibility as VP, so his management strategy was to randomly sample his teams looking for—you guessed it—places to leap.

The Leaper's skill lay in his ability to detect bullshit. Being bright, a former engineer, and familiar with the problem space, he could tell when he was being spun. He knew when he was hearing less than the truth. Generally he was understanding when he sampled ambiguity, but there was one sure way to get him to leap: answer a question with an excuse.

The Leaper attacked excuses as a personal affront. He wouldn't let anyone leave the room until it was painfully clear that the excuse card had been played, that it was unacceptable, and that the proper steps were taken to make sure it would never happen again.

For first-time excusers, it was a painful perspective adjustment. See, when the Leaper asked a question that the answerer wasn't comfortable answering, they did what I did when I ignored a mail: they made an excuse. It's a knee-jerk reaction with seemingly little consequence, but that's not what the Leaper saw. He saw the lame diffusion of blame and a weak defense.

An excuse is an abdication of responsibility. There are no healthy excuses. I'll explain.

On Delivery

"But Rands, it's really Antonio's fault! He owns the deliverable, he missed the date, it's his fuckup." Calm down. You're arguing about the wrong part of the excuse.

An excuse has two parts: the content and the delivery. Your Antonio content may be spot on, but the reason The Leaper is going to leap on you is your delivery. It sounds like you're redirecting, it sounds like you're spinning. You're delivering the facts, but what's being heard is the emotion. OK, maybe it is Antonio's fault, but why'd he miss the date? Do you know? No, you're stuck on the fact he screwed up and by association screwed up you, and that's what you're conveying and that's what is being heard.

Yes, with confidence, you can deliver weak content and not trigger a leap, but this only delays the inevitable. Your chutzpah may disguise the content, but since your content is weak and you don't actually know what you're talking about, you're eventually going to take the reputation hit...three times. First, when the crap content is discovered. Second, when everyone realizes you were pitching your facts on false confidence. Third, every time in the future when the same people will be listening to you and wondering, "Does he actually know what he's talking about?"

Well done there.

The irony is thick. In order to avoid looking like you didn't know what you were talking about, you opened your mouth and only added to the confusion. If you told the Leaper, "I don't know, but I will know tomorrow," he'd be cool.

Life in a big or small company is an information game where you are judged by the amount, accuracy, and timeliness of your information. This game becomes more complex as you leave the individual contributor role for management, but even as an individual, you are expected to be aware of your surroundings and honestly able to describe them to others.

I know that feeling when someone in authority spends 30 seconds looking at something you've been working on for six months and immediately finds a painfully obvious flaw. The mental conversation starts with, "There's no way he could…" and it finishes with, "Holy crap, how could I miss that?" It's disorienting, and when the question is asked of you, "Why didn't you think of that?" I know where the excuse comes from. It's alarmed spin, it's poor marketing, it's the uncomfortable admission of guilt.

So, what are you going to do? Clearly, there's a reputation hit here, so what's the right move?

Remember it is likely an excuse that got you here in the first place. Someone, somewhere abdicated responsibility for an important part of your product, and that's why everyone is staring at each dumbly at this conference table. Take a small amount of time to say something real. Honest, clear, and brief. Sure, these are executives and they might be pissed, but the last thing to do in that scenario is to add fuel to the fire by actively demonstrating your discomfort.

There are executives who like to see you squirm, who revel in the discovery of flaws. While they might be right, this does not give them the right to be cruel. I'm talking about that deliberate dead silence after the flaw has been exposed, and everyone sees it now and everyone is wondering, "How could we miss that?" In that moment, someone is expected to say something. This is your opportunity to say something of value.

Say Something Real

Working for the Leaper for years, I can now sense the moment before I'm about to employ an excuse. I can feel the chain of events that are about to occur as I construct my weak redirection of responsibility. I hear what I'm about to say in my head—*It's not my fault*—and then I stop.

I want you think of the very last conversation you had, and I want you to think of one thing that you did not say. Maybe you were in a hurry and you blew off someone's question. Maybe you were in a great conversation. Perhaps you were talking to your dad. What is the topic you should have brought up? What is the small thing you could have said to make that conversation more valuable?

This is everything that crosses my mind after I stop with the excuse. I think about all the throw-away phrases I use where I could have actually said something valuable. I once wrote, "Every time you say blah blah blah, a creative writing teacher dies," and I meant it. Each time you open your mouth, you have an opportunity to build something. That's the perspective you want during the uncomfortable dead silence, not the victim-based emotion of excuse.

I'm in a hurry, but being in a hurry isn't an excuse for not taking a small amount of time to say something real.

CHAPTER 12

The Enemy

The $150,000 mistake, the discovery of critical and unfixable architectural flaw three weeks before shipping, and the Really Bad Hire (aka, we're being sued).

These are not screwups,* these are fuckups, and they aren't about to happen—they're here. They're guaranteed. When you discover them, the air leaves your lungs, the back of your head tingles, and there's an odd metallic taste in your mouth. Your mind goes blank except for the crisp mental picture that is a fuckup of your own making.

Initial personal discovery is shocking, but what I want to examine is secondary discovery. This is when your boss learns of the fuckup, and you shouldn't be worried whether there's an odd metallic taste in his mouth; you should worry about who he's about to turn into.

Management Transformations

Ideally, your boss is the levelheaded type, and he'll manage your fuckup cleanly and easily using his years of experience, but fuckups knock people off their game and out of their comfort zone.

---

* _http://www.randsinrepose.com/archives/2004/07/10/what_to_do_when_youre_screwed.html_

Fuckups create unusual stress, and stress can mutate normally sane people into unrecognizable caricatures of themselves. Let's talk about some of them.

The Interrogator

The Interrogator's approach is an endless stream of questions: "When did the customer first call?" "Who triaged the bug first?" "What were the results?" "How did we proceed from there?" It goes on and on.

What's annoying about the Interrogator is that he actually only wants to ask one question—THE question—but he's putting you through the paces to build a sense of context. This stream of questions will demonstrate the relevance of the one question. The one question is the only question that matters, and when it shows up, it's time to start the meeting.

While you're being grilled, I want you to remember this: the Interrogator is blowing off steam while asking the endless list of questions. This process of question and answer is laborious, but with each piece of data you convey, you have an opportunity to paint a more detailed picture of your fuckup and increase the chance he can help.

There are Interrogators who don't actually have one question that they're driving toward, and these managers need managing. If you're 27 questions into your 1:1 with no clear direction and a total lack of context, it's time to dig in your heels and ask, "Hey, Boss, what are you really trying to figure out here? Are you just pissed, or are we trying to make progress?"

The Prioritizer

Meetings with the Prioritizer start with a complete inventory of the to-do list for your team. He wants to know everything that you're planning to do to resolve the fuckup, and if this list doesn't exist or isn't complete, you might as well reschedule the meeting, because there is no other way to satisfy the Prioritizer.

With that list in hand, the Prioritizer will now put you through the agonizing process of prioritizing every single task on the list. If he's in a really bad mood, he's going to want to talk through your mental process of prioritization for each task. What he's doing is sniffing for a lack of knowledge on any of these tasks, and if he finds it, you're screwed because any lack of knowledge or confidence this close to the fuckup erodes his confidence that you've actually got a plan.

Unlike the Interrogator, there is no obvious point where you're going to understand, "Oh, this is what he wants to know. This is the plan." He wants to know everything. Your fuckup has him freaked out, and his reaction to this is to gather as much data as possible. Feels like micromanagement, right? It is. More on this in a moment.

The Randomizer

The insane version of the Prioritizer is the Randomizer. This is the manager who is going to swoop into the situation with good intentions, but he's mostly going to randomize the team with his endless good intentions.

The warning signs of the Randomizer are easy to recognize: his marching orders to address the fuckup change every couple of hours. You might not initially see this, because the Randomizer is the boss. His sense of passion and urgency is intoxicating because everyone wants to get to the other side of the fuckup. They want to succeed. After the third drastic change to the plan of action, the team is going to start scratching their heads and thinking, "*How is running around bumping into shit actually helping us?*"

Your job as the minion of the Randomizer is to get back into the 1:1, close the door, and see if you can summon the Prioritizer. Your boss should be your strategic muse, not your tactical nightmare.

The Illuminator

The Illuminator is on the same mission as everyone we've already talked about, but he's subtle about it. You may not even know the Illuminator is in the room when you show up for your 1:1. I love the Illuminator. I love being the Illuminator.

See, you fucked up. The Illuminator isn't going to interrogate or prioritize you for an hour; he is elegantly, calmly going to get you to realize the magnitude of the fuckup and also get you to suggest a reasonable course of action. In fact, you'll be proud of yourself halfway through the meeting when you slap your forehead and say, "*Wow, this what happened and this is what we should do!*"

The transcendent Illuminator experience is when you don't realize the Illuminator is gently mentally course-correcting you and providing silent guidance. The cherry on top is, even if you do see this management manipulation, you realize, "Oh, he's trying to help."

The Enemy

On the opposite side of the spectrum of the Illuminator is the Enemy.

Like the Illuminator, the Enemy isn't going to reveal his colors immediately, but unlike the Illuminator, he will not revel in silently providing guidance; he loves going on the attack. The Enemy is pissed. The Enemy is angry about your fuckup, and the Enemy believes that dragging you through that anger is a useful learning experience.

Here's the terrifying reality regarding the Enemy: unlike all the other personalities I've talked about, the Enemy is not on your side. As long as your fuckup didn't involve breaking the law, your manager is part of your team, and even if he's furious with you, he should always be trying to lead and trying to help because you are his responsibility.

If the Enemy shows up, your fuckup has now doubled in size. You've got a fuckup and you've got a manager who doesn't believe in you. My hope is that the Enemy is a mood; it's the peak fury of your manager's reaction to your fuckup and, fingers crossed, it should fade into a calmer personality. Still, even when it does, you need to figure out why your manager doesn't trust you when he's freaking out.

The M Word

Yes, everyone except the Illuminator is a micromanager, and while being micromanaged sucks, see, you fucked up. It'd be great if your manager remained even-keeled, but we humans are a squishy, moody bunch, and how we react when a fuckup is thrown in our laps varies by the day.

Whether you're being interrogated, randomized, or prioritized, you need to remember two things.

First, it's your job to figure out how to bring your calm, levelheaded boss back into the room. Every personality save for the Illuminator is looking for the same thing: *explain to me what we're going to do to fix this, why this is a fix, and when is it going to be done?*

Second, as you stare at this strange person who was your boss, you need to remember that people with more experience can teach, you can learn from them, but you might need to wait for it.

While you wait for the storm to pass, might I suggest a healthy dose of proactive fuckup triage? Unless you're working for the Enemy, your boss will eventually help, but long-term success here will be taking an active role in understanding the full scope of your fuckup and determining what needs to change to make sure it never happens again.

CHAPTER 13

The Impossible

Right now, there's a CEO standing in front of his 85-person start-up at an all-hands meeting and he's saying, "In the next 90 days, we need to do the impossible."

The particular version of impossible doesn't matter. What matters is that everyone in the room is shocked when he says it. You can tell by the intensity of the silence.

"We're going to what in the what?"

What gives this guy the right to ask the impossible? Sure, he's the CEO, but does that mean he gets to stand in front of the room and ask the team to build a levitation machine?

Yeah, it does.

However, this does not mean the CEO isn't screwing up.

Asking for the impossible is an advanced management technique, and it's one that is particularly abhorrent to engineers. Engineers are very clear on what is and isn't possible because they're responsible for building and measuring all the possible. When you ask an engineer to do the impossible, they often laugh in your face, not only because they think it's an absurd, irrational request, but they also have the data to prove it.

Yet, given this irrefutable data, we are still going to consider this request. There is an upside to pulling off the impossible. Not only is it a great morale booster, it can also be incredibly profitable, because all your competition thinks the impossible is, well, impossible. Better yet, WHO DOESN'T WANT A FLUX CAPACITOR?

There are three measurements to take with regard to your CEO and his request when the team has been asked to do the impossible. These measurements aren't going to help you pull off the miracle, but they will help you size up the impossibleness of the miracle as well as the character of your CEO.

A Hint of an Insane Plan

First, let's figure out whether your CEO is insane. Listen carefully to the actual request. If your CEO is standing in front of the engineering team asking you to transform lead into gold, you should grin, nod, and start mentally editing your resumé, but don't bolt from the room just yet. Now, if he's asking you to reduce your release cycle from 90 days to 10, you can let yourself be shocked, but be relieved by the fact that you're not being asked to perform matter transmutation.

There's a subtle difference between insane and impossible.

You should respect your gut when that internal "he's insane" flag starts waving, but that doesn't mean you should stop listening. There's more data to gather, and there are times where an insane approach might be the right thing.

Our next assessment has to do with legwork. Has your CEO done any preliminary work to actually figure out whether the impossible idea is achievable? What is his strategic intuition about this crazy idea? Is he able to articulate, however vaguely, why this idea is a good idea for the company and how you might pull this off? You're not looking for a definite plan, more the strategic broad strokes, a point from which the managers can begin sketching in the details.

A word of warning: there are managers and executives out there who can pitch the impossible on confidence alone. They need no intuition or evidence regarding feasibility to get their teams' buy-in, and while these chutzpah-laden individuals sure are inspiring, you should trust that nagging feeling that shows up later when you're

driving home, the high fades, and you're left with a strategic emptiness. That emptiness is the practical result of the CEO's request lack-
ing everything but confidence. The absence of some thread of an
idea about how you're going to do the impossible means you might
be screwed.

The lack of a glimpse of a plan beyond the charisma translates to
a lack of hope.

Skin in the Game

Next, you want to figure out how much skin your CEO has in the
game. How much of the company is he betting on this request? If
this is a bet-the-company decision, I'm comforted by the fact that
he's backing this impossible request up with his job. He knows that
failure means everyone is looking for a new gig. That's motivation.

If the request is smaller, if this is a bet-the-department request, well,
the risk is more localized. The cost of failure will likely be born by
the senior guys and gals running the show. I'm not suggesting the
CEO thinks any less of the importance of this impossible request,
but trust me, he knows that it's not necessarily his job on the line if
the team blows it.

What you're assessing here are two things: size of the request and
level of executive commitment. Having a gut feel for these two
things is often a moot point. Depending on your seat on the org
chart, you might not even have a chance to choose whether you're
saddled with the impossible. However, developing this swag out of
the gate means when the impossible hits the fan, you can be one of
the first to act.

The Importance of Respect

The glimpse of a plan and confidence. These two fuzzy mental
assessments are in play when deciding to ask the impossible, but
there is one more that needs to be considered.

Remember, this is an impossible request. This isn't, "Hey, can you
fix these 10 bugs by Friday?" It's, "Hey, can you rewrite this major
component in half the time it took you to write it the first time?"
Forget whether it's remotely feasible. Forget whether the confidence

is oozing out of every pore of your CEO. You're not going to be convinced, and more importantly, you're not going to engage if you don't respect the person who is asking you to do something

Financial rewards, promotions, IPOs, promises of future interesting projects. All of these incentives matter and can be used to light a fire under a team, but an individual's decision to engage in the impossible starts with the question, "Do I respect this person enough to tackle the impossible?"

There's a book to be written about how to build respect in an organization. My brief advice is, when you are asked the impossible, carefully consider every hard request already made of you. Does he ask the impossible every month? Every Monday? Does he follow up on his impossible requests, or does he expect you to run with them? Have we ever successfully completed an impossible request? Is he there at 3 a.m. on Sunday morning with everyone else, looking like he hasn't shaved in a week?

I don't know how many impossible requests you get, but I do know that frequent impossible requests result in an erosion of respect and a decaying of credibility. And that means when the CEO is standing up in front of the troops asking them to perform magic, all they're thinking is, "This crap again?"

What He Really Wants

Nothing I've described is concrete. Nothing I've described is going to placate your initial intense, negative engineer reaction when your CEO asks you to do something utterly absurd and irrational.

It gets worse...I mean better.

There are times when your leadership should be unencumbered by your version of reality. There are times when it's important that your CEO isn't intimately familiar with a product space or lifecycle. Day to day, doing business requires reasonable expectations and an adherence to plans, but those things actually prevent the extraordinary from occurring. The extraordinary requires a catalyst like an impossible request.

What's important when the CEO asks for the impossible is that he's pushing the definition of possibility for what the team can accomplish. Maybe your CEO only has an idea and can only feel the possibility in what he's asking, but it's not his job to make it all happen. That's where you come in. You're the person responsible for transforming the feel, the intuition, the glimpse of a plan, and the confidence into knowing and doing.

You're the one who is actually responsible for delivering the impossible, and all I'm asking is that you consider the request because agreeing to engage in the impossible shatters normality and ignores fears, and I love that.

CHAPTER 14

Knee Jerks

There was a fight on the roller hockey rink this morning. Anaheim bumped into Philadelphia at speed, and Philly didn't like that so he elbowed Anaheim in the chest—hard. Anaheim pushed back, shoving Philly into the goal where he tripped and fell. Swearing, more shoving, and then we spent the next five minutes keeping them separated.

This hockey rink is a remnant of the first Internet bubble. Built by Netscape, the rink has held a game every Saturday since 1998. A majority of the folks who show up know each other, so the game is mellow. Finesse, not fighting. A fight is an unusual once-a-year thing.

When Philly, who I believed was at fault for this whole situation, got the bench, someone asked him what happened. His answer: "Anaheim ran into me and I protected myself."

One Eighth of a Second

I want you to think of the last time you were surprised. Good, bad, I don't care. When was the last time you were really surprised? Got it? OK, now think about the very first thing that you thought about the surprise. I don't want to know how you eventually handled it; I want you to think about your instantaneous first reaction.

How do you react when you're surprised? Is this how you always react when a surprise lands? My guess is yes.

On the hockey rink, Philadelphia puts up his shields when he's surprised. It's a natural reaction, protecting yourself, but what's interesting isn't Philly's very sensible reaction to the perception of being attacked; it's everyone else's interpretation. We all saw him hold up his arms in defense of Anaheim's unintentional attack, and we all thought, "Man, Philly. What a goon."

In any group of people larger than one, these instantaneous reactions to unexpected situations happen a lot, and understanding their range and impact is important to navigating awkward, tension-filled, and professionally tricky situations.

The Jerks

These are knee-jerk reactions, and the first thing you need to know about them is that they should be first viewed without judgment. I'm not a psychologist, and I don't know why some people are aggressive knee-jerkers and others are passive. I don't know if these reactions are a function of upbringing or genetics, but I do know that we as a species have little control over these initial reactions and there are many of them.

In my head, the complete set of reactions fit on a spectrum that is labeled Fight or Flight. The first step in understanding a knee-jerk reaction is first figuring out where on this spectrum the reaction lies. Is this a person who is going to take on the surprise, or are they going to let it wash over them? Will they bolt? Will they wilt? If there is one thing you want to know quickly about those around you, it's their penchant to fight the surprise or flee it.

Again, no judgment. A person who automatically has the fight instinct is not necessarily a jerk—it's just the default instinct when the world unexpectedly and rapidly changes. I know who on my team will attack a surprise. They'll leap on it. I also know the ones who will silently digest the surprise. I know who is going to come back three hours or three days later with a totally different attitude because they'll have actually processed the surprise.

The base assessment of fight or flight gives you a starting point regarding what might first happen when a surprise lands, but there are other instantaneous reactions that occur, and understanding them gives you an idea of what you need to do next, if anything.

For the sake of this chapter, my assumption is that a surprise has landed and it's bad news. These reactions apply regardless of the type of surprise, but let's assume it's professionally bad news with negative consequences, and it's being delivered in a group setting. Here's whom you might see across the table.

Dr. No

Denial. That's the reaction. Doesn't matter if the surprise is reasonable, understandable, or well-explained. Dr. No's only reaction is a fighting "No."

"No, I'm not going let her go."

"No, I'm not moving organizations."

"No, we're not shutting down this group."

Remember, knee-jerk reactions are not rational, they are not considered, and while they are tactically interesting, they are not strategically useful. Dr. No's denial is not her actual thoughts on that topic; it's her reptilian brain's reaction to a surprise.

No.

If this is a group surprise and Dr. No is sitting in a conference room full of people throwing down the No, there's a chance for everyone to go off the rails. Well, Dr. No said no and I agree, so NO AS WELL. The time immediately after the surprise goes down is not the time to take any action, except to allow folks to react. There are going to be Nos as well as a bevy of other reactions, and your job, if it's your meeting, is to let folks talk—let them react. The goal with Dr. No and everyone else in the room is to get their reaction out so that we can figure out what to do next.

The follow-up: The good news is that Dr. No has got it out of her system. She's expressed her displeasure, which is half of the game. The next time you chat, there will be residual No, but Dr. No knows that she's been heard and will be willing to brainstorm what to do next about the surprise.

Raging Bull

Perhaps the most dangerous of the reactions, Raging Bull wants to fight. They're taking the surprise personally, they're going to say No, and they're going to pick a fight. The Raging Bull is Dr. No with attitude.

The move with the Raging Bull is to know that it's coming, to know that you've got a Raging Bull on your hands. If you have any control over the surprise, you want to put the Raging Bull in a safe situation where he can react to his heart's content without afflicting psychological damage on others or sparking a mob mentality where he infects a mindless horde of mini-Raging Bulls. If it's a pure surprise and it's a group setting, my advice is to end the meeting as quickly as possible. Like Dr. No, Raging Bull is expressing his shock. Unlike Dr. No, the Raging Bull isn't going to feel complete until he's got the emotional satisfaction of picking a fight with someone else.

The follow-up: Everyone needs time to contemplate a surprise, but no one needs time more than Raging Bull. Each knee-jerk reaction scratches a particular psychological itch, and in the case of Raging Bull, he believes that getting someone else to participate in his mental and verbal freak-out is somehow going to help.

It's not.

Of all the reactions, Raging Bull's behavior is the one that I've found likely to repeat itself after the fact. Raging Bull will often continue to pick fights days after the initial surprise, which is why it's your move to get him thinking, as quickly as possible, about what's next. What are we going to do about the surprise? What specific thought does Raging Bull have that is crucial to successfully navigating this surprise?

Still Water

This reaction reads like flight because she's not fighting. In fact, she's just sitting there, but Still Water is taking it all in. She's not missing a thing, and in her complete silence, wearing her poker face, she is meticulously processing, evaluating all possible permutations, best- and worst-case scenarios, and potential impact on her day to day.

This processing results in one of two very different Still Waters. There's the true Still Water who is going to maintain the calm demeanor for the entire duration of the surprise. See, this Still Water's processing has resulted in a comfortable plan. She believes she knows what to do about the surprise, and this realization has brought her peace.

The second Still Water is mentally losing her shit. Sure, externally she looks calm, but internally her processing has resulted in increasingly loony nightmare scenarios regarding the surprise. Without quick action, Insane Still Water will find reason to become a Raging Bull.

The follow-up: You want to get to Still Water as quickly as possible in a safe location after the surprise, because Still Water isn't still. Unlike Dr. No and the Raging Bull, who had their opportunities to weigh in, Still Water is still in her head, and the longer she remains in her head, the higher the probability she'll tell herself a tale that will drive her insane.

You need Still Water to say out loud how she feels about the world suddenly changing. Like Raging Bull, you need to engage Still Water in the surprise and move the problem out of her head and onto the table where everyone can take action.

Distiller

This is my favorite knee-jerk reaction because the Distiller attacks the surprise with questions. Why did this happen? How come we didn't see it coming? OK, what's the impact? Right, what are we going to do?

This is a fight reaction, but a constructive one. The Distiller is as uncomfortable as anyone with the surprise, but his coping mechanism is aggressive understanding. He's not going to stop asking questions until he feels he has a complete understanding of what actually happened.

In a group setting, I let the Distiller have free rein during the landing of the surprise because his incessant questions are helping everyone in the room contemplate what actually happened. The Distiller focuses the surprise on facts rather than feel.

The follow-up: You're going to feel you've got a good idea where the Distiller is at because of his endless questions, but now's a good time to explain that everyone comes down from a surprise in different ways, which is why everyone needs that personal follow-up. Yeah, a Distiller can turn into Raging Bull after a night's sleep. Still Water might go Distiller. You just don't know who is going to walk into the building 24 hours after the surprise. This is why most surprises are engineered to occur late in the week; there's a belief that all the knee jerks are going to calm down over the weekend. Maybe. More on this in a bit.

The Handler

The first flight reaction sure doesn't feel like flight. The Handler is not surprised. In fact, she's fired up to handle whatever the surprise might be. She makes it appear that she knew this surprise was going to occur. How'd she do that?

The Handler is a calm facade. Where the Distiller understands via questions, the Handler's coping mechanism is the illusion she's got it all figured out—that she's 10 steps ahead of everyone else. This is a convenient reaction when you've got the Raging Bull standing on the conference table challenging anyone to hand-to-hand combat, but the Handler needs help.

The follow-up: The Handler crumbles hardest. The Handler is actually Dr. No, except without the denial. There will be a quiet moment in the middle of the night when the Handler realizes absolutely nothing has been handled, and then you'll see her actual reaction.

My Bad

This flight reaction is one of accountability. My Bad's impression is that he's personally done something to incur this particular surprise. He believes that if only he had done just one thing differently, no one would've had to deal with the surprise.

There's hope inside of My Bad's reaction. His empathy regarding the surprise is constructive, as opposed to the destructive social tendencies of Dr. No or Raging Bull, but you don't want him wallowing in his overdeveloped sense of accountability.

The follow-up: My Bad is not responsible for the surprise. While his sense of responsibility is admirable, My Bad needs to understand the actual cause behind the surprise. He didn't cause it, so he shouldn't feel it. The more he focuses on feeling responsible, the less energy and focus he has for making progress.

We're Doomed

The most common flight reaction is also the reaction that, I believe, everyone is going to experience as they digest the surprise. Despair.

In a room full of geeks hearing a surprise for the first time, one of their first thoughts is, "How does this surprise fit into my mental system of how things work?" Failure to map the surprise into the mental model results in an uncomfortable realization: "The world does not work as I expected. Therefore, other surprises are guaranteed to happen randomly. QED. I have no control whatsoever. Shit."

The follow-up: A perceived lack of control or understanding of our world is a confidence-shattering experience for the geek, and the best way to attack this despair is with a project. Doesn't matter if the project is surprise-related or not, the geek needs something to do. They need the blissful distraction of building something. It's during this constructive distraction that they'll actually figure out how they feel about the surprise.

I Quit

The last knee jerk is our strongest flight reaction. An extreme version of We're Doomed, I Quit does exactly what you'd expect: she threatens to quit on the spot.

She's not quitting. Well, she might, but not right now. You need to translate "I quit" into what she's actually saying: "I am very surprised, and I don't like being this surprised." It's unfortunate that this is her reaction, especially in a group setting, because I Quit's attitude can create mass professional hysteria, which means this needs to be handled immediately. You can't wait until after the weekend to explain to I Quit that her reaction at this moment might be vastly different after a night's sleep. You need to hold up a mirror in front of her and ask, "No matter the surprise, why in the world would you eliminate so many options by quitting on the spot?"

The follow-up: I Quit will calm down and land on another opinion, but her knee-jerk reaction is a sign of a larger problem. I don't know what your surprise is, but I know if someone wants to quit, first, it's a big surprise, and second, she values her job second to her peace of mind.

Stages of Jerk

With people, it's never as easy as just a name. These labels for the knee-jerk reactions are deliberately simple, but people are conspicuously complex.

As I hinted earlier, I've found it commonplace that you're going to see multiple knee-jerk reactions as a corporate surprise is comprehended. These reactions, like grief, have stages, and your job as a manager or a concerned coworker is actually not comparably complex. Your job is to listen.

The reason there's a knee-jerk reaction is because the unexpected occurred. It kicks off the process of assimilation, and that's what we care about—the understanding of the surprise, not the reaction to it. While everyone has a different reaction, they're all going to end up trying to figure out what just happened, and part of that process is having someone they trust sit there and listen to their assessment. Verbally walking through our thoughts is one of the ways we organize and understand them and begin the process of finding a comfortable, constructive conclusion.

I'm just as uncomfortable with a Raging Bull as anyone, but I know this knee-jerk reaction is not who they are; this is just how they react. Understanding these varied potential reactions is just the first part of digesting a surprise. It helps you understand what to expect so you can begin to figure out what to do next.

CHAPTER 15

A Deep Breath

I admit it. I love it when the sky is falling. There is no more delicious state of being than the imminent threat of disaster.

During these times, I've done great work. I've taken teams from "We're fucked" to "We made it." Yeah, we had to cancel Christmas that one time, and there was that other time I didn't leave the building for three days straight, but it was worth it because there's no more exhilarating place to hang than the edge of chaos. We're wired to escape danger.

There's a reputation you get after successfully performing the diving saves. You're "the Fixer." You're the one they call when hope is lost, and while that's a great merit badge to have, it's a cover story. It's spin. See, someone upstream from you fucked up badly. When the sky falls, it means someone, somewhere underestimated the project, didn't make a decision, or let a small miss turn into a colossal disaster, and while fixing a disaster feels great, you're not actually fixing anything.

Management by crisis is exhilarating, but it values velocity over completeness; it sacrifices creativity for the illusion of progress.

Still, right now, the sky is falling and rather than let it fall, immediate action is necessary, and my first bit of advice is that everyone takes a deep breath.

Sigh

When you see an impending crisis, your body has a distinct natural reaction. In your consideration of the crisis, you take a long, deep breath. You often don't notice this, but if I were sitting next to you, I would hear *sigh*.

A sigh is associated with despair. *We're screwed. Sigh*. My interpretation is different; this long, deep breath is one of preparation. Let's break it down: breathe in. Gather your strength. *Oh shit, how am I going to deal with this?* Hold it. Hold it. OK, breathe out. *OK, not sure what the plan is, but let's roll.*

The interesting part of the deep breath is when you hold it. Try it right now: take a deep breath and hold it. What are you doing when you're holding your breath? Well, first off, you're slowly asphyxiating, but in that moment of life-threatening tension you're doing interesting work. It's a subtle transformation from building tension to calm release. It can also be a deliberate moment of consideration.

You can let that breath out now.

It's a metaphoric stretch, but it's around the deep breath that I build my team's communication structure. I'll explain, but first, a story.

The team at the start-up was in a design crisis. The 1.0 version of the product was out and doing well and everyone wanted to do...well, everything. Every feature was being considered. Unbridled ambition is a good problem to have for about a week. After a month, we had three different design directions in play with various levels of support. The creative rush of developing a new release was degrading into useless design meetings where different camps were building strategic fortifications rather than talking. Decisions were being made and not communicated. Confusion was replacing creativity.

In times of crisis, a few human behaviors can make everything worse:

- In the absence of direction, people make shit up. Nature abhors a vacuum, and in the absence of solid information, people generate their own information to fill that vacuum. They're not lying, they have no ill will; they're just trying to build a semblance of structure amongst the confusion. This is only exacerbated by the fact that...

- Human beings provide mutual group therapy by endlessly talking about the crisis at hand. This isn't the creation of new content; it's just the regurgitation of the latest new. At the right time, this hallway cross-pollination is a great way to evolve an idea, but if all we're doing is talking about the crisis, all we're doing is scratching at the worry rather than dealing with it.

- Finally, everyone wants to know everything. Combine the communication vacuums and the group therapy creating a fire hose of additional questionable content and it's not surprising that everyone on the team wants to know everything. *Before I proceed, I want total disclosure. I have something unique to add, and I better get a chance to do so.*

It was an information communication disaster. There were brilliant ideas wandering the hallways, there were stickies with great ideas hanging from monitors, but in the confusion that was our communication structure, everyone was running around panicking and no one was taking a deep breath.

Three Meetings

Starting on a Monday, I imposed a new meeting structure. Let me first describe the meetings, and then we'll talk about the purpose. There were three types of meetings:

1:1s with my staff

Monday morning. First meeting of the week. Thirty minutes for the folks who are cruising. One hour for those in crisis. The agenda is a simple deep breath:

1. What are you worried about?

2. Here's what I'm worried about.

3. And discuss....

Staff

With air from our 1:1s still in our lungs, I have my staff meeting. Two hours, right after the 1:1s are complete. It sounds like a long meeting, but when this meeting is run well and full of the right people, it's almost always over before you know it.

Staff is where we can continue to publicly worry, but Staff is where I want to turn the corner, where we turn inhale to exhale. *OK, we're worried about a lot, but what are we going to do about it?*

The tone and content for this meeting vary wildly by where we're at in the development cycle. If we're early in the cycle, we're talking about the state of design. If it's late in the development cycle, we're looking at confidence in the quality.

There are three buckets of topics that I work through at my Staff, and they're increasingly slippery. We start with Operations (Where are we?), move onto Tactics (What are we going to do about that?), and finally, Strategy (No, really, what are we going to do about it?). I'll explain each.

Operations: Where are we?

> Operations topics are hard, nondebatable measures. How many bugs do we have? Where are we at with hiring? When are we moving? Any hard piece of data that we collectively need to know. No debate, no discussion, just alignment.

Tactics: What are we going to do about that?

> Now we're working. Tactics are changes, tasks, events, things we're going to do as a team over the next week to address the worry we found in our 1:1s. Like operational topics, tactics are measurable, consumable things, but these are not topics we're reporting on; this is where we're taking action. *We are going to scrub every bug in the next product milestone to make sure it belongs there. Jason is going to provide the new design by Thursday.* By defining these tactics, you're defining the agenda for the last meeting on my list, but we first need to talk strategy.

Strategy: No, really, what are we going to do about it?

> All of these well-defined tactics are great. They are real work that, hopefully by the end of the week, are going to define measurable progress. Go you. There are some organization, product, and people problems that you won't be able to tackle in a week… or a month. Strategy involves deep changes to policy or culture.

Our quality isn't great, so we're going to institute a code review culture. Our design is all over the place, so we're going to define a style guide. Strategic topics during Staff are my absolute favorite because they represent the biggest opportunity for substantive change in the group. They're also the hardest to define as well as the hardest to measure.

Worse, strategic changes are also tricky to implement during sky-is-falling situations because everyone is working to prevent the sky from actually falling—they're intensely and correctly tactical. This doesn't mean strategic discussions aren't important during Staff. You might not discover a strategic change, but just having the discussion around the idea of change will give a glimmer of future hope to those who are hyperventilating.

When my Staff meeting is done, I've not only taken a deep breath, I've also begun the process of calmly exhaling...*I now know what we need to do this week....* This is generally where people screw up. They confuse the relief associated with the exhale with having a plan, with actual progress. You haven't done anything yet, except sit through three hours of meetings, and we need one more.

"Look What We Built" meeting

4 p.m. on Friday. This meeting exists for one reason: to measure the tactics we defined at Staff. *Did we do what said we were going to do?* From an agenda perspective, this meeting is a no-brainer. The list of topics and measurements were hopefully well-defined on Monday. Again, the content varies as a function of where we're at in the development cycle, but some version of this meeting always occurs on Friday. *Let's review the design. Let's look at the bug charts. Let's confirm that we've made that big decision.*

The "Look What We Built" meeting is the time to demonstrate progress, to show that even when the sky is falling, we know how to kick ass.

Invest in the Boring

It's not just during a crisis that this calm, repetitive meeting pattern pays off—it's always. I know you've been working with your favorite designer for three years. I know you believe you're totally in each other's heads, but this psychic confidence doesn't mean you should ever skip your 1:1 with her, even when the sky isn't falling.

Communication in a group of people is an endless exercise in alignment. No matter how well you know your team, you can never predict where the internal dialogue of your team is going to wander. What this meeting structure does is set organization expectations:

- Everyone knows when they're going to get their moment to speak in private.

- Everyone, whether they're in the meetings or not, knows the system by which a lot of information moves around the building.

- Everyone knows, whether the sky is falling or not, how we're measuring success on a weekly basis.

Equally important to these meetings' existence is that they occur with obsessive, robotic regularity. Years from now, when your team has been disbanded, I want you to look at your clock at 10:15 a.m. on Monday and think, *I've got my 1:1 with my boss in 15 minutes.* This regularity is not a threat, it's not a stick; it's the basis for building trust in a team. *I know I have a say.*

And I haven't even told you the best part yet.

All of this structure, all of this boring meeting repetition, exists to make room for something else. Whether you're designing as an individual or as a team, when you're being creative, you need two things: an environment that encourages the random and time to live there. An obsessive meeting schedule is an investment in the boring, but by defining a specific place for the boring to exist, you're allowing every other moment to have creative potential. You're encouraging the random, and random is how you're going to win. Random is how you're going to discover a path through a problem that no one else has found, and that starts with breathing deeply.

CHAPTER 16

Gaming the System

On my list of creative management solutions to dire situations, I offer the rolling whiteboard.

The rolling whiteboard was a curiosity at the start-up. Not a full-size whiteboard, but a door-sized whiteboard on wheels, suitable for rolling into conference rooms and cubicles alike. I never knew who owned it; I just grabbed it in a moment of desperation.

It was end game. The time in the project where you pay for every single shortcut you've taken, for every specification you didn't write, and for all the warnings from engineers that you've ignored. All the data is grim. Bug arrival rates are skyrocketing while bug resolution rates are pathetic because, uh, well, engineers are still finishing features.

Like I said, grim.

The endless stream of bad news was grating on everyone. We were already three weeks into working weekends with no end in sight. A normally pleasantly pessimistic engineering staff had gone uncomfortably quiet. Everyone was staring at "the date we can't miss" and thinking, "I guarantee we're missing it."

I needed a game.

An Entertaining System

As I said at the beginning of this book, geeks are system thinkers. We see the world as a very complex but knowable flowchart where there are a finite number of inputs that cause a similarly finite set of outputs. This impossible flowchart gives us a comfortable illusion of control and an understanding of a chaotic word, but its existence is a handy side effect of a life staring at, deducing, and building systems. It's also why we love games—they're just dolled-up systems—and the more you understand this fascination with games, the better you'll be at managing us.

As with all mental excursions with geeks, there's a well-defined process by which we consume a game, and it goes like this:

- Discovery
- Optimization, Repetition, and Win
- Achievement

Discovery: From Confusion to Control

The initial joy of a game for the geek is discovery. This is a delicate balance of confusion and progressive disclosure. A game is initially attractive because it starts out chaotic and unknowable, but even in the chaos, there's always a hint of the rules...of structure. *What are the specific rules that govern this game? And how might I learn them?*

A geek is searching for a single source of joy in this initial state. It's the sense of discovery and progress toward a currently unknown goal. *I want to see the engine that defines this particular universe...I want to see its edges.* We're looking for those edges because as soon as we find this wall, we know this is a containable and knowable place, and that is comforting because the game becomes a controllable thing.

There's creative flexibility in rule discovery and pacing, and it tends to be a function of the size and the intent of the game. The beauty of *Tetris* is that the initial rules are immediately obvious. But the wonderful curse of a massive online game like *World of Warcraft* is that while there are rules, they are vast and, as we'll see in a moment, they are changeable.

This discovery is the hook where a geek is going to know in just a few minutes whether this particular game suits his particular appetite. But getting past the initial phases of discovery doesn't mean you've successfully engaged the geek. The real test is…

Optimization, Repetition, and Win: A Paradox and a Warning

With the basic rule set discovered and defined, the process of optimization begins. *OK, I get how it's played, but how do I win?* This is the phase where, now equipped with the rules, geeks attempt to use them to their advantage.

There's a discoverable structure to the rules. There's a correct order that, when followed, offers a type of reward. It's the advantage of thinking three blocks ahead in *Tetris* or holding onto those beguiling hypercubes in *Bejeweled*. This is the advanced discovery of the system around the rules that leads to exponential geek joy.

There's a paradox and a warning inside of optimization and repetition.

The paradox involves the implications of winning. Geeks will furiously work to uncover the rules of a game and then use those rules to determine how they might win. But the actual discovery of how to win is a buzzkill. The thrill, the adrenaline, comes from the discovery, hunt, and eventual mastery of the unknown, which, confusingly, means if you want to keep a geek engaged in a game, you can't let them win, even though that's exactly what they think they want.

Think of it like this: does it bug you that there's an absolute high score to *Pac-Man*? It bugs me.

To get around this entertainment-killing paradox in subscription-based games like *World of Warcraft*, game designers freely change rule sets as part of regular updates. The spin is, "We're improving playability," which translates into, "The geeks are close to figuring it out, and we can't have that, because they'll stop paying."

This paradox does not apply to all games. It's hard to argue that there is much more to learn about *Tetris*, but folks continue to play it incessantly, which leads to the warning.

There's a socially frightening act inside of optimization that normal humans don't get, and it's the calming inanity of intense repetition. In a game like *World of Warcraft*, many of the tasks involve an exceptional amount of repetition. Repetition like, "Hey, go kill 1,000 of these guys and come back, and I'll give you something cool." Yeah, 1,000. If each kill takes a minute, you're talking about 16 hours of mindless hacking and slashing. This is not a task that requires skill or thought…and that's the point.

If you walked in and looked over my shoulder at troll kill #653, you'd think I'd dropped into a twitchy, fugue-like mental state, and I have. *I am…a machine.* Machines don't have a care in the world, and that's a fine place to be. This is the act of mentally removing ourselves from a troubled planet full of messy people, combined with our ability to find pleasure in the act of completing a small, well-defined task. This is our ability to lose ourselves in repetition, and it is task at which we are highly effective.

In the defense of game designers, there are no quests that read, "Go waste 16 hours of your life doing nothing." They are more elegant with their descriptions; they splice all sorts of different tasks together to distract you from the dull inanity of large, laborious tasks. But they know that part of what makes us tick is the micro-pleasure we get from obsessively scratching the task itch in pursuit of the achievement.

As I've never designed and shipped a game, I can confidently and ignorantly say the compelling magic in games comes from the design in optimization and repetition. This is the portion of the game where we spend the most time and effort and derive the most pleasure. It is this abstract mental state we long for when we're not playing.

But there is one last phase to consider: achievement.

Achievement: Who Cares if You Win by Yourself?

Once a geek has learned the game by discovering how to win, they become interested in advanced winning. They're interested in how their win fits into the rest of the world. They want to compare and measure and answer the social question, "Is my pile of win bigger than yours?" They believe they've mastered the game, but reputation—achievement—is nothing unless someone else can see and acknowledge it.

Before the Internet, winning was a private thing. You entered your three-letter name into the local *Pac-Man* machine and then anonymously stumbled off in search of *Donkey Kong*. In an interconnected world, games became social, and once we discovered each other in these virtual worlds, we looked for a means to compare our feats. We began to understand that achievement was not just becoming great at a game, but also being recognized for being great.

Achievement can be as simple as a score, a numeric means of comparison, but the more sophisticated the game, the more complex the achievements. In *World of Warcraft*, you'll be busily into your seventh hour of mind-numbing troll extinction when you see that night elf run by with...what's that? A staff...where the hell did she get that staff? It's sweet. *My world will not be complete until I own that staff.* Now, what was four more hours of troll killing becomes the quest for the staff.

There's no well-defined rule that says, "To win, you need this staff." Sure, it might make those next 200 kills easier, but that is not your entire motivation. For you, the staff is your own personal badge of mastery, and you don't wear a badge for yourself; you wear it for others to see.

Most achievements do have an empirical value, but that's not what makes them important. The point of an achievement is to have someone you know or don't know look at your Violet Proto-Drake and say, "Holy crap, do you know what he had to do to pull that off?" It's wondering exactly how far you'll go to get the Legendary badge on Stack Overflow.

In a world where we spend a ton of time with people we'll never meet, achievements are the currency of respect and identity.

The Rules of the Game

Now that we understand how games float the geek boat, we can tease out rules you can use to build your own business-centric games. This is will take a creative leap on your part, because I don't know in what way your particular situation is grim. Perhaps your bug count is crap like mine? Maybe you can't hire fast enough? Maybe you can't measure how screwed you are? I don't know what game you need, but I know you need to follow the universal rules of games.

The rules need to be clear.

Whatever game you design must stand up to scrutiny. Test the rules with selected geeks before you roll it out. Find the holes in your game before you're standing in front of the team describing a game that makes no sense. Ambiguity, contradiction, and omission are the death of any good game.

The rules must be inviolable.

Enforce rules with an iron fist. A rule not followed is twice as bad as a poorly defined one. A violation of the rules is an affront to a geek. They react violently to violations of the rules because it's an indication that the system is not working. Rules make a game fair, and when they stop being followed, the geeks stop playing.

The playing of the game must be inclusive, visible, and broadcasted.

Include everyone on the team. Those not on the team should be aware of the progress and implications.

Use money as a reward only as a last resort.

It's a knee-jerk management move to use money as an incentive. Problem is, money creates drama. Money makes everyone serious, and while you may be in dire straits as you design your game, you don't want the team stressing about who is getting paid; you want them to stress about the work.

This is not to say that rewards in a motivational game are verboten, but step away from the money and think about achievements. One of the best trophies I've awarded was a horrifically ugly ceramic blue rhino the size of a pit bull. The winner proudly displayed the rhino achievement in his office for years.

It's not a game.

Just because I'm using the word "game" all over this chapter doesn't mean it's trivial, simple, or something not to be taken seriously. Your geeks will treat the game as a motivational tool as seriously as you choose to treat it in building and rolling it out—because they want to win.

The Whiteboard Game

Everyone was working on a Sunday night as I stared at the blank portable whiteboard in my office. A weekend of hallway conversations, bug scrubbing, and informal testing confirmed what I already knew: the product was shaky, the bugs we were discovering were alarmingly bad, and there were too many of them.

OK, a game. The game will be called *Focus*, and it will concentrate and structure our attention on the worst parts of the product. I thought of the 10 worst bugs I'd found during the weekend and listed them on the board. Next to each bug, I drew four boxes:

- Root cause

- Fix identified

- Fixed

- Tested

I grabbed a handful of dry erase pens, rolled the board into the architect's office and said, "This is all we're working on."

He stared at the board for 10 minutes and finally nodded, "Good, but each person needs their own color, and you should assign points for each of the boxes. 10 points for root cause and fix identification, 5 for fixes and tests."

"Points for what?"

"Points for points. We're geeks."

"And everyone has their own color?"

"Yeah, so we know who has the most points. Give me a blue pen, I've already got root cause on bug #3."

"Blue?"

"Yeah, I'm always blue."

CHAPTER 17

Managing Werewolves

If I move a muscle, I'm dead. Jane, who I'm pretty sure is a Werewolf, is jumping from one player to the next, testing will and looking for weakness. She's looking for a sign of guilt or discomfort, and it's not just her. The room is full of people looking for someone to lynch.

The game is *Werewolf*, and I'm both exhilarated and terrified, which is odd because I'm paid to play this horrific game every day.

A Dangerous Scenario

Werewolf is a party game described by its creator as "a game of accusations, lying, bluffing, second-guessing, assassination, and mob hysteria." Understanding the basics of how it's played is important to understanding why this game will help your critical thinking skills at work.

A moderator begins by handing players cards that indicate their role: Villager, a Seer, or Werewolf. With all the cards distributed, each player announces his role in the village, and everyone says the same thing: "Hi, I'm *MyName*, and I'm a Villager."

Now, some people are lying. There's a bunch of Werewolves, and they're not going to admit that, because the Villagers want to kill the Werewolves before they kill us.

The moderator then announces that it's nighttime, and all the players close their eyes. The two things that Werewolves are afraid of are, obviously, cows and zombies, so all the players make one of the following sounds: "BraAaaaaaaaAaaaains" or "MooOoooooooOooooo."

These sounds are an auditory cover for what really goes on at night when the moderator asks the Werewolves to awaken and pick a Villager to kill. Once the Werewolves have silently selected their victim, they go back to sleep. The moderator then awakes the Seer who points at one player. Via a thumbs up or thumbs down, the moderator confirms for the Seer whether that player is a Werewolf or not. With everyone back to sleep, the moderator then awakens the village and announces who has died.

Then the game begins. The village must collectively choose someone to lynch, whomever they decide is a Werewolf based on whatever meager information they've gathered from either the Villager introductions or the previous night's killing. It's not much information, but they must kill someone because, each night, each turn, that's exactly what the Werewolves do, too. And when there are more Werewolves than Villagers, the Werewolves win.

We can't let the Werewolves win.

I've explained the mechanical basics of the game, but I have not explained its beauty. I love *Werewolf* because it's a game where you can safely learn how to deal with the worst people you're going to meet in the most dangerous scenarios possible.

People Lie, Some Are Evil, Others Just Want to Screw You

I have a long-standing policy of optimism. It's my leadoff mindset. I assume that we're a team working collectively to do the right thing. As a strategy, optimism has served me well, but here's the bad news:

- People can vary from being poor communicators to being outright liars.

- Politics and process often screw up people's value systems beyond recognition.

- Evil things happen. Sometimes randomly.

In your career as either an individual contributor or a manager, you are going to be faced with these unexpectedly shitty situations involving other people with devious agendas. While the HR department is furiously working on cleverly named workshops about conflict management and situational leadership, there's really no replacement for having someone lie straight to your face and having to figure out what to do next.

This takes us back to a critical part of *Werewolf*: the accusation phase. In the morning, the Villagers wake up and must select someone to lynch. What's the process for this? Who leads this process? How is this potential Werewolf selected? While the moderator keeps track of time, it's the Villagers who organically guide this process.

Invariably someone in the village jumps into the leadership position. They start questioning people and guiding the accusation process. Why are they leading? What's the motivation? Every word and every movement in this situation has differently perceived meaning. This is, effectively, your boss's staff meeting, except in this meeting, people die.

When the group has selected a potential victim, the moderator asks the initial accuser why they think this Villager is a Werewolf. The reasoning can vary from "He's twitchy" to "Well, we have to kill someone." The victim is given a chance to defend himself against this accusation, which, in the case that he actually is a Werewolf, means he sits there and comfortably lies to the entire room.

This is why I love *Werewolf*. Where else can you hone some of the sketchiest but most important skills you need in groups of people?

Rapidly size up a person based on how they deliver a single sentence

"I...am a Villager." Where was he looking when he was speaking? Did he make eye contact? Was he fidgeting? Is he usually fidgeting? Why'd he stutter? *That strikes me as...wolfy....*

Observe the rapid evolution of roles in high-pressure scenarios

Who comes forward to lead? Are they challenged? Do they last? Why is she leading now? *She was quiet last time.* Who does she question? What kinds of questions is she asking? What kind of nonverbal language is she using? And why does she appear to be aligning with him?

Figure out how to fluidly integrate yourself into a group of strangers

How do they develop alliances based on little information? Who already knows each other? How are they communicating? Who is really playing, and who is just trying to figure it out? Who am I instantly connecting with? Why I am being let into this particular clique? *I don't trust her, but for some reason she's got my back.*

Learn how to lie without the guilt or getting caught

What's the difference between sinning by omission, twisting the facts, and outright, blatant lying? When is lying just temporarily convenient versus long-term trouble? How much lie can you tell and still keep your story straight? What are the keys to a convincing lie? What does this particular group of people want to hear? *"You can't kill me. I'm the Seer and I know where the werewolves are...really."*

Aggressively turn the spotlight off you and onto someone else using nothing but chutzpah

Who is the weakest in the room, and how did they make themselves weak? What's the balance between sounding credible and desperate? When is answering a question with a question the right move? Can they sense you're aggressively trying to hide? How do you defuse the leader's authority and credibility? *"No, I'm not a werewolf, but I'M CERTAIN SHE IS!"*

Perfect the poker face

Can you hide your emotions and reactions? What is the right type and amount of eye contact, body language, and tone of voice? When is calm believable? When is it not? Who can you look in the eye while maintaining your cool? Who is a liability? When is it time to completely shift your personality to make a point? *"I...am a Villager."*

This Isn't Role Playing; This Is Life or Death

Werewolf is a game, and games are fictionalized simplifications of life designed with a mythology and a rule set that allow you to explore in ways you normally cannot.

In real life, there's a subtle, detectable flow to how a group of people interact. There are standard roles that people will adopt. There are discernible rules to how people will act. Unfortunately, it's an impossibly long set of rules because the rules vary as much as each person is different.

In *Werewolf*, there's a very small set of rules:

- Villagers kill Werewolves as best they can.
- Werewolves kill Villagers as best they can.
- Sleep when you're told to.
- Survive.

Interwoven within these rules is the actual game, and therein lies the brilliance of a solid game of *Werewolf*. It's a crucible of people dynamics, improvisation, and intellectual combat. In just a few short hours of game play, you realistically experience some of the worst possible meeting scenarios you can imagine paired with the agility and amazing motivation to handle these situations because, well, you don't want to die.

Now, I'm optimistic and, sometimes, realistic. I don't actually believe someone will deliberately lie under normal circumstances or that they are purely evil. I think there are those who have an agenda that doesn't align with mine, which gives them incentive to work against my interests. But they're not just out to screw me; they're out to succeed…just like me.

In reality, I know most meetings aren't these high-pressure, survival-of-the-fittest lynchfests. Many meetings are well-structured affairs with hardly a drop of blood spilled. I also know that each time you speak in a meeting is a moment in the spotlight to explain that, yes, you understand what's going on, you are clear about the fuzzy rules of this particular game, and you're in it to win.

We Can't Let the Werewolves Win

I suspect Jane is a Werewolf because she's running the show this round. She's keeping the spotlight on herself, and that means she's excited, she's got a lot of energy, and, I suspect, a thirst for blood. I'm waiting for her to make her way to me, to accuse me, and I know she will.

I'm being quiet. Intentionally. I'm setting a trap because I've played with her before, and I know that she believes what I believe:

"We kill the quiet ones because they aren't helping."

CHAPTER 18

BAB

My management team was bickering. Two managers in particular: Leo and Vincent. Both of their projects were fine. Both of their teams were producing, but in any meeting where they were both representing their teams, they just started pushing each other's buttons. Every meeting on some trivial topic:

Leo: "Vincent, are you on track to ship the tool on Wednesday?"

Vincent: "We're on schedule."

Leo: "For Wednesday?"

Vincent: "We'll hit our schedule."

Leo: "Wednesday?"

Endless passive-aggressive verbal warfare. Two type A personalities who absolutely hated to be told what to do. My 1:1s with each of them were productive meetings, and when I brought up the last Leo'n'Vincent battle of the wills, they immediately started pointing at their counterpart: "I really don't know what his problem is."

I do. They didn't trust each other.

On the Topic of Trust

There's a question out there regarding how close you want to get with your coworkers in your job. There's a camp out there that employs a policy of "professional distance." This camp believes it is appropriate to keep those they work with at arm's length.

The managerial reason here is more concrete than the individual reasoning. Managers are representatives or officers of the company and, as such, may be asked to randomly enforce the will of the business. Who gets laid off? Why doesn't this person get a raise? How much more does this person get? Professional distance or not, these responsibilities will always give managers an air of otherness.

Here's my question: do you or do you not want be the person someone trusts when they need help? Manager or not, do you see the act of someone trusting you as fitting with who you are?

Yes, there's a line that needs to be drawn between you and your coworkers, but artificially distancing yourself from the people you spend all day, every day with seems like a good way to put artificial barriers between yourself and the people you need to get your job done.

Is that who you are or who you want to work for?

The topic of trust is where I draw a line in both my personal and management philosophy. My belief is that a team built on trust and respect is vastly more productive and efficient than the one in which managers are distant supervisors and coworkers are 9-to-5 people you occasionally see in meetings. You're not striving to be everyone's pal; that's not the goal. The goal is a set of relationships where there is a mutual belief in each other's reliability, truth, ability, and strengths.

It's awesome.

And it's something you can build with a card game.

BAB

It's pronounced how you think. Rhymes with crab. It's an acronym for a game that, with practice, will knit your team together in unexpected ways. It's Back Alley Bridge. The rules are included as an appendix at the end of this book, but before I explain why this game is a great team-building exercise, you need to understand a few of the rules.

BAB isn't bridge

The game does have a few important similarities with bridge. First, it's a game for four players, involving two teams. The folks facing each other are on the same team and share their score. Second, it's a trick-based game where the goal is for each team to get as many tricks as possible. A trick is won when each player turns up a card and the highest wins, unless someone plays a trump suit, which, in the case of BAB, is always spades.

Bidding

Also like bridge, BAB has bidding, meaning each team bids how many tricks they think they're going to get after the cards have been dealt. Scoring is optimized to reward teams who get the number of tricks they bid and heavily punishes those who don't get their bid. Bidding is a blind team effort—you have no idea what your teammate has in his hand other than what you can infer from his bid.

Decreasing hand count

Unlike bridge, the number of cards each player gets decreases with each hand. Each player gets 13 cards in the first hand, 12 in the second, and so on. Play continues down to a single card and then heads back up to 13. A work-friendly modification I've made is to only play every other hand (13-11-9, etc.). This number of hands fits nicely into a lunch hour.

There are two special bids: Board and Boston. A bid of Board indicates the team is going to take every single trick. A bid of Boston indicates the team intends to take the first six. Achieving a Board or Boston can be an impressive feat and is rewarded handsomely from a scoring perspective. Failure results in a scoring beat-down. Both of these special bids allow for wild variances in the score, which can be handy for teams who are falling behind.

Scoring, game play, and other information are in the complete rules. Now, let me explain why I picked this game as a recurring weekly lunch meeting.

In BAB, you talk shit.

I've landed BAB in three different teams now, and in each case, the amount of trash talking that showed up once players became comfortable with the game was impressive. This is a function of my personality, but it's also a byproduct of any healthy competition amongst bright people. It's also a sign of a healthy team. I'll explain.

Trash talking is improvisational critical thinking—the art of building comedy in the moment with only the immediate materials provided. As I'm looking for candidates for my next BAB game, I'm looking for two things: who will be able to talk trash and who needs to receive it?

The art in talking trash is the careful exploration of the edges of truth. When someone effectively lays it down, they say something honest and slightly uncomfortable. The ever-present risk with trash talking is when *that* line is crossed. It's that one thing that is said that goes too far and offends, but it's the presence of that line that makes talking trash so much fun.

It's these honest and dangerous observations that form the basis of trust. When a coworker makes a big observation about you and shares it with the other players, you take note—someone is watching. It sounds problematic, but remember, we're just sitting here playing cards. It's safe.

In a new BAB game, it takes players time to get used to the trash talking, especially in a situation like Leo and Vincent's. Adversarial coworkers playing on the same team need to learn to ditch the business for the game. They need to understand there is a relationship outside of the daily work, and there's nothing like a comedic verbal beat-down to remind them to lighten up.

In BAB, you learn things unintentionally.

Once you've got an established game with regular players who all know the rules, you'll learn two things: people get better at trash talking with practice, and information travels in unpredictable ways in groups of people.

It goes like this:

- Player #1: "I bid 3."
- Player #2: "I bid 1."
- Player #3: "Pass."
- Player #4: "Kevin's quitting. I'm sure of it."
- Player #1: "Yeah, I know."
- Player #2: "Sucks to be you."

Out of nowhere, in the middle of the game, you're suddenly assessing the departure of a coworker. I see this as a sign of a thriving, healthy BAB game because the team has begun to trust each other more. In the safety of the game, they're letting the worries of the moment spill onto the table for all to see, which is impressive, since everyone knows that anything on the table at BAB is fair game for talking shit.

In BAB, you're having work experiences without the work.

Relationships need time to bake. Trust doesn't magically appear; it's cautiously built over time via shared experience. The majority of these experiences are created during the regular work day, and I'm certain there are a great many healthy professional relationships that are defined and maintained in this manner, but I want my teams closer. I'm not suggesting group hugs and voices united singing "Kumbaya." I'm looking for each team member to have the opportunity to understand each other slightly more than through what they see when they're at work.

The more you understand how your coworkers tick, the better you're able to work with them. You'll stop seeing them as the role, the title, or the keeper of a particular political agenda. They are just...Phillip. And you know what I know about Phillip? He's the manager who used to wait too long to speak in a meeting. He had plenty to say that mattered, but he used to be too shy to say it.

Two months of trash talking over BAB showed me his reservations, so I learned to pull Phillip into the meeting conversations as quickly as possible. After a few pulls, he started to do it himself. After a few weeks, you couldn't get him to shut up.

The Second Staff Meeting

The inspiration for the game came from a regularly scheduled bridge game at Netscape, and there's nothing special about BAB that makes it the perfect lunchtime game. I chose BAB because it's a team-based game that fits nicely in a lunch hour.

You bet I maneuvered Leo and Vincent onto the same team for weeks on end. There was no magical moment during one game when they suddenly understood each other. Leo and Vincent continued to bicker in meetings, but over time the tone changed from the passive-aggressive to the playful talking of trash. They turned competition into something healthy and fun.

In the safe competition that is BAB, you learn how to work together better by understanding that winning doesn't always mean hitting your dates, getting paid, or receiving a promotion. Winning can be a simple, playful thing: "We were awesome as we kicked your ass."

More importantly, BAB is a regular forum for experiencing that relationships are not defined just by the work we do together, but who we become with each other when we aren't looking.

CHAPTER 19

Your People

In your career as a geek, there's a list of essential career intangibles. These are the things you need to do in order to be successful, which are also maddeningly difficult to measure. There is no direct correlation between completing these activities and a raise. It's unlikely that accomplishing these indefinite tasks will end up in your review, but via organizational and social osmosis, you've learned these intangibles are essential in order to grow.

I want to talk about one: networking.

There are two types of networking. Basic networking is what you do at work. It's a target-rich environment with coworkers, your boss, and those of interest in close proximity. It's work, but it's easy work because your day is full of those you depend on, and you've learned that professionally befriending these people keeps you comfortably in the know.

I'm going to call the other type "people networking," and it's harder work. This is when you put yourself out there. It's attending a conference where you know no one. It's driving to the city to sit in a coffee shop with 10 strangers bonded by a programming language. It's a leap for the socially awkward, but the infrequent reward is that you discover Your People.

I don't have a good definition for these people, so I made a list. My hope is that as you read this list you'll think of at least one person you know who is already Your People:

- Your connection with Your People is instant and obvious; it transcends age and experience.

- The best way to discover whether someone is Your People is absence. If, when they return, it's as if they never left, they are Your People.

- There are more of them than you expect, but their number is disguised by the ebb and flow of their presence in your life.

- An investment of time with them will be repaid, but not in a way you can predict or expect. That is the point.

- Your People will piss you off because the relationship is genuine. They do not coddle and they do not spin. Consequently, Your People error-correct you in ways that others cannot.

- You may call on each other without reason, randomly. During these random visits, hours of time will vanish, and neither you nor Your People will notice.

- Conversely, long silences are also acceptable and comfortable.

- Your People have a knack for showing up when you need them, even if you didn't know you needed them prior to their arrival. I don't know how they do this, but the more People you have, the more likely it is that this will happen.

- Your People rarely demand anything. But when either you or they make a request, neither the request nor the agreement to do it is ever in question.

- Your People keep in you in balance. Their presence reminds you first that you're never flying solo and, second, that there are two sides to every story.

- Your People instinctively know who you are and are able to say accurate and valuable things to you and about you with stunningly little data.

- You get mail all day from everyone, but you always stop to read mail from Your People.

- Your People will always be Your People—even if they leave and never return.

When I'm talking about Your People, I am not thinking of your best friend. Sure, your best friend might be Your People, but I'm talking about a larger population who aren't necessarily your friends and who isn't your family. These are a strange lot of people you've discovered in a motley array of places because you were searching for them.

Furthermore, I am not suggesting that those who are not Your People are somehow less valuable. In fact, the majority of the folks in your life are going to be extraordinarily more work than those who are instantly familiar. The work in bridging the gap between you and those who are harder to know is also an essential intangible skill.

Lastly, while Your People may be less work, they are harder people to have in your life. These are not people that let you sit in place, these are people who hold a mirror up to your fuck-ups, and who explain, in excruciating detail, exactly what you don't want to hear. If they did not do these things, they would not be Your People.

Share What You Build

As a geek, it's going to take quite a shove to get you out of your Cave and into a situation where you're likely to stumble upon Your People. A list twice the size as the one here isn't convincing you to move an inch, because strangers are, well, strange. They're unpredictable nobodies who have no idea they're supposed to be your new genuine friends.

My end run around my social insecurity has always been my hobby: writing. It's late on Monday night and I'm blaring *Thriller* because I'm still missing Michael Jackson while I'm transforming this article from a blog entry into a chapter for the book. The lights are all off, and I'm wearing a hood because this month I'm a better writer when my head's covered. Go figure.

This writing hobby, this wonderful, dark, antisocial place has the fortunate upside of appealing to people I do not know, and when I'm not looking, I find ways to use the writing to find more people. I publish a blog entry and carefully read every comment for a sign of a person who I need to follow up with. I turn a chapter into a presentation. A presentation that I give to a room full of strangers who, when I'm done, occasionally approach me to talk about these things I write when I'm alone. These presentations are often at conferences that I've discovered are target-rich environments for people I need to know.

Geeks build stuff. I'm not sure what you build, but when no one is looking, you build something. I'm not talking about what you're paid to build; I'm talking about what you build for yourself. You have a different relationship with this work than the work you've been asked to do. You have more confidence about a work that is entirely yours. I see no reason why you can't parlay that confidence into conversation with others who share your interest in the intimacy of that which you build for yourself.

More good news. Likely candidates are nearby. You probably already know who they are, and you likely already talk with them daily, but you've also likely never seen them.

Just because you have hundreds of Twitter followers or an instant messenger list chock full of names doesn't mean you've found Your People. The final addition to my list is, "They're Your People because you know them." I'm not suggesting your Facebook pals aren't an important part of your life, but until you've sat in a bar arguing about the relative benefits of your favorite programming languages until 2 a.m., you don't know how someone is built.

The Web connects us, but the medium also filters out the aspects of humanity that make us interesting and knowable. You're not going to know me until you see that I talk with my hands. I'm not going to know you until I realize that when you're really thinking about a thing, you can't look anyone in the eyes, because it distracts you.

You Tell Stories

All day. It's a constant story being composed in your head. You're doing it right now. You think you're reading this paragraph that I've written, but what you're actually doing is telling yourself the story of reading this paragraph. It's your inner dialog, and it's often full of shit.

I'm not saying you deliberately lie to yourself. OK, maybe I am, but we're all doing it. We're all gathering data through the course of the day and creating a story based on that data, our experience, and our moods. It's a perfectly natural phenomenon to guide the narrative in our favor. We see the world how we want. A carpenter sees all problems as a nail. I see problems as finite state machines.

As we edit our days into these stories, there is always a risk of fiction. This is why you need to identify and nurture Your People.

You tell these stories to Your People without reservation. Your People love your stories—fiction and all. They love how you tell them, they laugh about the lies you tell yourself, and then they stop and they tell you the truth.

Networking is the art of finding those who are willing to listen to and critique your stories, so go look at your Inbox. Better yet, go look at your Sent box. Check your phone and see who you call the most and who calls you. I'm certain that, right now, one of Your People wants to hear a story and they have one for you, too.

CHAPTER 20

Wanted

Jesse walked.

Monday is the day we set aside for new hires. All the new hires spend the morning learning about the company, figuring out how to create accounts, and becoming indoctrinated in company culture. When lunch time arrives, managers pick up their new employees and take them to lunch.

Their morning starts at 9 a.m., and at 9:15 I got a call from HR: "Jesse's not here."

Bad traffic, miscommunication, there were a dozen good reasons he wasn't here, but I instantly felt a rock in my stomach: "Jesse walked."

A quick call to my recruiter and the mystery began to unfold. "Oh, yeah, he called just before 5 p.m. on Friday and said he wanted to chat. I was off Friday, should I call him now?"

Yeah, call him. Tell me what I already know.

The recruiter discovered that Jesse was firmly ensconced in a cone of silence because his Friday call was his cold feet call. After three months of phone screens, interviews, offer negotiations, and acceptance of said offer, Jesse was calling to tell us that while he had resigned two weeks ago, a last-minute counteroffer had shown up, and he'd decided to stay...at 4:45 p.m. on his last day.

Jesse walked.

As I sat at my desk, lightly tapping the phone headset against my forehead, I thought how simple it would be to be pissed. In terms of respect, trust, and professionalism, Jesse had screwed me in just about every manner possible, but in this case, the fault would be mine.

I had not explained to Jesse that he was wanted.

The Requisition Situation

This chapter talks about the beginning and the end of the hiring process. Whether you're a manager or not, I'm going to make sure you know two things: first, that you understand how urgent it is to hire, and second, how to make sure those hired actually show up. There's a huge pile of work in the middle of this process involving phone screens, interviews, and offers, but for this chapter we'll just focus on the beginning and the end.

Let's start by understanding where this whole hiring process starts. We need to talk about requisitions.

In many companies, jobs are ruled by requisitions ("reqs"). These imaginary pieces of paper give you, the hiring manager, the permission to hire, but they serve two other purposes. First, they document and formalize the process of hiring a new full-time person, and more importantly, they give executives visibility into the state of the company's growth.

It varies by company, but reqs, specifically open, approved reqs, are one of the more popular organizational levers the execs have to control the growth of the company. In software development, one of your larger corporate expenses is base salary, which means the moment uncertainty appears on you company's horizon, reqs (read: potential large expenses) are one of the first things to vanish.

This leads to the most important rule regarding requisitions:

Reqs vanish randomly, often without notice, without reason, and at the least convenient time.

In larger companies, the bureaucracy involved in actually getting an approved req is impressive. When the req is finally approved by the 17th person you don't know, you have a false sense of accomplishment. You believe this req is yours, but there is really only one way to make it yours—make the hire.

It's not just corporate nervousness that causes reqs to vanish. Your boss, whom you love, is a likely req-stealing culprit. *Anton's got a guy right now who is perfect for his team and we've only got one req. He can hire him right now, and I swear we'll get you a req when you find someone.*

You believe your boss. You trust your boss, so you give him your req, and Anton's a happy guy and you feel like you've done the team a solid. Except that when you actually find someone, guess what, you don't have a req. Neither does your boss, because some time between when you gave your req and actually found someone for your position, the first rule was invoked: every single req in the company was frozen.

I'm guessing 50% of the reqs I've managed to get approved in my career have resulted in a hire. Meaning, a flip of a coin would as accurately predict whether or not I'd be able to hire someone.

From the moment there's a hint of an idea of a req in your future, you need to work on improving your chances that you'll be able to hire. And that means, as quickly as possible, you need to: find the person, phone screen them, interview them, interview them again, negotiate an offer, get that offer accepted, and get them in the building. Think of that as you're staring at your shiny new req. Think that the industry average for hiring against an approved req is 90 days—three months—and each of those days represents a day that someone, somewhere can steal your req. This why you need to...

Spend an Hour a Day on Each Req You Have

We'll talk about how to make sure they'll show up in a bit, but to start you need to get the pump primed. A former boss helpfully suggested, "Spend an hour a day on each req on your plate."

An hour?

If you've got an approved req, you have approval to grow your team. To add new skill sets. To build more stuff. In your role as a manager, I ask: "What's more important than growing your team?" No, this isn't a draconian hour; this is a daily reminder that you need to grind away at this req until you've hired someone.

Rands, I have no candidates yet. The req was just approved. I...

Again, reqs vanish. Randomly. At the end of each workday, you need to think, "Phew, no one stole my req."

Here's how to start:

- Search the Web for candidates. *Show me a stranger who will be perfect.*

- Mail friends who might know the perfect person. *Know anyone? How about you?*

- Annoy your recruiter. *Where are my resumés?*

- Ping folks who have turned you down in the past. *Are you ready now?*

- Scan your Inbox and Sent folders for folks you need but may have forgotten. *Really, are you ready now?*

- Read your job description for additional inspiration. *Do I actually know who I'm looking for?*

But isn't this why I have a recruiter?

It's terrific that you have a recruiter. They're going to streamline your entire hiring process, but you still need to spend an hour a day for each req. A quality recruiter is going to find candidates and do time-saving phone screens, and they can keep in-flight candidates warm. When it comes to offer negotiation, they're great at providing you essential compensation telemetry, and they're good at playing bad cop, but as we'll see, it's your job to demonstrate that the candidate is wanted.

I Found Them! I'm Done!

No, you didn't, and no, you aren't.

No, really! He verbally accepted, and he starts in two weeks. It's a done deal.

No, it's not. If randomly vanishing reqs are painful lesson #1 of hiring, painful lesson #2 is:

People lose their flippin' minds during job transitions.

Think back to your last job transition. Think about the mental turmoil. When did you actually fully believe that you were going to accept the new gig? For me, it's about two months after I started.

You keep recruiting; you keep searching for the perfect employee until your new hire is sitting in their office. It's not common for an accepted offer to be declined, but it needs to happen once for you to learn the lesson, to suddenly realize, "Oh, I need to start over. Crap."

Until he's sitting in the seat, in the building, badge hanging from his belt, you haven't hired anyone.

Deliberate Want

Michele's team was embarking on a new technology direction, and while she had the basic talent in place, she needed two more hires and we had the reqs. In a recruiting brainstorm, I sketched out the type of person we needed. "OK, we need Alex. He's the Sr. Architect at this other company, but he's the right combination of technical brilliance and architectural jerk. We need someone with that technical ability and the will to enforce it because we're starting from the ground up."

Her: "Why not hire Alex?"

Me: "He'll never leave his start-up."

"Have you asked?"

"No."

"I'll ask."

She did, and although it took six months, Alex, the perfect fit for the team and for the project, joined the team. Halfway through the recruiting stint with Alex, when it looked like he might not budge, I threw another perfect candidate on her plate and said, "Maybe ask him, too?" Sean was on the team a month after Alex.

Two hires I thought we had absolutely no chance of hiring. Both on the team in a matter of months. Your question is, "What's her secret?" And the answer is dangerously simple—deliberate, consistently expressed, and reinforced want.

Both of the positions we had were attractive. Senior engineering gigs working on a 1.0 product in a name-brand company. But these guys were the top of the field. Recognized names. There were any number of opportunities across the Valley that would be attractive. How'd we win?

We continually and consistently explained that they were wanted.

The idea of a new gig, a fresh start, is appealing because of its simplicity. You know nothing about your future team; you have no idea about potential death marches, or that guy down the hall who just bugs you for no particular reason. It's simple to think about the future optimistically because the future hasn't screwed you...yet.

This optimism fades in the middle of the night when you open your eyes, startled, and think, "Why in the world would I leave a solid gig with people I know and a bright future?" The reasons are myriad, but that's not the point. The point is for any big decision, you're going to question it from every single angle. You're going to have endless inner dialogues with yourself. You're going to talk yourself into the gig, and then you're going to talk yourself out of it.

It's exhausting.

Michele's message during the entire hiring process was, "You are the best person for this gig. We want you." Remember that we're not talking about random, anonymous candidates; we're talking about handpicked candidates.

Before any interview, she'd drive to them, explain the gig, and begin, "You are the best person for this gig. We want you." After the first round of interviews, her message was the same: "See, this gig is perfect for you. We want you."

When we started the offer negotiations, she worked with the recruiter and knew exactly what we'd need to do to lure the candidates. She knew that base salary was a big deal for Alex. She knew Sean was going to be a stickler about stock. There was no offer negotiation, because Michele constructed offers that were going to be accepted. She presented them: "This is the offer you wanted. This gig is perfect for you. We want you."

Once the offers were accepted, Michele didn't change her tone or message a bit. She'd had rockstars walk before, and she knew the slippery inner dialogues that were going on. She knew that change begets more change and that the easiest time to lose someone was during that post-courtship purgatory between gigs. She had her team take them to drinks. She planted seeds of future work that would need to be done. She reminded them, "We want you."

This strategy reads like a massive ego-stroke for an attention-starved engineering rockstar, but it's not. Whether you have pre-identified a candidate for your gig or you're lucky enough to randomly find a great fit in a pile of anonymous resumés, the strategy is the same: you consistently remind the candidate that they are wanted. In the mental chaos that is a career change, you and your gig are unchanging in your message. You're not coddling them; you're a constant amongst mental chaos.

Hire for Your Career

The strategy I'm proposing steps on a lot of recruiter toes. Recruiters are professional relationship people and their instinctive reads on candidates can be eerily accurate, but their job is the hire and once the hire shows up, the recruiter vanishes. The relationship is ended because the job is done.

Your professional relationship with those you hire and work with is never over. If you're hiring well, you're hiring people not just for this job, but for your career. These are the people who, for better or worse, will explain to others what it is like to work with you. They'll explain your quirks, your weaknesses, and your strengths. When they eventually leave the group, they're taking your reputation with them. You may never talk to them again, but they'll continue to talk about you, and my question is: what stories are they going to tell?

Your daily, hands-on management of your hiring isn't just going to improve your hiring process; it's going to improve your career because from the first moment you interact with your future employee, you demonstrate that you care.

Jesse didn't decide to turn us down at 4:45 p.m. on his last day. The decision began long before that, and I wasn't listening. I didn't hear the parts of his current job he loved, because I didn't do the phone screen. I didn't understand his concerns about leaving the first job since college that he loved, because I didn't build enough trust in the interview. I didn't hear him drifting away during the offer negotiation. The last thing I heard about Jesse is that he walked.

CHAPTER 21

The Toxic Paradox

Everyone is an adjustment. When you're interacting with anyone, you leave the core you and become slightly them. This is not a betrayal of who you are; this is the middle ground we define between any two people. It's a place of compromise so we can communicate.

There are those people with whom this is an easy, natural place to reach. It's that friend you haven't seen or heard from in six months, and how you know it will take 12 seconds for both of you to get back into a familiar place where the six months vanish. It's the easy Now.

Then there are those people who are more work. They require a protocol of context setting, translation, and cautious check-ins. *Hi, I said this, is this what you heard? OK, good.* This set of abilities, of communication skills, is more work and is a skill you refine over the years. It is a requirement of seasoned managers who are constantly thrown into meetings with strangers where they need to move quickly and efficiently past the "getting to know you" phase and into the "we've got work to do" portion of the meeting.

My guess is the majority of our relationships fall into either the natural or slightly-more-work buckets. The majority of the folks you surround yourself with both inside and outside of work are manageable. Not all are natural, so they are work, but you can live with them and are willing to do the work to maintain the relationships.

Then, there are those you can't handle. These are the folks who, for reasons you may never understand, behave in a way that you'll never grasp, can't define, nor will ever like.

These people are toxic.

Big Fat Toxic Assumptions

This chapter is going to end with someone getting fired, and it makes two large, uncomfortable assumptions.

First, as I explain the serious issues with toxic coworkers, I need to remind you that when it comes to disconnects between two people, there are always two vastly different stories regarding perceived toxicity. If I were to say that Veronica had a toxic personality, you would do well to spend some time with Veronica and learn about her perception of me. While I might have done as much due diligence as possible to examine every possible personality angle regarding Veronica, there would still be essential data to be gathered directly from her.

A declaration of toxicity is a judgment. Sometimes defined by a group, sometimes spearheaded by an influential individual who simply cannot find a healthy way to relate to this person, but regardless, never trust a toxicity label without doing your own research.

Second, this chapter isn't about fixing this toxic person, but rather your perspective of them. I'm assuming you're done trying to bridge the gap between you and this person. If you're a manager, this is hopefully the end result of months of careful negotiating, delicate compromise, and hardcore communication.

There are entire parts of your organization dedicated to providing ideas and skills about how to interact better with anyone on your team, and this chapter assumes you've employed all of them.

I'm not going to walk you through strategies for dealing with toxic people, because you're past that. This person is infecting the team with their toxicity, and you're vastly underestimating the daily damage this person is doing to the group.

This chapter is here to convince you it's time to make a change.

Go Team!

A toxic person kills, and by kills, I mean totally destroys teamwork.

"Teamwork" is one of those painful managementese buzzwords that is blindly used at inopportune times as a means of motivation. "We need better teamwork to improve efficiency and productivity." Ew. I just threw up in my mouth. Fact is, teamwork—teams of people actually working together—is kinda magical.

Listen, it takes all I can muster to get along with my brother who I've known my entire life, so the fact that a group of people sitting in close proximity to each other can build a product without killing each other is a fucking miracle.

It's not actually a miracle. It's years of practice, starting in elementary school where you learned the basics: raise your hand when you want to speak, say "please" and "thank you," and don't eat the glue. In school, you learn just as much about how to deal with different types of personalities as you do about the world, so when it comes time to jump into the workforce, you already have years of experience in social interactions with a variety of personalities.

However, all of these hand-raising, glue-free pleasantries barely prepare you for a toxic personality.

Let's go back to the personality buckets I described earlier: natural, work, and toxic. Let's say the cost of natural relationships is 1x. It's the base unit. It's no work; it's simple. Let's say that the work relationships are 2x. It requires twice as much effort on your part to bridge the communication and social gap. It's not difficult; it's just work. You reduce this cost as you gather more experience and as you get to know people a bit, but these relationships will never be totally natural. Fact of life.

A toxic relationship cannot be measured in terms of these work units, because, at its core, it does not work. You never get to a state of comfortable communication in these relationships. They are never predictable, nor very productive, because you are in a constant state of social corrosion. There are brief moments of clarity where you have a lightning strike of insight: *she's this way because I said that, and this is how she always reacts to that...so I won't do that. Brilliant!*

These moments of respite are short-lived. For reasons you may never understand, you are incapable of reverse engineering this personality, or your patterns of reaction to it, and it's only a matter of time before you rediscover this basic disconnect and move back to thrashing around, trying to figure out the unknowable.

Yes, this is a worst-case scenario.

Groups of people get along because they all subscribe to a similar culture. Yes, these people are all unique, but they get along because they have a similar belief system and buy into the same goals. This similarity of beliefs has a lot of benefits, but the biggest win is that it reduces organizational friction. There are heated arguments, but they are arguments based on similar beliefs, and the presence of these beliefs means these arguments have a chance of resolution.

Now, think about your base interaction with this toxic person. You sit down in the conference room across from them, and the topic at hand is easy. *"We're discussing a small change to the architecture, and since you own a big part of it, I wanted to get your opinion."*

Reasonable. Professional. Respectful.

"THIS ISN'T A SMALL CHANGE. YOU HAVEN'T THOUGHT THIS THROUGH. WHY WASN'T I CONSULTED EARLIER? HOW COULD WE CONSIDER THIS GIVEN WHAT I SAID 14 MONTHS AGO ON THIS VERY TOPIC WHEN I WAS IGNORED...?"

It's a flood of incomprehensible toxicity. Now, inside of the flood is a bunch of historic fuckups on everyone's part, but go back and read that previous paragraph. Are you seeing any of the content, or are you seeing the toxicity?

Do the math. This is one meeting, and while you might pull off a meeting win when everyone's calmed down, you're spending the first 30 minutes of the meeting in ALL CAPS, and here's the bad news: a majority of the team is having similar experiences. Most of the folks interacting with this person are spending their time trying to figure out how to keep this person from going ALL CAPS rather than actually getting work done.

After a time, this results in even more damage. People stop scheduling meetings with this person. They stop traveling to this person's part of the building. And again, I'm not talking about one or two people here, I'm talking about the majority of the team.

My definition of toxicity isn't based on the idea that you are incapable of getting to a professional place with this person; it's based on the idea that the culture of your group, your company, is literally rejecting this person. Everyone is avoiding this corrosive person, and this avoidance is affecting productivity and morale across the board. It's a daily emotional tax of frustration and demoralization.

A culture rarely changes for one person, and in the case of a toxic person, a culture will protect itself through rejection.

A Toxic Paradox

Rands, he's just not getting along with the right people.

No.

This is not high school. I'm not talking about cliques here; I'm talking about culture. Cliques are inevitable micro-collections of people who like the look and sound of each other. Culture is the foundational broad strokes of beliefs, values, and goals in a group of people, and a healthy culture is inclusive. It seeks out new members who evolve the culture into something new and better. It's constantly growing in interesting ways because of the people it's built on.

A rejection by the culture, while not pleasant for anyone involved, is not a rejection based on individual taste, and it's not because someone doesn't like someone else. It's a rejection because of a lack of shared core beliefs. Vastly different personalities get along famously when they share a common goal.

Yes. People get petty and people dislike each other for seemingly inane reasons, and yes, it's a manager's job, along with HR, to figure out how to build a constructive working relationship among these people, but this is not the situation I'm describing. I'm talking about trying to shove a toxic square peg in a cultural round hole. It doesn't work. Keep pushing all you want, but…it's not happening.

It's hard to remember this when a toxic person is yelling at you, but they're not actually yelling at *you*. They're yelling at the culture. They're pissed because their belief structure isn't a fit with just about everyone else's and they know it. They know that they're not winning this argument…ever. They know that in order to win this argument, they'd need to restart the culture of the company, and such an endeavor makes a re-org look like a walk in the park.

And, here's the worst part: they might be right.

The history of the Silicon Valley is full of stories of toxic people who were, well…right. These people were physically removed from their respective companies, but their agenda, their ideas, however unpalatable to the existing cultural regime, were actually the right thing to do for that particular company.

The paradox is that we need these toxic people. We need these self-centered assholes to totally ignore cultural conventions and to mix things up beyond recognition. They don't need social grace and they don't need charisma. Both help, but their value lies in their intense belief in their own culture.

We need these folks, but it can't be at the cost of the existing culture. Yes, this toxic person might have a core cultural contradictory belief that is key to the future of the business, but assess the risk. What if the cost of integrating that idea is half the team quitting because they can't work with the idea's toxic architect? Is that a viable solution?

No? Maybe?

The deportation of a toxic asset is a judgment call, and it's based on the fundamental idea that fitting in is easy, but real change is hard.

Everyone Is an Adjustment

Your career is defined by two tasks: what hard problems have you solved and whom have you joined in solving these problems? For me, the harder the problems, the trickier the people, the better. In an impossible challenge, I believe, there are invaluable lessons.

A truly toxic person is not a disruption; that person is a disaster. When you're measuring the damage and the emotional anguish caused by a single person, the question isn't, "What am I going to do?"; the question is, "How quickly can I do it?"

CHAPTER 22

The Pond

"Can I work remote?"

I cringe. It's Ian, and Ian is a senior engineer. He's a rock. He gets it done. I never have to ask him twice, and after six years, Ian has every right to ask to work remote. But I'm still freaked because my first thought when anyone asks to work remotely is, "This fine person is a year away from either quitting or being fired." Why? Because they're asking to leave the Pond.

The Unspoken Royal We

When I think of communication in a large group of people, I imagine a pond. Small, round, slightly green water. You can see the edges of this pond, and there's a willow tree over there looking both informed and sad. Metaphorically, all the people in the organization are standing somewhere on this pond. Our positions are based on whom we know and where we are in the organization chart. When something happens in the company, when something noteworthy is said, a drop falls in the pond and creates a ripple.

The ripple is the piece of information traveling from one person to the others. Big drop, big ripple...travels farther.

With me so far?

There is a constant flow of information in your company. That means there are constant drips in the Pond, creating various-sized ripples traveling every which way, bumping into each other, and transforming each other into slightly mutated ripples. These mutated ripples are the rumor mill, gossip, and all those small pieces of slightly bizarre information that cross your path during the course of the day.

If you're in the Pond, you're gathering data, whether it's intended for you or not. It's inevitable. It's what we do as curious humans; we receive information, digest it, alter it, and then send it on its way, tweaked to our own personal wavelengths.

A remote employee is not in the Pond. Yes, he's on the mailing lists and he aggressively updates the wiki, but the subtle, unintentional, tweaked, quiet information that is transferred throughout the Pond doesn't leave the Pond. There are those whose job it is to look at the Pond and attempt to relay the interesting ripples, but while these program and project managers are well intentioned, they relay poorly because they're just single observers of ripples. Real information is never conveyed by the individual; we understand by listening as a group.

The group forms a collective picture of the state of the Pond—a distributed picture understood by everyone, but never completely known by one. It is the unspoken royal "we," and this intricate, immeasurable thing is absolutely essential to how a group gets things done well.

Do You Mean It?

Remote has to work. It's not just Ian. There are bright people in your building right now who are going to want to return home to Colorado, and you're going to let them because losing them is not an option. Also, there's a planet full of talented people who will always be at a distance, but who represent huge, untapped productivity for your team. Your challenge is how to augment the remote employee's absence from the Pond.

This chapter is about how to decrease the risk that you will have to fire your favorite employee who decides to become remote. I'd like to give advice from the other side, on how to work remotely, but I've never done it. I don't have the personality. My professional satisfaction comes from being able to look those I depend on in the eye and ask, "Do you mean it?" There is essential content to be discovered in that stare that will never be fully conveyed in an email, IM, or tweet.

My belief is that without deliberate attention, the remote employee slowly becomes irrelevant to the organization. Through no fault of their own, they can be gradually pushed to the edge of what's important. And when you're at the edge, you're an organizational shudder from falling over it. Failure happens at the edges.

Avoiding failure involves asking four questions before they leave:

- Do they have the personality?
- Do they have the right job?
- Does the culture support it?
- Do you have a remote friction detection and resolution policy?

The Personality

Whether the employee has the right personality to be a productive remote worker is a tricky call because most of your data about this person is based on working with them. What's going to happen when you can't see them? How are they going to react when you forget to include them in the staff call? How are they going to feel when the product launches and they aren't there to celebrate?

This is what I consider.

Are they eloquent in email?

Every bit of communication is more expensive with remote folks, so they'd better be good at it—no matter the medium. Can this person construct and convey a complex argument in a single email? Can this person make an important point...via iChat? Written communication is bereft of much of the intangible value of the Pond. It lacks the nuance of face-to-face communication, which means the author needs to be painfully explicit about the details. Can this person do that?

Are they self-directed?

How do they deal with ambiguity? If you've given them crap direction, do they bump around for a bit before admitting defeat, or do they immediately ask for clarification? Many of the subtle ways you check in and error-correct coworkers leave with them. If they're in the weeds, are they going to ask for help? How long until they ask for help?

How detail-oriented are they?

If self-direction indicates how they start a thing, their detail orientation is how well they finish. Is this a person who needs help across the finish line? Do they get lost in nonessential details? When you ask for a thing, are you getting the end result you expect?

How well do they know the Pond?

We'll talk about their job in a moment, but whatever that job is, it will have dependencies on people they are leaving behind. Does this person know how the organization communicates? Do they know both the organizational structure as well as the social structure? Are they asking you who to follow up with, or are you asking them? Are they instinctively aware of whom they might piss off and proactively account for this in the first mail rather than after the flame-o-gram?

Do they need the Pond?

Knowledge of the Pond is great, but does this person thrive because of the Pond? How much of their day do they spend talking with coworkers? Is this conversation essential to what they do or purely social? Which part of them are you going to socially amputate when they're no longer in the building?

Are they reliable?

I imply at the beginning of this chapter that it's a senior employee who has a better chance at being successful remotely, but that's not true. The ability to work remotely is not entirely a function of seniority; it's also genetic. There are those who do it better solo. Their standard operating procedure is to simply get it done. Seniority can improve personal efficiency and the quality of the finished product, but I've discovered innate reliability at all levels of experience. There are people who simply do what they say they're going to do.

The Right Job

Typical corporate logic dictates that a remote employee should work on a project that is separable from the rest of the team's. The reasoning here is flawed. The belief is that the inconvenience of communication and decision-making latency around their distance means they should be separated and placed on nondependent work.

Every part of that reasoning is wrong. Every part is another reason that remote fails.

My most successful remote employee was a perfect anomaly. He wrote standards—protocols. The heart of his job was to define a structured means of communication where the primary goal was the removal of ambiguity. He was a phenomenal communicator. He went out of his way to completely and promptly answer every email. 24 hours a day. When he visited, he took the time to do a complete circumnavigation of the Pond, vetting all the ripples he could find. He instinctively knew that the skill in defining a protocol is creating a structure that is going to meet the needs of right now, but also the unimagined needs of five years from now. And he applied that not only to what he wrote, but also to how he worked. He was a wonderful anomaly, and he taught me that a remote job must be perceived, in all ways, as equal to a local one.

There should be absolutely no consideration of a person's location on the planet Earth when considering the work you need of them. Each time the concern "Well, they're remote" comes up, you need to turn the concern around and ask, "What about my company, my people, or the work makes remote an issue?" because that is what needs to be considered locally.

The Culture

How are those back in the Pond viewing the remote employee? The means by which Pond-based employees discriminate varies from the discreet to the direct, from the passive to the aggressive. The reason for this discrimination always boils down to a single, fundamental tension: remote creates productivity friction.

The friction sounds something like this:

- "I don't know what the hell this remote person is doing, so I'm going to assume he's stumbling around the house in his underwear."

- "This remote person is messing with my deadline or deliverable."

- "He doesn't answer his email."

How long does it take to build a thing of quality? There's a cost and the question is how the remote worker affects this cost. Anything higher than the cost of a local employee creates friction. What was a 27-second walk down the hallway to yell at Bob about his crap code is now 30 minutes constructing an email. Staff meetings start with a wasted 10 minutes trying to get the videoconferencing to connect. Every single communication with a remote worker costs more and generates more ripples in the Pond, and both their job and yours is either to make this cost go away, or to justify it.

Respect comes from knowledge, and the question is: does your culture support a constant and consistent flow of knowledge to and from the remote worker?

Let's find out:

- Have you created or implemented specific communication media for the team? Wikis? IRC? Are they used? Do different teams need different media? Are there too many and, if so, how are you going to anoint the one true medium?

- Other than the job, how are you encouraging other random interactions between local and remote folks?

- How often are you seeing these remote folks face-to-face? My vote is at least monthly.

Friction Detection

Remote friction is going to crop up. Just like interpersonal tensions randomly appear in the building, so does friction around remote employees. What are you doing not only to detect these, but also fix them?

An example: I hate meetings, but the brilliant thing about a meeting is that it's full of people, and in a room full of people you never quite know what the hell is going to happen. The knee-jerk reaction to bridging this meeting gap when there are remote workers is always, "We need good videoconferencing software."

After 10 years of hearing this argument, I'm calling fail. Videoconferencing works when you need to talk to your kids during that trip to Chicago. It fills that visual gap, but all of the video-conferencing solutions I've been a part of relative to a meeting create friction rather than remove it.

Yes, I can see Anne on the screen, but she's flat. She's also got this 1/10th of a second lag on the conversation, which doesn't sound like a lot until you're in the middle of that strategic rant about design and Anne chimes in, mid-sentence, with a bright thought that completely disturbs the creative cadence of your rant. That 1/10th of a second. Her inability to inject her essential thought at precisely the right moment. These micro-disturbances of the Force are a constant reminder that Anne's not there. She's being projected on the conference room wall like a well-intentioned screensaver. This isn't just hurting the tempo of the meeting, it's eroding her credibility.

In this case, surprisingly, less technology, rather than more, is better. Skype's proximity to my computer and the usual lack of lag is far superior to videoconferencing for 1:1s, and spending a little money on a quality Polycom is a fine solution for the staff meeting, but technology is a tool and never the answer.

Friction detection is paying attention to all the ways a remote employee interacts with the group and constantly asking, "Is this working?"

Another Pond

You, as the manager of people, are responsible for making the remote call regarding a person, putting them in the right job, and making sure the culture supports remote people. But the responsibility of delivering while remote is squarely on the remote employee. Yes, a remote employee answers to himself. At four in the afternoon when they run into an impossible problem, it's almost entirely up to them to develop their plan of attack.

Working remotely isn't a privilege; it's work. And it's the same work we're all doing back at the mothership…fully clothed…in the Pond.

YOUR DAILY TOOLKIT

The list of essential daily skills you need as a software developer that high school and college did not prepare you for is impressive.

It's great that you can explain Big O notation, but what class taught you about presenting to the CEO? I'm happy you're an Emacs zealot, but do you know who in your 2 p.m. meeting is out to professionally screw you?

The stereotype regarding engineers is we want to code—we want to hide in our caves, far from people, and code. And we do. Coding is awesome, but that's not all you want to do. You're halfway through *Being Geek*, and that means you now understand there is a larger set of skills necessary to being a successful developer.

Manage your time—it's an invaluable commodity—obsess about the tools you use, and take the time to understand the people around you. Figure how to speak their language so you can learn how to convey your bright ideas to anyone.

CHAPTER 23

The Nerd Handbook

OK, we're halfway through the book, so it's time for a break. Much of this book is focused on you. Your current job and your plan for your career. This wonderfully narcissistic journey is not one you're going to complete alone; you have an extensive supporting cast.

It's not just your boss and your coworkers, but also your friends. Angela, who you've known for years, who you must meet for a drink and a professional vent every three months. There's Ryan, the annoying guy on the train who somehow randomly lands that quip that changes your day. And Lorraine. She runs the coffee shop, and her mood and her coffee can set the tone for the start of your day. You are surrounded by folks who support you, whether you realize it or not, and I haven't even mentioned the most important—your significant other.

The following chapter is not for you; it's for them. My hope is that you can look up from this book and see them sitting there on the couch. They have questions about you. They don't know how you can sit at the computer for five hours straight. They find you funny, but they don't know where that funny comes from.

Stand up and hand them this chapter right now. If they're not in visual range, turn the corner of the page as a reminder that part of your success will be the understanding of those who support you.

Understanding Your Nerd

Hi. You've just been handed this book by someone important to you who also happens to be a nerd. This nerd would like you to read this chapter so that you can better understand those strange quirks you've already recognized but may not understand.

See, a nerd needs a project because a nerd builds stuff. All the time. Those lulls in the conversation over dinner? That's the nerd working on his project in his head.

It's unlikely that this project is a nerd's day job, because his opinion regarding his job is, "Been there, done that." We'll explore the consequences of this seemingly short attention span in a bit, but for now this project is the other big thing your nerd is building, and I've no idea what it is, but you should.

At some point, you, the nerd's companion, were the project. You were showered with the fire hose of attention because you were the bright and shiny new development in your nerd's life. There is also a chance that you're lucky and you are currently your nerd's project. Congrats. Don't get too comfortable, though, because he'll move on, and when that happens, you'll be wondering what happened to all the attention. This handbook might help.

Understand Your Nerd's Relation to the Computer

It's clichéd, but a nerd is defined by his computer, and you need to understand why.

First, a majority of the folks on the planet either have no idea how a computer works or they look at it and think "it's magic." Nerds know how a computer works. They intimately know how a computer works. When you ask a nerd, "When I click this, it takes a while for the thing to show up. Do you know what's wrong?" they know what's wrong. A nerd has a mental model of the hardware and the software in his head. While the rest of the world sees magic, your nerd knows how the magic works, he knows the magic is a long series of ones and zeros moving across your screen with impressive speed, and he knows how to make those bits move faster.

The nerd has based his career, maybe his life, on the computer, and as we'll see, this intimate relationship has altered his view of the world. He sees the world as a system that, given enough time and effort, is completely knowable. This is a fragile illusion that your nerd has adopted, but it's a pleasant one that gets your nerd through the day. When the illusion is broken, you are going to discover that...

Your Nerd Has Control Issues

Your nerd lives in a monospaced typeface world. Whereas everyone else is traipsing around picking dazzling fonts to describe their world, your nerd has carefully selected a monospace typeface, which he avidly uses to manipulate the world deftly via a command-line interface while the rest fumble around with a mouse.

The reason for this typeface selection is, of course, practicality. Monospace typefaces have a knowable width. Ten letters on one line are the same width as any other ten letters, which puts the world into a pleasant grid construction where X and Y mean something.

These control issues mean your nerd is sensitive to drastic changes in his environment. Think travel. Think job changes. These types of system-redefining events force your nerd to recognize that the world is not always nor entirely a knowable place, and until he reconstructs this illusion, he's going to be frustrated and he's going to act erratically. I develop an incredibly short fuse during system-redefining events, and I'm much more likely to lose it over something trivial and stupid. This is one of the reasons that...

Your Nerd Has Built Himself a Cave

I've written about the Cave elsewhere, but here are the basics. The Cave is designed to allow your nerd to do his favorite thing, which is working on the project. If you want to understand your nerd, stare long and hard at his Cave. How does he have it arranged? When does he tend to go there? How long does he stay?

Each object in the Cave has a particular place and purpose. Even the clutter is well designed. Don't believe me? Grab that seemingly discarded Mac Mini that has been sitting on the floor for two months and hide it. You'll have 10 minutes before he'll come stomping out of the Cave—"Where's the Mac?"

The Cave is also frustrating you because your impression is that it's your nerd's way of checking out, and you are, unfortunately, completely correct. A correctly designed Cave removes your nerd from the physical world and plants him firmly in a virtual one complete with all the toys he needs. Because...

Your Nerd Loves Toys and Puzzles

The joy your nerd finds in his project is one of problem-solving and discovery. As each part of the project is completed, your nerd receives an adrenaline rush that we're going to call the High. Every profession has this—the moment when you've moved significantly closer to done. In many jobs, it's easy to discern when progress is being made: "Look, now we have a door." But in nerds' bit-based work, progress is measured mentally and invisibly in code, algorithms, efficiency, and small mental victories that don't exist in a world of atoms.

There are other ways your nerd can create the High, and he does it all the time. It's another juicy cliché to say that nerds love video games, but that's not what they love. A video game is just one more system where your nerd's job is to figure out the rules that define it, which will enable him to beat it. Yeah, we love to stare at games with a bazillion polygons, but we get the same high from playing *Bejeweled*, getting our Night Elf to Level 70, or endlessly tinkering with a Rubik's Cube. This fits nicely with the fact that...

Nerds Are Fucking Funny

Your nerd spent a lot of his younger life being an outcast because of his strange affinity with the computer. This created a basic bitterness in his psyche that is the foundation for his humor. Now, combine this basic distrust of everything with your nerd's other natural talents, and you'll realize that he sees humor as another game.

Humor is an intellectual puzzle: "How can this particular set of esoteric trivia be constructed to maximize hilarity as quickly as possible?" Your nerd listens hard to recognize humor potential, and when he hears it, he furiously scours his mind to find relevant content from his experience so he can get the funny out as quickly as possible.

This quick wit is only augmented by the fact that...

Your Nerd Has an Amazing Appetite for Information

Many years ago, I dubbed this behavior NADD, or Nerd Attention Deficiency Disorder.

How does a nerd watch TV? Probably one of two ways. First, there's watching TV with you, where the two of you sit and watch one show. Then there's how he watches by himself, when he watches three shows at once. It looks insane. You walk into the room and you're watching your nerd jump between channels every five minutes.

"How can you keep track of anything?"

He keeps track of everything. See, he's already seen all three of these movies…multiple times. He knows the compelling parts of the arcs and is mentally editing his own versions while watching all three. The basic mental move here is the context switch, and your nerd is the king of the context switch.

The ability to instantly context switch also comes from a life on the computer. Your nerd's mental information model for the world is one contained within well-bounded, tidy windows where the most important tool is one that allows your nerd to move swiftly from one window to the next. It's irrelevant that there may be no relationship between these windows. Your nerd is used to making huge contextual leaps where he's talking to a friend in one window, worrying about his 401k in another, and reading about World War II in yet another.

You might suspect that given a world where context is constantly shifting, your nerd can't focus, and you'd be partially correct. All that multitasking isn't efficient. Your nerd knows very little about a lot. For many topics, his knowledge is an inch deep and four miles wide. He's comfortable with this fact because he knows that deep knowledge about any topic is a clever keystroke away. See…

Your Nerd Has Built an Annoyingly Efficient Relevancy Engine in His Head

It's the end of the day, and you and your nerd are hanging out on the couch. The TV is off. There isn't a computer anywhere nearby, and you're giving your nerd the daily debrief. "Spent an hour at the post office trying to ship that package to your mom, and then I went down to that bistro—you know, the one next to the flower shop—and it's closed. Can you believe that?"

And your nerd says, "Cool."

Cool? What's cool? The business closing? The package? How is any of it cool? None of it's cool. Actually, all of it might be cool, but your nerd doesn't believe any of what you're saying is relevant. This is what he heard: "Spent an hour at the post office blah blah blah...."

You can be rightfully pissed off by this behavior—it's simply rude—but seriously, I'm trying to help here. Your nerd's insatiable quest for information and the High has tweaked his brain in an interesting way. For any given piece of incoming information, your nerd is making a lightning-fast assessment: relevant or not relevant? Relevance means that the incoming information fits into the system of things your nerd currently cares about. Expect active involvement from your nerd when you trip the relevance flag. If you trip the irrelevance flag, look for verbal punctuation announcing his judgment of irrelevance. It's the word your nerd says when he's not listening, and it's always the same. My word is "Cool," and when you hear "Cool," I'm not listening.

Information that your nerd is exposed to when the irrelevance flag is waving is forgotten almost immediately. I mean it. Next time you hear "Cool," I want you to ask, "What'd I just say?" That awkward grin on your nerd's face is the first step in getting him to acknowledge that he's the problem in this particular conversation. This behavior is one of the reasons that...

Your Nerd Might Come Off As Not Liking People

Small talk. Those first awkward five minutes when two people are forced to interact. Small talk is the bane of the nerd's existence because small talk is a combination of aspects of the world that your nerd hates. When your nerd is staring at a stranger, all he's thinking is, "I have no system for understanding this messy person in front of me." This is where the shy comes from. This is why nerds hate presenting to crowds.

The skills to interact with other people are there. They just lack a well-defined system.

Advanced Nerd Tweakage

If you're still reading, then I'm thinking your nerd is worth keeping. Even though he's apt to vanish for hours, has a strange sense of humor, doesn't like you touching his stuff, and often doesn't listen when you're talking directly at him, he's a keeper. Go figure.

My advice:

Map the Things He's Bad At to the Things He Loves

You love to travel, but your nerd would prefer to hide in his cave for hours on end chasing the High. You need to convince him of two things. First, you need to convince him that you're going to do your best to recreate his cave in his new surrounding. You're going to create a quiet, dark place where he can orient himself and figure out which way the water flushes down the toilet. Traveling internationally? Carve out three days somewhere quiet at the beginning of the trip. Traveling across the U.S.? How about letting him chill on the bed for a half-day before you drag him out to see the Golden Gate Bridge?

Second, and more importantly, you need to remind him about his insatiable appetite for information. You need to appeal to his deep love of discovering new content and help him understand that there may be no greater content fire hose than waking up in a hotel overlooking the Grand Canal in Venice where you don't speak a word of Italian.

Make It a Project

You might've noticed your nerd's strange relation to food. Does he eat fast? Like really fast? You should know what's going on here. Food is thrown into the irrelevant bucket because it's getting in the way of the content. Exercise, too. Thing is, you want your nerd to eat healthily so that he's here in another 30 years, so how do you change this behavior? You make diet and exercise the project.

For me, exercise became the project 10 years ago after a horrible breakup. When the project was no longer the Ex, I dove into exercise every single day of the week. There were charts tracking my workouts, there were graphs tracking my weight, and there was the exercise. Every single day for two years until the day I passed out in a McDonald's post-workout, after not eating for a day. OK, so time for a new project. Yeah, nerds also have moderation issues. That's a chapter for another book.

Significant nerd behavioral change is only going to happen if your nerd engages in the project heart and soul; otherwise, it's just another thought for the irrelevant bucket.

People Are the Most Interesting Content Out There

If you've got a seriously shy nerd on your hands, try this: ask him how many folks are in his buddy list. How many friends does he have in Facebook? How many folks are following him on Twitter? My guess is that, collectively, your nerd interacts with 10 times more people than you think he does. He can do this because the interaction is via a system he understands—the computer.

Your nerd knows that people are interesting. Just because he can't look your best friend straight in the eye doesn't mean he doesn't want to know what makes her tick, but you need to be the social buffer—the translation layer. You need to find one common thread of interest between your nerd and your friend, and then he'll engage because he will have found relevance.

The Next High

As you discovered when you were the project, your nerd's focus can be deliciously overwhelming, but it will stop. Once a nerd believes he fully knows how a system works, the challenge to understand ceases to exist, and he moves on in search of the Next High.

While I don't know who you are or why in the world you chose a nerd for your companion, I do know that you are not a knowable system. I know that you are messy, just like your nerd. Being your own quirky self will be more than enough to present new and interesting challenges to your nerd.

Besides, it's just as much a nerd's job to figure you out, and maybe someone, somewhere is writing an article about your particular quirks. Good news; he's probably reading it right now.

CHAPTER 24

The Taste of the Day

Think of this. You have a job where, whenever you need to, you can find the absolute truth. When someone asks you, "Phil, why is this happening?" you are 100% confident that you can figure out the precise answer.

This is the idyllic situation many engineers on the planet Earth live in, and, well, it's just a great gig.

I exaggerate. Engineers do have blind spots, but for their work, for their specific pile of bits, they are omniscient. They're their bits, and they constructed them into their specific system where they are intimately familiar with the rules because they defined them.

Outside of my career as an engineer, I've been a store clerk, a butcher, a video rental clerk, a lawyer's assistant, and a bookseller, and although it's been over 15 years since I've done any of these jobs, I remember the sense of naive pointlessness: "What do I build? Well, I sell stuff, cut stuff, or type stuff. I don't really build anything, I... do stuff."

This made the first engineering gig a revelation. "You. We are building a database application and you own this specific part. It is entirely yours. Don't fuck it up."

Delicious, delicious structure. Sweet, sweet definition.

These basic and essential elements of job satisfaction are at the root of why many engineers make horrible managers. They are trained as and love to be control freaks.

The New Gig

Now you have a new job. You have an office and you have a door. On your desk, there's a timer that tracks the number of seconds that it's just you alone in your office. Whenever someone else walks into your office, the timer magically resets to zero.

Today's record for consecutive uninterrupted seconds is 47.

This is not a world an engineer is used to, this interruption-driven day full of people and political calculus. This is where the reputation that your manager does nothing begins. It's your manager who thinks it. It's the close of the day and your manager wonders, "Did I actually do anything today except contend with a constant stream of people coming into my office?"

Try as you might, the structure and definition of your quiet engineering gig is gone. Your days of digital omniscience are over.

This is the big switch between the engineer and the manager. You are leaving the comfortable world of bits for one of bafflingly configured atoms, where you need to figure out how to trust those you work with. Where you need to train folks to make decisions for themselves, but also help them understand it's OK to escalate for help. It's a gig where you need to keep track of everything, constantly reprioritize, but remain strategically limber.

And to do all of this, you need a task tracking system that allows you to strategically forget.

The Taste of the Day

This is my system. Yes, I'm a manager, but there's no reason this system wouldn't work for anyone who feels buried. This system is a mix of my ability to be a systematic thinker with the fact that there is more to do than I can ever complete. I've been using some variation of it for 10 years now, and it's how I run my day and my week.

It all orbits around a task system. Your first question will be: "What task tracking system do you use, Rands?" The answer is a simple: "Whatever works for you." I've used a homegrown Excel system, Tasks, and I'm currently using Things, but as you'll see, the strategic key here is not identification of the task tracking system, it's using it—all the time.

This system is designed to create a living, breathing, manageable list of things you might actually do, and it starts with...

The Morning Scrub

The first task of the day is to set my head. What kind of day am I getting myself into? A quick glance at the calendar gives me the first hint of what to expect. Is this a quiet get-things-done day? A meeting hell day? Or a sky-is-falling day? Each day has a different taste, and the Morning Scrub forces me to set my head appropriately. It gives me a rough sense of my capacity, the people I'll meet, and what they might need. More importantly, it reminds me that *Priority is Relative.*

Humans suffer from a bright'n'shiny complex, where we're titillated by the new. Think of it like this: have you actually done anything with that last domain you bought? No. You had the idea for it on Tuesday morning and you got all fired up, so you bought the domain the moment you got in to work. At lunch you furiously doodled your design in your notebook, fully intending to get home and get started on the HTML/CSS, and then you got home...and watched *Lost.*

Take the bright'n'shiny complex and apply it to your entire group, where everyone is prioritizing their day by their particular inspiration, and it's shocking that we collectively get anything done.

By taking a deep breath and considering your entire day, I'm attempting to ditch all the bright'n'shininess and gather perspective: "What is going to matter today?" With this rough priority scale in mind, I do a complete scrub of the to-do list. Yeah, the whole thing. If you can't get through this list in five uninterrupted minutes, your list is either too long or you're bad at scrubbing. Don't worry about that yet.

The purpose of the Morning Scrub is to land each task into one of three buckets:

Today

> This task must be completed today.

Later

> Not today. Later.

Never

> Yeah, I'm never going to do this task. It's gone. This is an important, essential decision that we'll talk about in a moment.

Initially, getting through this list is tricky because, invariably, a task will be so delectable that you'll want to jump into immediate action. Don't. The point of this scrub is not forward momentum; it's complete prioritization. Any deviation from the scrub decreases the chance you'll get through the whole list.

How many Today tasks are left when you're done with the scrub? I don't know, because I don't know who you are or how granular your tasks are, but I usually end up with between 10 and 20.

With the Morning Scrub complete, I create the Parking Lot. This is a blank legal-size piece of paper that sits directly to the left of the keyboard. New sheet. Always legal-size. Every morning.

Anyone who has sat through an offsite knows exactly what this paper is for. It's the landing spot for any idea/task/thing that is worth remembering but, if acted upon at the moment, will derail the productivity train. Like the Morning Scrub, the art of capturing a bright'n'shiny idea and landing it in the Parking Lot is an acquired skill. You're going to want to move on the new, and sometimes that's the right move, but you need to honestly and quickly answer the question, "Is moving on this new thing more important than finishing what I'm doing right now?"

Practice Productivity Minimalism

This is not a chapter where I'll debate the pros and cons of various productivity tools. You get to find a tool that fits your personal quirks, but whatever that tool is, I have some brief advice on how to use it relative to assessing your personal Taste of the Day:

- My task list has no hierarchical organization. I've used systems before that allow me to lump tasks by projects or by theme and, inevitably, I end up maintaining the structure rather than getting shit done. This pisses me off.

- I do use tags within the Things applications, but only to track who the most important person is, if anyone, for a given task. This is a handy way to run 1:1s. "Show me all Bob-related things."

- No priorities. Really. Again, priority is relative, and while slapping a priority on a task when you create it feels right, it's wrong because two days from now the priority will be different. Priority is a big deal—as a manager you want to get the right stuff done at the right time, but the priority that matters is the one sitting in your head right now rather than the one you dreamed up a week ago.

- No dates. I'm pissing off productivity nerds now. I don't track due dates, either. I fully scrub my to-do list every day, which means I'm constantly making real-time decisions regarding scheduling tasks.

As an engineer, your natural inclination is to build an increasingly complex system for tracking your tasks. The risk is the more structure you put into your list, the more you need to maintain it, and the more you maintain it, the less time you'll have to actually get work done.

The Evening

After work, after dinner, or just before I go to sleep, I complete another scrub. The process for the Evening Scrub is slightly different.

First, I scrub the Parking Lot into the Later bucket. This is the first taste I get of how the day actually went. Lots of new tasks? OK, what kind? With the Parking Lot scrubbed, I take a moment to size up the day. How'd I do on taste? My original read was "meeting-infested nightmare"—was I right? This is another priority-leveling exercise. It doesn't matter if I made the right call on the day; the point is to again set your head appropriately.

Finally, I scrub unfinished items in the Today bucket. For each item remaining, I ask, "OK, why didn't I get this done?" Very often, the answer is, "Not enough time," so the item gets thrown back into the Later bucket, but sometimes it just gets deleted. Your question is, "How did a task that was scrubbed into the Today bucket this morning suddenly become irrelevant?"

The efficient, version-control-loving information pack rat in you is going to have a problem punting a task into oblivion. Your thought is, "Sure, it might not feel important right now, but WHAT IF!?"

Stop. Delete it. We've already wasted 37 seconds noodling on this semiessential but tasteless task. Nuke it. By getting this task off your list and out of your head, we're making space. Don't worry, if the task is actually important, it's going to find its way back to your Parking Lot.

This deletion is advanced task management kung-fu, and it's based on insight I don't like to give to new managers, because it's a total productivity buzzkill. The insight is: "You will never complete everything you should."

I can do anything!

Of course you can.

Don't tell me what I can't do!

I'm not. What I'm telling you is that management is the art of choosing what *not* to do, which means you need to be ready and willing to look at the task at the end of a day and ask, "OK, I made this urgent this morning. A day has passed and I had time, but never got to it. Does it matter?"

Priority is relative. What felt so important last Wednesday loses importance five days later when the larger context of your week, your month, and your career shows up. You need to develop a practice of strategic information shedding where you are constantly and intelligently jettisoning ideas and work.

A well-maintained to-do list gives you a daily sense of professional well-being. It constructs the pleasant illusion that you have a degree of control in a world where you have no idea how tomorrow will taste. The system I've constructed to maintain this list is lightweight, built from the practical use of constraints, designed to sift through an endless crapload of information that passes me during the day, but it's a system that is incomplete.

A glance at my current Parking Lot demonstrates this incompleteness. It's a list of things I need to do. It's a list of tactics that I need to use to keep the management engine running, but dutifully following these to-dos isn't management; it's task execution. You need another list, one that represents the strategy for your team, your career, and your values.

And as we'll learn in the next chapter, that one is called the Trickle List.

The Trickle List

There's a gaping hole in the prior chapter, "The Taste of the Day." Yes, it's a handy task management system, but it's incomplete. It describes a process for constant scrubbing of a task list, as well as a handy place to keep distractions out of your way via the Parking Lot, but at the end of the day, what exactly is it helping you do?

Here are three tasks from my current list:

- Headcount Asks
- David Lunch
- Move Europe Trip

These are tasks for today. They are well-defined, measurable, tactical, and they need to be done today. While it's professionally terrific that I'm actively making sure nothing is falling through the cracks, these are still just tasks. What am I accomplishing when I complete them? I'm getting things done.

Is that what you want to do all day? Things? Stuff?

No.

You're a Senior Development Engineer or an Engineering Manager or a Project Manager, and while things and stuff are part of the gig, if it's all you're doing, you're productive, but you're vigorously running in place. You're tactical, but not strategic. Tasks are an incomplete picture of what you do and what you need to do.

The curse of any effective task management system is that you get really good at capturing, prioritizing, and executing tasks. To the point that you start to believe that merely completing a task is helping your career. After a solid decade of rampant task management, I realized I needed to augment tasks with a system that would strategically guide and remind me that my job was not to do things, but to remember the interesting words in my title: manager, engineering, and products. That's what I do.

What I needed was a guiding force behind these tasks, a way to remind me that I was pushing toward a goal and defining and refining a strategy.

I call it a Trickle List, and it looks like this:

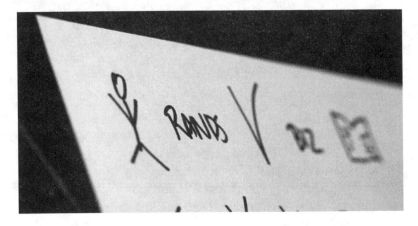

Trickle Creation

My first excursion into the word "trickle" was an idea called Trickle Theory. The argument was simple: you can do more than you think with small, consistent investments of your time.

To understand the Trickle List, you need to first look at the headers at the top of the list. These are the heart of the list, and how you define them is how you define what you want to do.

A good place to start is figuring out what your current job is. If you need a reminder, go scrub that task list again. The question I want to start the Trickle List with is: "What should your job be?"

OK, got it? You want to be a manager. Good, we can work with that. What simple, regular tasks are going to point you in a managerial direction? Do you need to network? Do you need to file more bugs? Write more specs? Strategically, I don't know who you work for, or where you're headed, or what your company values, but here's the good news with the Trickle List: you don't have to be perfect. In fact, imperfection is a great place to start.

Here's my current list:

- People — Have a random chat with someone in the hallway
- Write — Write something, anything
- V — Take a vitamin
- Biz — Learn a part of the business
- Book — Read something in a book

"Rands, these are simply recurring tasks."

No. They're not. You're doing more than stuff and things with your trickles; you're designing moments of high potential. I'll explain.

Having a random hallway chat usually isn't going to be a career changer. Nine out of ten of those conversations are lightweight, but those are nine conversations I wouldn't have had otherwise. Plus, it's hallway visibility, and in a gig where 90% of the days are spent holed up in meetings, that's time well spent. And there's the 10th conversation where I learn something huge:

Wait, the project is HOW FAR behind?

Hold it, you're thinking about QUITTING?

By choosing to create a moment where I leave my structured day to have a random conversation, I'm creating informational opportunity, and while these moments may appear to have low initial return on time investment, you're playing a numbers game. You're counting on the fact that, over time, over many moments, you're creating unexpected potential.

The items on your Trickle List don't need to be huge. In fact, as we'll learn in a moment, the bigger they are, the less likely you'll do them. What they need to be is aligned with where you're headed. However small, they need to be a daily ⟶ eaded somewhere. The size and the impact of the trickles will come from repetition. Here's three months:

That's not just 90 vitamins I remember to take; it's 47 random hallway conversations that not only increased my hallway visibility, but also resulted in the discovery of some sweet gossip, gave me a chance to deliver some quiet career advice, allowed me to unearth an impending, avoidable disaster, and, oddly, taught me a lot about high-definition TVs.

The Trickle Process

With a couple of defined trickles, let's talk about how to work them into the day. Remember the Taste of the Day process: the Morning Scrub, the creation of the Parking Lot, and finishing the day with an Evening Scrub. The Trickle List integrates with all of it.

After I've done the Morning Scrub and after I create my fresh, new legal-sized Parking Lot, I pull out the Trickle List for a look at the previous day. Anything that didn't get checked off yesterday gets brief consideration. Any clue why it didn't get checked? Offsite all day? That makes sense.

This is not a guilt-inducing list. I'm not beating myself up when I'm looking at unchecked items. I'm looking for data. Didn't check anything? So I was buried, right? Haven't checked off one item for a week? Is this a trickle I should be trying to do? Yes? OK, why isn't it happening? What larger thing do I need to change?

If your Trickle List becomes a Must Do List, you'll stop looking at it. The weight of Must Do will slowly transform into "I didn't do it, so I suck, and I don't want to suck, so I'm going to move my Trickle List out of my line of sight, like, say, to the trash."

The last step of the morning is adding a fresh new line to the list, starting with today's date, and then I put the list somewhere where I'm going to visually stumble on it during the course of the day. We're off.

Hopefully, during brief moments of calm, I glance at the list and it gives me a motivational shove. "Now is the time to learn something about the business, and I've got the bookmark right here."

The Evening Scrub shenanigans, like the morning's, involve assessment. It's the end of the day and what'd I get done? "Hey, I haven't done this trickle in a week? Why?" Again, the point is not guilt; it's assessment. I want you to add and delete from your Trickle List with glee. In fact, if you're not regularly adding new trickles to the list and removing others, I'd argue that you aren't really using the list. What you need to do as part of your evolving career is, well, evolve. Perhaps you no longer need to focus on the hallway chats, and that's why you haven't checked it off in a week. Fine. Remove it. Move on.

Maybe your trickles are too meaty. I keep trickles deliberately simple and vague because tasks that take more than a few minutes to think about don't get checked. You need trickles that you can easily do. I design trickles for likelihood of completion, rather than perceived impact. Again, impact is going to come from repetition.

Finally, as you can see from my Trickle List, I often use letters and glyphs as my column headers. My thought is that by giving them less definition, I make more room for me to be creative about how I complete them.

Structured Improvisation

My constant struggle with productivity and task tracking systems is a struggle with structure. My natural tendency is to build systems that track everything, and that's a silly goal. There's no way I'm going to keep track of and complete everything. I can look at my calendar and tell you what I think I'm going to be doing tomorrow, but the fact is, I won't actually know what I'm going to be doing until I'm doing it.

This is why I'm particularly choosy about the structure I use in task tracking. I need just enough structure to not lose important tasks, but never structure that collapses when the sky randomly falls.

Because the sky always falls. There's always a crisis. If two days pass and I don't feel blindsided, I start to worry that I'm not paying enough attention. This is my other requirement for my productivity system: it needs to encourage improvisation.

There's a reason I'm scrubbing my task list twice a day. There's a reason I've got the Trickle List taped to my white board. I want both lists front of mind all the time, not only because I want to constantly seek opportunities to complete a task or tackle a trickle, but also because I want to be aware of the larger themes present in both my lists. This 360-degree awareness is going to improve my ability to improvise, and that's where I'm really going to kick ass.

Your job is not to check off one thing on your list. It's to cross three things off—at once. It's to have an epiphany so big that you add a column to your Trickle List in the middle of the day—I MUST DO THAT. A LOT. The only way you're going to come to massive strategic realizations is to have a sense of your entire task list and Trickle List in your head. I'm not talking about memorization; I'm talking about a complete feel of things you need to do and the ability to improvise odd strategic conclusions.

It's the moment in a meeting where I see a hint of opportunity in that thing Phil said. I see the opportunity because I know I've got 12 Phil-related tasks and 2 trickles that, in a way I can never describe but only feel, intersect with that thing Phil just said.

Strategic insight only comes from well-informed chaos, and you can take a stab at building a productively ephemeral perspective with the tactical information you gain from a structured task list combined with hopeful strategy provided by a slippery, healthy Trickle List.

The point of your productivity system is not to keep absolute track of your tasks. The point is to keep the important information in the front of your brain where it will improve your improvisation and inform your whims. A task tracking system gives you just enough information to calculate your chaos while reminding you to create and act on random moments of high potential.

CHAPTER 26

The Crisis and the Creative

If you polled my team about my daily agenda, they'd say, "He's either running to meetings or in meetings." Glancing at my calendar confirms this: 14 meetings this coming Monday—double-booked for five of them. Sweet.

Yes, I go to meetings all day, but it's more than that. I'm also managing a constant, distracting flood of interesting decisions that find me no matter where I'm sitting. When they arrive, I must make an instant prioritization call: Crisis or Creative?

A Spectrum for Everything

This will be the third chapter where I've described prioritization. The Taste of the Day describes how I deal with tactics, identifying and recording tasks that need to be done, as well as a system for punting tasks that are lingering aimlessly. The Trickle List goes strategic and imparts direction for my day: what are the daily investments I want to make in my people and myself?

The Crisis and the Creative is less a system and more a mental model for all of the work on my plate. It's similar to The Taste of the Day in that it's a lens by which I look at the health of everything I'm responsible for. The model looks like this:

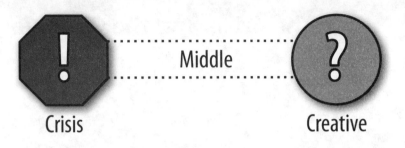

As my day moves by in a rapid progression of people, tasks, and meetings, I often need to stop and make a snap decision regarding whether or not to engage in whatever is sitting in front of me. In that moment, I place this thing in the model and assess. This is what I'm thinking:

The Crisis

This is any item I'm responsible for that is in Crisis. The definition of Crisis varies on a daily basis and can mean anything from "Word on the street is the quality of this feature blows" to "The program managers say we're going to miss our date." Crisis means it's not working and I need to pay constant attention. Oddly (or sadly), there's always something in this category. More on this aspect of management in a moment.

The Creative

The title for the other side of the spectrum should be The Strategy, but I'm incapable of not using alliteration, so it's The Creative. This is anything I'm responsible for that, by investing in or completing, means I'm growing, I built something, I took the team toward new. The Creative are my responsibilities that take us places either because I have the experience to recognize that they will, or because I will make them so through pure force of will. They rule.

These edges are the main reason I'm running to all of those double-booked meetings. Whether it's Crisis or Creative, activities in these buckets run hot. Whether I'm making sure someone isn't going to quit or I'm jump-starting a brand-new project at a time when no one has a free second, when I'm working the edges, it's fast and furious. The issue is that I'm responsible for a lot more than just the work that's running hot.

See those boring lines in the middle between Crisis and Creative? That's an important part of the model. Items in the middle are the silent non-Crisis, non-Creative responsibilities that are my team just making it happen. It's all very important work, but it's work that occurs with very little investment from me because I've hired, manage, and work with competent people who excel at what they do. The middle doesn't represent responsibilities that I've delegated and need to check up on, this is work the team just does, and to understand how to get the work there, you need to understand the edges.

The Crisis

There are those who love the panic associated with the Crisis. They love the motivating threat of imminent disaster. This is especially true for managers because a Crisis gives them super powers. When it hits the fan, the team can be freaked to the point that they are incapable of making a decision because they don't want to make it worse. This is why, when the manager shows up and starts making decisions, the decisions are often followed without question. The team is happy, they're thinking, "Whew, OK, good. Someone is driving us out of this mess."

The larger question is: where'd the mess come from?

There are two standing goals when managing work that is in Crisis. Goal #1: Make sure the sky doesn't fall. Goal #2: Figure out how to prevent future sky-falling situations. It's a balance. You can't truly perform a post-mortem while holding the sky up, but then again, you can't truly remember what it's like to hold the sky up a month after it happens.

When I'm standing in the middle of a Crisis, I'm doing two things at the same time. First, I'm frantically trying to fix the issue by any means possible. I'm also carefully looking to identify the root cause of the Crisis. This is information that vanishes in the joy of no longer being screwed once the Crisis has passed. Sure, we'll still have a debrief once everyone's caught their breath, but I'm going to learn more about what actually happened by asking questions at 10 p.m. on a Saturday night after two weeks of not having a day off.

The thing I remind myself throughout the Crisis is: if I'm responsible for resolving this Crisis, there's a good chance I'm just as responsible for its creation. I don't want to be grilling anyone at 10 p.m. on Saturday. I want the Crisis to never occur again, which means being Creative.

The Creative

The panic junkie is the person who is addicted to Crisis and, in the absence of it, will manufacture drama in order to create additional Crisis. Their intent was originally good; they wanted to get stuff done quickly and discovered that the umbrella of a Crisis removed traditional organizational roadblocks. Problem is, they've become addicted to the power and momentum granted to them by driving the crisis. As soon as the current Crisis appears to have passed, they deflate, thinking, "Blah, back to the normal," and immediately start looking for another Crisis. If they don't find one, they create it.

I was one of these people and burned a lot of calories getting a lot done, but management by Crisis is a losing strategy. You become a corporate arsonist—burning through people and process in your apparent endless hurry, but not actually building anything.

There's always a Crisis in progress. It's a statistical fact that in any decent-sized group of people there is one person who needs help with some part of a Crisis. Get used to it. The question I ask myself each morning as I stare at the day's selection of Crises is: "Am I going to play in the Crisis or the Creative?"

I'm not talking about being Creative about solving a Crisis such that it never occurs again, I'm talking about work that is purely Creative—where you're actively improving or building a thing. It's writing that piece of code that nobody but you wants; it's spending two hours recruiting that guy you're never going to get; it's standing in the design room with a variety of dry erase markers and just filling that whiteboard with random.

I'm not talking about impossible tasks; I'm talking about Creative ones. I'm talking about inspired investments in an uncertain future. These are often hard tasks to measure, which means they are equally hard to justify to those sitting around you, but they occasionally, infrequently hit. You get the guy. You find the idea. You build something new.

Given the constant presence of Crisis and things to do, the act of choosing to devote part of your time to a purely Creative activity can be rough, but if you're going to grow, there have to be times where you let things go further to hell in the now, because you're choosing to invest in the Creative for the future.

That's right. You are going to actively ignore a burning Crisis so that you can hide in the design room and doodle on a whiteboard. The panic junkies are going to be pissed. They're going to walk by, laptops in hand, and wonder, "Why the hell isn't he all over the Crisis? Doesn't he know it's, ya know, A CRISIS?"

Yes, it's a risky move. Yes, there are crises that can't be ignored. Yes, if you piss off the wrong panic junkie, you're going to hear about it—quickly—but the bigger risk is a panic-filled career reacting to disasters, instead of one where you're recognized for what you've built versus what you've fixed.

A Personal Model

The Crisis and the Creative isn't a productivity system, it's an identification system. It's your personal view of your world, and for me, it's a set of reminders. First, I choose how I invest my time. Second, I know that a Crisis is an opportunity not only to save the day, but also to make certain that future days never see this Crisis again by Creatively moving something into the predictable Middle.

And I want more Middle.

The more Middle, the happier I am because that's more time for the edges, and undiscovered opportunity always hides at the edges.

CHAPTER 27

The Foamy Rules for Rabid Tools

The brother-in-law lives in the 'burbs and needed five trees removed. Not big trees—10 to 15 feet tall, six-inch trunks. Not a problem.

I live on the edge of a redwood forest in Northern California. There are sturdy oaks, playful maples, lovely madrones, weed-like bay laurels, and of course, giant redwoods. But the pleasure of living in a forest has a tax. Trees fall and trees die, and in a forest of any significant size, this is always happening.

You need a chainsaw. In my case, I need three. There's Junior, who is great at handling the small jobs. He's light and ladder friendly.

Then there's Marty. He's the everyday mid-sized saw that is enough to handle almost any job. Marty would be perfect for a job in the 'burbs.

Last, there's the Rocket. Any tree is the Rocket's nemesis.

Even if you've never handled a chainsaw, you've probably used a handsaw. It's a physical, grinding affair. It's fun for about three minutes, and then you start wondering…am I making progress? The brother-in-law had taken it on himself to use a handsaw on one of the trees. In his three minutes he'd sawed off…a branch.

When Marty and I showed up, we dropped all five trees, cut up the trunks and branches, and stacked them into disposable piles in an hour.

The lesson: the correct tool is exponentially more productive.

That's a long introduction to say an obvious thing, but I'm going to make it even longer. Take a moment and step inside the mind of the brother-in-law. *I've got several trees I want to get rid of...and what do I have in the garage? Two hammers, a paint can full of nails, some leftover wood and...a saw. Perfect. A saw.*

Context shapes perspective, so thanks to the contents of his garage, he knows of no universe where there are chainsaws. He's heard of them and suspects they're much faster than the laborious, sweaty grind of this sawing, but there's no chainsaw here, so he's semi-happily hacking away. To me, standing there with my arsenal of chainsaws, it's absurd. It's a criminal waste of his time.

The lesson again: the correct tool is going to make you exponentially more productive.

The Foamy Rules

As an engineer, there is a short list of tools that you must be rabid about. Rabid. Foaming at the mouth crazy.

This is an obvious list of tools, and there's nothing here that you haven't heard before. The news is that you need to care. You need to be able to explain in great detail why using green-colored text on a black background is THE ONLY WAY TO CODE. You need to be a zealot about your tools, and zealotry starts with fit.

I was a database guy, then I was a shrink-wrap guy, and then I became a web applications guy. Each of those professions came with their own set of bright and shiny tools, but the tools were not important. Even a specific feature inside of that tool is not that interesting. I believe you can be just as productive sitting inside of a rich development environment such as Xcode as you can inside of TextMate and a slew of terminal windows. The point is not which tool; the point is that the way that tool—your tool—looks, feels, and functions fits how you see, move, and work.

These are my foamy rules, and they may differ wildly from your list. That's cool. My development experience is different than yours. I started working with computers before the mouse, which means I trust my keyboard more. Integrated debuggers had just landed when I began developing, which means, yeah, I like debugging at the command line. Again, the point is to get foamy, because what makes you foamy makes you your best.

My foamy rules:

My Tools Appear Deceptively Simple

TextMate. Terminal. Transmit, LaunchBar, DropBox. The mean time to get one of those tools set up is just a few minutes. I can build out my development environment on a new machine in a half hour. This has a couple of handy implications. My tools are readily available and lightweight. I can download and install everything except for an operating system in a short amount of time. Similarly, setup and configuration of these tools is close to zero.

You might think this setup means I'm expecting my computer to randomly explode. No. These tools are not simple; they are well-tuned. A TextMate user knows it's an onion application. You can keep pulling back the layers and finding new functionality, which is going to make your development experience faster. The same goes for Terminal and LaunchBar. The base functionality just works, and if you have a particular development itch you want to scratch, the tool can scratch it.

My Tools Do Not Care Where My Work Is

How many times have you experienced this? You write a quick script on your local machine to do something clever. You fine tune it and then plop it on your server and rediscover the rule—there's nothing quite like production.

Any tool that does not allow me to develop live in production is slowing me down. When someone showed me how to set up Transmit to do editing on remote files, I saw hours of heretofore unknown production debugging issues vanish.

Yes, editing locally is fast, especially when you live on the edge of a redwood forest where DSL latency blows, but a tool that doesn't allow me to develop over the wire isn't a tool; it's a debilitating hindrance.

Rands, edit? In production? Are you insane?

No. The tangential background rule is: "If you don't know what you're doing in production, you don't belong there."

There's a corollary, which is: "I don't care where my work is." This is recent foaminess brought on by Dropbox. For nonproduction work like, say, writing a book, I don't want to think about where the most recent version of the work is sitting. Yes, I'm talking about version control. But shh, don't call it version control—just call it Dropbox. Provided I have a network connection, this tool magically refreshes a shared directory sitting on each of my machines. I can't think of the last time I worried about which version of a document I was on, and that means I'm spending more time working than worrying.

My Tools Are Designed to Remove Repetitive Motion

One of my first algorithmic holy shits was during my second computer science class as we were learning sorting algorithms. The professor elegantly walked us through the construction of different algorithms, explaining the pros and the cons, and then he landed Quicksort. Holy shit.

It wasn't just the elegance. It wasn't the recursive simplicity; it was the discovery that with imagination there were approaches that were wildly more efficient—and simpler. Whether you're formally trained as a computer science nerd or not, you've learned the value of efficiency—to make each action that you take mean something. You know that when you're efficient, you have more time to do what you love.

This is why I have a simple requirement that any tool I rely on has complete keyboard support. I will fall back on using the mouse for one-off activities, but for any action I take that I know I'm going to do again, my question is, "How do I make this action cost less?"

Think of it like this. What if I told you that each time you wanted to save a file, you had to stand up, climb up on your chair, and jump up and down, yelling, "I would like to save my stuff now!" The first time you had to do it, it'd be kinda fun, but after that it'd drive you batshit crazy. It's a similar feeling each time I reach for my mouse. I feel I'm engaging in an unnecessary task, which is always going to waste my time because with a mouse sometimes you miss, and missing is a tremendous waste of time.

Finding *any* file or application is, ideally, four keystrokes. Cmd-Space (LaunchBar), Letter #1, Letter #2, Return. Sometimes I get lucky; sometimes it's three, and you know that puts a smile on my face *every single time it happens*.

My Tools Do Only What I've Told Them to Do

Back when Dreamweaver first landed, I wanted to love it. I was so tired of the repetitive motion of developing HTML pages, and the idea of a tool that was going to visually handle that laborious process was appealing. Problem was, Dreamweaver changed my code...without asking.

It what?

Dreamweaver was attempting to be helpful, but the moment it reformatted my code, I threw a fit. YOU TOUCHED MY CODE. Dreamweaver never recovered from that horrendous first impression.

My impression and my opinion of robust integrated development environments is that they can do a lot of good in terms of helping you visualize what the hell is going on. Borland developed some of the best environments for building code back in the day, but I still find myself with extremely primitive development environments where I'm tweaking code in TextMate and debugging inside of a couple of Terminal windows.

Yeah, I know all about the glory of integrated debugging, and I see all you Eclipse guys having a ball, but what I found in many years of development is that embracing the fancy tools means spending time tinkering with your tools to get them to behave how you want.

The corollary to this rule is: "My tools don't have a lot of moving parts." Dreamweaver-grade code offenses are few and far between with solid development tools, but the fancy still comes with a cost. You may be fully willing and foamy to embrace that cost, but I'm not.

Am I more efficient than you? Maybe. Do I know where I stand relative to my tools? Yes. Do I have to relearn my development process when the people behind an elegant tool shoot for more elegance? Nope.

My Tools Are My Tools

Choosing a thing makes it yours. The choice is the result of that unique mix of logic, superstition, stubbornness, and experience that fits you.

You read that right. Green text. Black background. I'll tell you why right now. I'm an old-school DOS guy. My first word processor was Wordstar, and that's the word processing program I came to associate with the fugue-like state of maximum productivity: the Zone. This is why I continue to favor colored text on a black background in my current favorite editor, Textmate. The coloring reminds me of a primal, safe place where the tool is serving its purpose—to get the hell out of the way so I can go be exponentially more productive.

This is why, as engineers, we stick with something that works for us. This is why the ancient likes of vi and Emacs continue to flourish. Once we find a tool that works for us, once we've chosen that tool, it becomes ours and remains ours. It allows us to get foamy.

An Evolving Foaminess

My brother-in-law doesn't need a chainsaw. When I took out his five trees, I eliminated half of the population of trees on his property. While a chainsaw is a delicious combination of sound, power, and sawdust, my brother-in-law didn't choose a home where the trees are on the offensive, so he doesn't need defensive weaponry.

He does need to know about a universe where chainsaws exist because every moment of his time is valuable. What differentiates us from the monkeys is not our ability to pick the right tool for the right job, but to pick the best tool.

And you never stop looking. This is why the last foamy rule is the most important: *my tools are always fighting for their lives.*

My current tool set is influenced by all of my experience. Yeah, the elegant simplicity of vi is attractive to me—it reminds me of the uncomplicated early days of development—but vi can't compete with the holy shit moment I experienced when I first ran into TextMate. *This tool is always five steps ahead of me. I love that.*

But TextMate, like all of my tools, must evolve.

Try this right now. Stand up and walk into the office of the best developer in the building. I promise two things: he will be happy to, at length, foamily show you his development setup, and you are guaranteed to learn at least one thing about moving faster. Perhaps it's a tool you've never heard of, or maybe it's the way he deftly manages a tool you've taken for granted.

I don't know what you're going to learn, but I do know you'll see one thing that will instantly and obviously make your universe a smaller, more productive place.

CHAPTER 28

Up to Nothing

In Silicon Valley, you burn a lot of calories.

It's not just the daily burn of your gig; it's everything else involved in staying afloat in a valley that is constantly reinventing itself. You sign up for every new service and spend the prerequisite 3.7 minutes to determine, "Does this matter?" You surf the Web, you tweet, you update your Facebook...all of which brings a constant flood of new data that needs to be sifted, sorted, and assessed.

You have compatriots in this caloric consumption. They randomly walk into your office or your life and with them they bring additional reasons to burn more calories. *Have you seen this? You have to try it. In fact, I'm not leaving until you're jumping up and down excited about this very important thing.*

We are part of an industry that is addicted to enthusiasm, to getting things done, and discovering the new, but sometimes the right move is stopping and putting this world on hold. You need to learn how to build quiet moments of nothing as a measure of balance.

Which is why I go to a bookstore.

An Essential Exercise in Inactivity

The moment I walk into a bookstore, I remember what I love about them. They are an oasis of intellectual calm. Perhaps it's the potential of all the ideas hidden behind those delicious covers. Or perhaps it's the social reverence for the library-like quiet. You don't yell in a bookstore; you'll piss off the books.

A bookstore is where I rediscover that while I might be addicted to the nonstop calorie-burning Silicon Valley lifestyle, I also need the serenity only found in the deep quiet of the consideration of nothing. Considering nothing takes work and practice, and the act contains a contradiction: the more I think about what I need to do, the less I'll discover the thing that I don't know I'm looking for.

It's confusing, but you need these skills because you have days full of somethings. Your day is probably spent at one of two sides of a spectrum. You're either reacting to whatever is showing up on your doorstep, or proactively looking for new things to place on your doorstep so you can figure out what to do with them. Reactive. Proactive. It's how you spend your entire day.

Excursions to the bookstore are essential exercises in inactivity where the whole world stops being a thing to do. My most recent trip to my local Borders was in the middle of a two-week period where I'd spent time in both Tokyo and London. Forty hours of flying, resulting in five days of meetings that required constant thought, creativity, and focus. During a brief stint back in normality in the States, I had instructions to acquire a children's book for a nephew.

Now.

The children's book section at my local Borders has been voted "Most Likely to Be a Total Fucking Disaster" for three years running. Combining this unique cluttered chaos with a head full of jetlag means my head is overflowing with disorganized somethings, and I'm predisposed to be annoyed. Even worse, I'm not looking for a specific book. I'm running on "get something he'd like" orders, which means I need a modicum of inspiration in order to be successful.

I need to discard everything in my head that's preventing me from looking and being inspired.

This is a surprisingly hard mental maneuver because you and I are both used to days that are not only full, but full with well-defined things to do. A lack of structure, direction, and measures throws your brain into fits, and usually this is when I throw my hands up in frustration and walk out of the bookstore. My brain is rejecting the unstructured ambiguity involved in the search for the unknown.

Look in my head when I start: *Where am I? This looks like the children's section, but this part is full of toys and I need books. I haven't read a good book in forever. OK, keep moving until something looks right. Since when did they sell candy at a bookstore? Edward Cullen Sweet Tarts? Please. You know, I don't even know what day it is. OK, dinosaurs, he likes dinosaurs. Wait, can he read?*

My analysis is *"this place is fucking confusing,"* and I think I'm talking about the bookstore, but I'm actually talking about my brain.

Up to Nothing

Go back to work and think about your average day. How often are you not clear what you're doing? How often is the goal of the next 30 minutes completely undefined? Yes, you've suffered through meetings where there was no clear agenda, and you felt like you were wasting your time, but that's still a known quantity—*I'm currently in the poorly run meeting scenario.* Been there, done that.

What happens when there is no meeting, no burning task, no one in your office? You wander, you surf the Web, you stare at that calendar on the wall and think, "Why do we have leap years again? I forget." And then you feel bad. *I should be working. I should be doing something. They're not paying me to reverse engineer leap years. I have things to do.*

You've built this guilt into your office. It's why your screen is not facing folks who walk through your door. You're worried: "They might see me doing nothing."

You're not up to nothing. You're aimlessly mentally wandering— an act made famous by every bright idea ever had in the shower. Think of that moment. Your body is busily on task with the cleaning, and what does your brain do? Sure, if you're stressed about layoffs, you're going to worry about layoffs, but those mornings when nothing is pressing—what happens?

Your brain builds something from whatever mental flotsam and jetsam is in your head. Perhaps it's a useful thing, an answer to a question you didn't know you needed. Perhaps it's just an interesting combination of thoughts put into a story. It's dreaming, but you're awake.

Back to the bookstore. Remember my orders, a good book for the nephew....

If I survive the mental rejection of ambiguity, the next moment I need is one of discovery. In order to ground myself in the silence, I need to discover a single bright and shiny thing, and there's absolutely no telling what that thing is until it shows up. It might be based on my mood, the last 10 things I cared about, a random word someone said to me, my favorite color...the list is endless, indefinable, and entirely locked in my head.

But there is nothing ambiguous or unclear about the discovery. It's obvious. It fills an immediate gap I did not know I had.

In this bookstore excursion, it's a black book. It's odd to see a black book in the endless rainbow of the children's section, but there it is. Black cover with masking tape surrounding what looks like a handwritten title: *Wreck This Journal*. OK, interesting. I flip the book open to the handwritten instructions:

1. Carry this with you everywhere you go.

2. Follow the instructions on every page.

3. Order is not important.

4. Instructions are open to interpretation.

5. Experiment. (Work against your better judgment.)

And there it was. Exactly what I needed. A reminder of why I go to the bookstore in the first place—to mentally stumble around, defying my better judgment, in a nourishing environment of nothing.

Wreck This Journal was created by Keri Smith, who calls herself a guerilla artist, and I've no idea what her book is doing in the clutter of the children's section. It's a journal dedicated to its own destruction. One page instructs you to "Rub Dirt Here." Another asks you to scribble wildly using only borrowed pens (and document where they were borrowed from). The journal is full of ideas to create unstructured moments of seemingly meaningless activity designed to get you to stop and let something else in.

Don't Look for It

Stop and let something else in. It's a confusing skill, which starts with a question: how are you going to find what you don't know you need by not looking for it?

A day in high tech rarely encourages the activity of doing nothing. Nothing is not cost effective. Nothing is not something you'll put in your review. Nothing gets a bad rap, and the more I attempt to define it, the less useful it will be to you because what I need out of nothing is different than what you need.

Moments of nothing are not moments of creativity or consideration. (They might be.) These moments don't last long, because your brain can't sit still; it's been trained to burn calories all the time. (The longer it sits still, the better.)

Your brain instinctively and naturally attempts to build something given whatever world it's currently in. In a bookstore, with effort, I can shed the somethings of my everyday life and find the nothing that I don't know I'm looking for. (And that rules.)

CHAPTER 29

How to Not Throw Up

As soon as you decide to become a professional nerd, either via a university degree or simply because you sit up all night writing Python to scratch your particular technical itch, you think you absolve yourself of having to stand up in front of a group of people and make a presentation.

And you might be right.

Then there's a chance you're going to build or think something brilliant, and no mailing list, weblog, or wiki is going to be able to contain this brilliance. Those who want to hear about your brilliance are going to insist that you stand in front of them and explain this bright thing that you did or thought.

Conflict. Yes, you want to explain your brightness, but, um, the last time you stood in front of people and told a story was Ms. Randall's 11th grade English class, and you stumbled through an incoherent ramble about Henry David Thoreau and some pond.

Unlike that pond, you are immensely qualified to talk about your topic, but you're totally unqualified to present in front of a group of people. It's not just that you haven't had the practice, but that lack of practice has given you the erroneous impression that there's a good chance you might throw up if you have to stand up and tell a story in front of 500 people.

Not Throwing Up Is a Two-Phase Process

This chapter is about presentations, not content. Both are equally important, but I'm not here to help you write your content; I'm here to transform that content into a presentation that doesn't suck.

Let's say you've written your 30 slides. A rookie presentation move is to: a) have too many slides and b) stuff your slides with clutter, like wordy bullet points. Filling each slide with as much content as possible. This is your feeble attempt to get out of actually presenting. Your thought is, "Fill the slides with information and read the slides." This makes sense to you, since I know you're nervous, but my question is, "Why are you nervous?"

"I've never presented in front of 500 people."

"So, you're not confident you can do it?"

"Right."

"OK, so let's focus on the confidence rather than creating more horrible slides."

Phase 1: Practice Endlessly

Confidence is going to come not when you memorize your slides, but when you move the content from one side of your brain to the other. Right now, your slides are sitting in the linear left side of your brain, the practical side. This is a fine place for the slides to be while you're creating them, but before you get up on stage, you need to move them to the right side of your brain, the creative side. You need to be able to feel your slides.

Your presentation is storytelling. It's a performance. It's you on stage telling me and 499 of my friends a story about why you're brilliant. That's not a comforting thought, since I know you're already nervous about standing in front of 500 people and bumbling through your slides. *And now you're saying it's a performance? My presentation regarding huge performance wins in garbage collection is NOT a performance.*

Of course it is. Why else would there be 500 people sitting here wanting to hear about it? I promise there's some art, some performance, in your presentation, and the best way to find it is to practice endlessly. The best way to do that is to stand up, walk around your office, and give your presentation to no one. Over and over again.

It takes some getting used to—pacing around your office or hotel room listening to your own voice—but that's exactly what your audience is going to hear. You need to figure out how to listen to yourself tell a story while also critically listening to the story. You're the presenter and the audience. Yeah, it takes practice.

Start with those three slides there about that one specific topic. Talk through it, and listen to how it sounds. Does it make sense? Does it flow? Are you reading the slide, or are you telling a story? How does it transition into the next point? After you've heard yourself verbally walk through a topic a few times, you start to hear what you're trying to say, and you make discoveries like, "Uh, I'm making no sense," "This is supposed to be funny, but it's lame," or "This topic doesn't have any relation to anything near it."

We're talking hours of practice here, but you'll slowly start to notice that you're not just memorizing the content; you're also memorizing the flow. You'll start to notice where you're repeating yourself, you'll find key points in the strangest places, and you'll stop to reorder and rewrite slides...a lot. Good. Keep practicing.

When you can sit at your desk with your eyes closed and talk through any one of your slides, you're going to stop worrying about what you need to say and focus more on how you're going to say it. This intimate knowledge of your content is going to give you confidence.

But you still might throw up.

Phase 2: Throw-Up Avoidance

A few years back, I gave a recruiting presentation at two different universities on the same day. Same presentation, same general age group of students, morning versus evening.

The morning presentation was in front of a packed room. Just after 10 a.m. I was three cups of coffee into the day and so was everyone else. Three slides in, and I knew this was going to be an easy presentation. Heads were nodding, laughs were coming from the least expected slides, and folks were actually taking me up on my offer: "Stop me if you have a question." Captivated. Forty minutes of slides. Twenty minutes of intense, engaged questions and answers. Mission accomplished.

Five hours later. I'm in another conference room 50 miles away in another university, and everyone's coffee has worn off. The room is half full, and I'm a little tired, but I've done this presentation 30 times in my head, so when I start on slide #1, it's on. I know this presentation, so why is everyone falling asleep on slide #3? There's no laughing, and by slide #10, someone gets up and walks out. Ouch.

Hopefully, this is normally when you consider throwing up. I say hopefully because there are a great many presenters who don't have a clue when the presentation is going badly. This is certainly a rookie mistake, but I've sat through a fair share of presentations by seasoned managers where they just flopped and didn't have a clue.

You need to stop and listen to what your audience needs. If your presentation isn't going swimmingly, stop five minutes in and look around the room. Is the audience looking at you? Or are they staring at their laptops? Has there been nodding? I know it's been 10 seconds now, and you're still looking at the audience saying nothing. It's OK; they're just sitting there wondering if you're about to throw up. You're building tension.

More importantly, you're figuring out the most important part of your presentation: which audience showed up? Here's the rub: you can write brilliant, compelling slides, you can practice your slides 40 times, but you can never predict who is going to show up, and your presentation must be tailored to those who show up.

OK, now throw up.

Improvise

Changing your deck on the fly is hard, and this is where our senior managers, with hundreds of presentations under their belts, screw up. First, they've stopped fretting, which means their presentations lack any sort of energy. Consequently, they don't listen to the audience, so when the audience indicates via their bored silence that they want more, the presenter is deaf. They make no adjustment to engage the audience, which is why they sound like bad used car salesmen; they're just reciting the sales pitch, and they don't care what you think.

How do you need to improve? What is your audience going to ask for? They want one thing: they want to participate. No, they don't want to get on stage and present your slides; they want to be included in this presentation—in this performance. I'm not talking about waves of applause, I'm talking about looking at a sea of people and *knowing* these people are listening to your every word. It's a constructive silence directed squarely at you, and when you learn how to read it, it's a high.

So, what are you going to do? How are you going to adapt? Maybe this crowd wants you to wake them up? How about accentuating your points loudly? How about a bit more walking around the stage waving your hands furiously? Perhaps you're too amped, and they want you to slow and pause between your words. Give them time for your words to soak in.

When someone walked out of my university presentation, I immediately stopped. I began reminiscing about my college years and the complex protocol I'd worked out for when it was OK to walk out of a lecture. This five-minute irrelevant segue did two things: first, it reminded my semi-lucid audience that I was one of them, and second, since my segue was timely (person walking out) and humorous (maybe), we reconnected. They woke up, and I dove back into my slides with my new college buds, who were now clear that I cared about what they thought.

Fret

No lying. The ability to improvise takes experience, and you're going to have to live through and recover from a couple of horrific presentations in order to build up your improv repertoire. For these early disasters, I have three pieces of advice:

- When you're presenting, talk like you're talking to one person who happens to have a thousand eyeballs. Don't get lost in the sea of faces; pick a person and tell them the story. Not for the entire hour, just a few seconds. Then move on.

- Use silence as punctuation. This is my favorite trick in the book, especially since I'm a fast talker. When you hear yourself gaining verbal momentum, stop. Count backward from 5. Walk across the stage. Resume. These breaks are going to give both you and your audience a chance to mentally regroup.

- They want you to succeed. This piece of advice is in every presentation guide out there—because it's true. Your audience is expecting you to rock their socks. They're expecting an A+. That's where you're starting in their heads, and walking on stage knowing this helps.

I don't want you to throw up.

I want you to fret about this presentation, and if you're not losing a little sleep, you don't care. You're not going to be motivated. You're going to end up perpetuating the idea that nerds can't tell a story. If you've been handed the responsibility of a presentation and aren't the least bit concerned, give it to someone who is going to sweat this thing, and then be prepared for that person to end up as your boss.

Out Loud

If you're looking for advice on giving a presentation, the Internet is chock-full of endless advice. If you're looking for tips on writing the presentation, the Internet goes dark for a fairly simply reason. To think about how to write a presentation, you need to think about how you speak, and that's not what you're doing when you read or write. I'll demonstrate. Say the following out loud right now:

I am reading this out loud to no one in particular.

Were you surprised to hear your voice? I was. Did you actually read it out loud? No? Why not? Sitting in a coffee shop? Worried that the guy next to you will think you're a freak? This basic discomfort is the reason it's tricky to explain how to present in a piece of writing. The skills involved in writing a clever paragraph are completely different from those used for developing and delivering that clever paragraph to a room full of strangers.

You still haven't read it out loud, have you?

Presentation or Speech?

Developing a compelling presentation involves a series of decisions and exercises to align your head with the fact that you're delivering your content directly to people. No Internet. No weblog. Just you.

Your first decision: speech or presentation? Wondering about the difference? Take a quick look at two entirely different appearances by Steve Jobs. The first is his *"Three Stories"* speech at Stanford,* and the second is part of his *MacWorld 2007* keynote.†

You need to watch only a few minutes of both to get a feel for the difference between a presentation and a speech. My guess is you only viewed the Stanford video, because everyone has seen Steve Jobs at MacWorld and the Stanford video is a shocker. Clearly, it's Steve Jobs. It's his voice, he's got his trademark bottle of water, but the delivery is completely anti-Jobs because he's reading his compelling stories from a piece of a paper.

It freaks me out.

In Steve Martin's autobiography, regarding his stand-up comedy years, he writes, "If you don't dim the lights...the audience won't laugh." This subtle, paradoxical observation is the core difference between speeches and presentations. In a presentation, half of the art is figuring out how to create an environment where your audience can actively participate without knowing they are participating. In a speech, the audience may laugh or cry, but they are not required nor encouraged to participate, because, during a speech, the spotlight never leaves the speechmaker.

For a presentation or a speech, you need your audience; otherwise, it's just you in an empty room talking to no one in particular, and we already have a word for that...it's called writing.

---

* *http://www.youtube.com/watch?v=D1R-jKKp3NA*
† *http://video.google.com/videoplay?docid=3206653149996743169#*

CHAPTER 30

The Unforgivable Mistake

There is one unforgivable mistake when giving a presentation. You've heard it before: "Don't read from your slides." As you'll see, my approach for presentation development is designed around avoiding this cardinal mistake, and it starts with picking the right tool.

For all of my presentations during the past three years, I've done all my content creation inside of my presentation software, which, thankfully, is *Keynote*. In the back of my mind, I've wondered if this is the right tool to iterate a presentation. Shouldn't I follow the same process as writing and drop all my thoughts into TextEdit, where I can easily slice and dice complex thoughts? No.

Start with and stick with Keynote or whatever presentation software floats your boat. First, presentation software is effectively designed to be outline software, and that's a great tool for organizing and editing your thoughts while not allowing them to become a book. By keeping your presentation in slide format, you're forcing your content to remain a presentation, not an article. Where each slide is a thought. Where moments of undiscovered brilliance are sitting between bullet points. We'll talk about how to find this brilliance in a bit, but for now, iterate in the slides.

Your job is to get as much of the meat as possible into outline form so that you can begin to transform it into a presentation. Don't worry about how you're going to say something or whether folks are going to get it. If you're worried that the outline doesn't allow you to capture the essential detail that you could with a blank piece of paper, start taking notes. I like the stickies in Keynote for random small thoughts. I like the speaker notes for bigger ones.

What's going to happen as you edit and re-edit is that an initial structure will emerge from your outline. Better yet, since you've stuck with presentation software, I'm guessing you're already starting to hear your voice in your head on certain slides...

- "This is a key point. I need to say this one reeeeeeeeallly slowly because it needs to stick."

- "Good data that needs to be conveyed, but...dull. Needs hip."

Once you've got what looks like a rough outline of your presentation, it's time to invoke the Disaster.

The Disaster

This is the second time I'm going to ask you to do something, and this time I just want you to do it. No questions asked. I want you to go to the first slide of your presentation, stand up, and give your presentation.

Wait, what, whoa Rands, this is rough and it's missing thoughts and uh....

Quiet. Give it a shot. Beginning to end, each slide, I want to hear your presentation.

Done? How'd it go? There's a reason I call it the Disaster, you know. There are three reasons you should tough out your rough presentation with zero prep:

- Get a feel for how it fits all together.

- Hear yourself speaking. This is more reinforcement that you aren't writing a book, you're writing a presentation.

- Build confidence. You now know the absolute worst-case scenario regarding this presentation. There is no way it could be worse than what you just went through.

Did you notice as you stood in your office talking to no one in particular how thoughts in your head sounded different than on the slides? Did you discover flaws in logic? Mysterious new gaps in content on the slides you've been staring at all morning? That's progress.

During the Disaster run-through, I take a ton of notes. I do this on a piece of paper next to the computer because, as much as possible, I want to stick with the idea that I'm giving my presentation. If I stop to edit my slides, I lose track of tempo and momentum, or worse, I end up rewriting my presentation rather than giving it. These handwritten notes look like this:

- No clue what slide #2 is trying to say.

- Segue between #4 and #5 is nonexistent

- #10: Repeating myself

Your first job after your Disaster is to integrate your notes as quickly as possible. For me, the post-Disaster edit is also the single biggest change I'll make to the presentation. In addition to major structural changes, I also find new content that needs to be added.

Reduction

This is a good time to remind yourself how to not throw up. For those *N.A.D.D.* afflictees out there, I present this chapter in three slightly revised bullet points:

- Practice endlessly (so that you can)

- Improvise (but never stop)

- Fret(ting)

In terms of developing your presentation, I'm going to further modify bullet #1 for this chapter. It's now, "Practice and edit endlessly." This is the largest piece of work where I have the least advice because you need to stare at your slides at 2 a.m. for three nights in a row. You need to soak in your presentation. So, mix it up. Invoke another disaster. Pitch a friend. Print your slides, and pitch a tent in the woods.

My best piece of advice is a threat: an audience can smell an immature presentation on the very first slide. It has nothing to do with the quality of the content; it's you standing lamely in front of your slide and silently conveying the "OK, what am I going to talk about here?" vibe, and it's presentation death.

During this endless editing and practice, you're looking for a reduction and consolidation of slides to occur. It's not that you're saying less, it's that you're beginning to internalize the content so you no longer need all those words to remember your point. It can be disconcerting to delete your fine ideas, so use the speaker notes or stickies if you feel you're going to forget something important. You aren't going to need them, but if it makes it emotionally easier to prune, terrific.

This consolidation is one of the reasons I usually don't send my slides to folks who ask after the presentation. My slides, standing on their own, rarely make sense without me standing in front of the room furiously waving my arms.

Second, as part of your consolidation, you'll want to start thinking about where you want to use images rather than words. Remember, a presentation is a visual and auditory medium, and a slide covered with words is, well, a cop-out. If you're only going to use words to describe your fine idea, why don't you just send everyone an email instead of wasting an hour of their time reading the same thought plastered on the wall behind you?

This presentation is only partially about you and what you think. Yes, you are the guiding force, but the goal is to present an idea with space around it. In this space, your audience is going to pour their own experience and their opinions; they're going to make your idea their own. Pictures, charts, and graphs create structured, memorable space. I use them in two ways: either to replace an entire thought wholesale or to augment a word slide that needs more space.

Note

A design aside: the visual design of your slides is an important topic that is outside the scope of this chapter, but know this—I've seen people lose their minds tweaking animations and transitions on slides. They try every single animation in the hope that just the right transition will add that certain something to their presentation, but what they don't know is that an animation fixation is usually a sign that your content blows. The same rule for typefaces applies for transitions and animations. The less your audience sees your design decisions, the more impact they'll have.

Third, you're looking for an underlying structure to your presentation that you're going to want to share with your audience. During all of this endless practice, you're going to develop a feel for how your presentation fits together, but this structure may not be initially obvious to your audience. For any reasonable-sized presentation, you need to design a visual system that allows audience members to instantly know where they are.

Fourth, and finally, you're looking for audience participation opportunities in the flow and tempo of your presentation. Where are you going to turn the lights up a little bit and remind the audience that they're sitting there, soaking in your thoughts? Let's talk a bit more about this.

Presentation Punctuation

Participation is presentation punctuation. You're going to use participation to accentuate parts of your presentation. You're going to use it to break up complex thoughts into digestible, comfortable ideas. But you only have partial control of when folks will actually participate.

The most common participation technique is the show of hands opener. It's usually done at the beginning of the presentation as a warm-up:

"Show of hands—how many of you own a Mac?"

"Quickly, how many of you think you're paying too much for term life insurance?"

As a warm-up technique, I'm a fan of the opener. It's an up-front reminder that this is not a speech, it's just an opening salvo, and you've got another hour to fill. As you're endlessly practicing your slides, look for sections that are idea-heavy and give your audience a shot in the arm with a question. You don't even have to ask for a show of hands; just direct the spotlight at them for a moment.

Tell me exactly what you do with your fingers when you read at your computer.

You're going to be able to plan only so much of your audience's participation, and therein lies the beauty of actually giving a presentation: you don't know when your audience is going to show up. Dull, wordy slides I considered deleting often got the biggest laugh. Visual slides that I've poured my heart into are often complete duds. You won't know until you're there.

Something for Their Pocket

What do you want your audience to remember? I should've asked this at the beginning, but I'm asking it now because you're almost done with your presentation and I want to know what you're giving your audience that fits in their pocket. I want to know what part of your presentation is actually going to leave with them.

There's a really easy and cheap way to do this, and it's the Lessons Learned slide. It's the bulleted list of important points slide that, when displayed, invariably results in a slew of cameras and iPhones appearing in the audience because they know this slide fits in their pockets.

Regardless of whether or not you use it, the Lessons Learned slide is a handy one to have at the end of your deck during the entire presentation development. It defines the basic structure of your presentation and represents a goal. Could you give your entire presentation from a single slide? Fifty minutes, a room full of people, and you with your single slide with six bullet points?

That's your goal, and you can have a wildly successful presentation without achieving it, but a one-slide presentation represents the ultimate commitment to your audience. It says, "This isn't about slides. This about me telling you a great story...out loud."

CHAPTER 31

Bits, Features, and Truth

There's a meeting going on right now. It's a cross-functional meeting, which means that not only are multiple departments in the organization represented, but also multiple expertise types, attitudes, and agendas. The cross-functional nature of this meeting means a program manager is present, and she is likely serving in her role as translator.

See, good program managers speak all the regional dialects of the company, so when engineering says, "It's done," they jump right in and translate, "Done pending function testing, production testing, and final documentation review," so that product management doesn't tell sales, "It's done," and they start selling something that actually isn't done.

In this well-attended, multilingual meeting, a decision is on the table, and it's a decision that's happening in every single software company right this second. It's not really a decision, it's a negotiation, but it's on the table, and people are tense because this decision is under heavy scrutiny:

Product management: "What's it going to take get this feature done?"

Program management: "What he's asking is...."

Engineering: "Quiet, I know what he's asking. The answer is, do you want to sacrifice TIME, QUALITY, or FEATURES?"

Program management: "What HE's...."

Product management: "Yeah, I've heard this before, and I still want it all."

More talking. More translating. Action items are assigned, which gives everyone the illusion that progress was made. And we all return to our respective regional offices and wait until we have the same meeting again, where we attempt to communicate intelligently with each other. But all we really do is schedule meetings...when what we need to do is figure out who makes decisions.

That Damned Triangle

Time. Quality. Features. It's usually described as a triangle, which somehow represents the state of your product or your feature. I believe the idea is that in an ideal and unattainable world, this triangle is perfect, equilateral, and seemingly at rest. There is balance between the time you have to release, the quality you are seeking to attain, and the features you want to ship.

In reality, this triangle is never at rest. It's constantly shifting and, well, I don't think it's actually a triangle. It's simply a mental model that gives you just enough ammunition to lie. The conversation goes like this:

Product management: "We need this feature to be competitive."

Engineering: "OK. We need four extra weeks to do that feature since it's new, and you're asking late."

Product management: "The date can't shift; we made commitments."

Engineering: "So did we. Listen, something has to give. You're adding more work or features, which means we need more time or, if you want, less quality. Make a choice."

These black-and-white arguments don't hold water. The idea that there are three simple levers that define a feature or a product is passive-aggressive professional absurdity. There are myriad levers the team can adjust, but to understand them you need to understand the people who are actually building the software.

Bits, Features, and Truth

Let's start with an exercise. I want you to think about the project that you're working on, or if your project is ginormous, I want you to think of the feature that you're developing. Relative to this product or feature, I want you to walk up to your nearest whiteboard and draw three large circles:

Now, a name belongs inside each of these circles, and it's the name of a specific role on your team. The traditional titles for these roles are engineering manager, product manager, and program manager, but I don't want you get to get hung up on titles. I want to you to think about the person who is best qualified to make a decision regarding the bits, the features, and the truth.

Bits

Who is the engineer who has the most influence on the bits? There are likely influencers, but who is the engineer that everyone goes to when they have a question? Your manager's name is a good knee-jerk name to put up here, but just because they have "manager" in their title doesn't mean they know what's going on as well as where to go. I want the name of the person who not only gets the call in the middle of the night when there is a bit-related emergency, but also the person who makes the large bit-related decisions. I want to know the name of the person who, when they say no, the debate stops. Got it? OK, next.

Features

Who is the person who defines the content for the product or feature? This is the name of the person who is constantly asking for more without regard for cost. This is the person who can eloquently and calmly explain the need for this feature with an argument stronger than, "Wouldn't it be cool if...?"

Truth

This might be the hardest to define because it's a role that could live anywhere in the building. While it took years to form this opinion, I believe the person who is responsible for the process is the one most likely to be the keeper of the truth.

There's a constant ebb and flow of information in any group of people. Important decisions are made in the morning that can take hours or days to move to the other side of the building. Information is tucked away for nefarious purposes. Information is laundered, adapted, and misinterpreted.

The truth is the aggregate best set of information that exists in the building, and the person who consistently has it is the keeper of the truth. You know this person; it's the person you go to when you're wondering, *"What the hell is going on here?"* This is the person who knows the politics and the players, they know the real reason the product is late, and this is why this is usually the job of the program manager.

The complaint I hear most about program management is the same complaint I hear about managers: *what do they do all day?* What do they actually own? Practically, the most important part of the product they own is the schedule, but their larger contribution is information management.

Yeah, I know you start-up folk believe you're doing just great without a semblance of program or process management. You believe that these types of folks are going to slow you down with their agendas and to-do lists. Here's the deal: just because no one has the title in your garage doesn't mean the role doesn't exist. In any group larger than one, someone has taken the role of keeper of the truth, and this person's key skill is information wrangling. They constantly gather the information from the group, synthesize it, translate it, and, sometimes forcibly, present this information to the folks who are busily lying to themselves.

Me: "We have six weeks to shipping, so we're good."

Keeper: "Feature complete was two weeks ago, and we're still writing code."

Me: "But the team is fired up, working weekends, and...."

Keeper: "Steve and Ryan are on vacation for two weeks starting tomorrow."

Me: "Oh."

A good program manager cares about the program and the product, but they also have a calm professional ambivalence. They have to; they're always uncovering and then surviving the worst-case scenarios. These discoveries often give them the most complete picture of how the product is doing. Their ability to survive them has made them unflappable—they don't freak out, because they've lived through it and know there's always a way out...somehow. All of this experience is why they usually end up owning the schedule. I'll explain why when we get to analysis.

So, who is this calm, truth-oriented, well-informed person on your team? Who is the person who doesn't lose it? Who is the person you go to when you need to understand the intent of the other parts of the organization? They very well might not have the title of program manager, but they are there.

Circle of Comfort

Before I analyze your circles, I need you to do one more pass where you ask yourself two questions.

Great, you've got a name in each circle. Maybe the same name is in two circles. We'll talk more about that in a moment. My first question is: for each name, what's the person's circle of comfort?

It's fine that you put Ryan in both Bits and Features, but where does his heart lie? What is his professional background? Which circle is he going to instinctively optimize for? For each circle, if you think the occupant's natural circle is different, write that name underneath their circle.

My second question is: have you picked leaders? Look at the Bits circle. The name you put in there is the brightest engineer in the building, and any time anyone needs someone to explain the architecture, he's the guy paraded across the building, but is he the leader? Does he make decisions about the direction of the product? He has incredibly strong and informed opinions about where it's going, but when it comes down to the commit, is he the guy? No? OK, who is?

Leaders have deep experience in their circle. It's not chutzpah, it's not spin; it's the knowledge and analytical skills developed from doing the job. It's because you can walk up to them, present a hard problem, and have an immediate, informed, and comforting answer. That's the name that belongs in the circle.

Leaders make decisions. Sometimes it appears they're doing it with little data. Some decisions are great, others are crap, but for the purpose of this circle exercise, you need to identify the three leaders relative to the Bits, the Features, and the Truth.

Circle Analysis

OK, what've we got? Let's walk through different circle scenarios:

Something is empty.

> *We don't have program management, nor do we have any product managers.* Again, don't get hung up on titles. Just because your company hasn't hired these folks doesn't mean the work isn't happening. Someone is picking features. Someone is designing the schedule. In fact, if you're really small, there's a chance the same name fills all three circles. Let's talk about that.

Same name. All three circles.

> *Edgar is the man. He's our one-stop decision machine. It's awesome.* While I appreciate your velocity as well as your enthusiasm, I have concerns.

I believe an effective team eventually needs each of these roles clearly defined and owned by three separate people. *Rands, where's QA? What about design? HELLO SALES. These are essential parts of the business. WHERE ARE THOSE CIRCLES?* This model is not about describing an effective business; it describes an effective team. Sales, design, QA, marketing, customer support—the list goes on. You need some version of these in order to have a business, and yes, they feed essential data into the product, but my assumption is that one of the reasons you wrote Mitchell's name in the Feature circle is that he has a solid relationship with the design team; he knows that an essential part of his features is the design.

Three leaders. One who makes decisions regarding the bits, another who is responsible for the features, and another who cares about the truth. The theory is that these leaders are sitting in these circles because they have the ability to make good decisions relative to their expertise, and the reality is that these folks do not get along.

Program management believes engineering will never ship, product management believes the product would be nothing without them, and engineering thinks everyone else is useless because they don't know how to code. It sounds pretty hostile, except when it comes to these three leaders. See, in addition to decision-making authority, these folks have healthy tension with their circle peers.

I divide healthy tension into two equal and opposite beliefs:

- First, there's the reality-affirming belief that most everyone in the building shares. It's the belief that *my job is the most important job in the building and in my absence it'll just fall apart.* It's a quiet belief that we tell no one, but it's a silent, strengthening belief that gives folks the confidence to make a decision. *I'm an expert, I'm brilliant, and I'm right.*

- Second, and specific to our circle denizens, there's the grudging respect for the other circles and the trust of their expertise. This is a tenuous arrangement given the first belief, but part of leadership within the circle is the ability to step back from a massive decision and say, "He knows better than I."

The idea is that the ability, skills, and experience that define each of these leaders are fundamentally different. An engineer who has seven years of coding experience has a vastly different perspective regarding features and products than a product manager who has transformed an MBA into a product management gig. You can fake it—an engineering leader can have a passionate opinion about a feature or a product—but there is a skill to defining, explaining, and justifying a feature that years of development won't give you.

If you're staring at your three circles and the name is the same in all three, I have two questions:

Are they all that?

> Can they consistently make correct bit-related decisions along with feature decisions while realistically balancing the truth? Really? If it's just the two of you in that garage, I get it, but if it's 100 of you and one person is responsible for all three circles, I bet they are optimizing for their circle of comfort, and that means two other circles aren't being represented.

Who do they argue with?

> Without the healthy tension of between Features and Bits, there's no debate about feature roadmaps and technical realities. A diversity of opinion takes any idea and, hopefully, shapes it into something unpredictably better. We can see good examples of this by looking at two other circle configurations.

Bits and Features are the same.

So Ryan, an engineer by training, is making both engineering and feature decisions. Great. That gets rid of a lot of those pesky feature prioritization meetings, right? What other meetings aren't happening? Where else is the feature set of your product not being debated because Ryan is making unilateral decisions as owner of the bits and the features?

Again, I'm being an alarmist and I'm exaggerating, but I believe you cannot effectively (and don't want to) remove yourself from what you do to make a well-informed decision outside of your circle. Think of it like this: is Ryan the customer or does he have direct access to the customer? If the features are for engineers, there's a solid argument that he could make decisions for both the bits and the features, but if the product or features aren't targeted for engineers, why do we believe Ryan can make informed decisions about them?

I'm not saying that anyone outside of the feature circle can't have an opinion about the product. You want a culture that encourages everyone to care deeply about the product you build, but if you're developing software for regular human beings, then you need a regular human being to speak to their needs.

Let's look at another variant.

Truth is the same as Features.

Tony the business guy owns both the features and the schedule. This is a pretty common configuration because the belief is that those who make feature decisions for the user should also make scheduling decisions. *We need feature X in May.* What's the hitch?

Well, you've got the truth bundled with the features, and I'm uncomfortable with that because the truth needs to be neutral. The truth needs to be unbiased, and with Tony's name in both circles, you've got the guy who is calling the shots for the features almost making the schedule decisions. He might have solid, healthy tension with your Bits circle, but how is Bits going to argue with the guy who owns the levers for both content and time?

The healthy tension created by having three distinct leaders creates diverse debate about your product. Yes, this is the same debate I talked about at the beginning of this chapter, but the difference is when you have three leaders equally representing a well-defined viewpoint along with a sense of ownership, it's a balanced debate in which the needs of the technology are weighed against the desires of the customer and the realities of the schedule. When one leader is representing two circles, their two votes are pushing decisions in their favor.

Let the Negotiation Begin; It's About the Debate

This is just another model. I've replaced the Time/Quality/Features triangle with circles. There are just as many ways to screw up and misrepresent this model with politics, inexperienced people, and poorly defined features. The difference here is that I believe this model not only realistically describes the forces that pull your product in different directions, but that it also gives those forces a proper name.

Let's go back to the endless debate where the Bits, Features, and Truth are equally represented:

Features: "I want feature X, and I want it on the same schedule."

Truth: "We need more time, and since I know all the moving parts, I know that we're ahead of schedule for one feature. I think we've got two weeks of wiggle room."

Bits: "Two weeks isn't enough. Can we cut this one feature that we haven't started and no one cares about in half?"

Features: "I can live with that."

Truth: "Sold."

Software is built by people. The best Gantt chart only tells you half the truth about the schedule, the most complete marketing requirements document can never describe why a feature is compelling, and the most detailed technical specification will never tell you what makes for beautiful code. These are only tools, and they tell little about the people who are building the software.

These people have names, and they've earned them by not only consistently making great decisions for their area of experience, but also knowing when to ask someone else for advice.

CHAPTER 32

The Reveal

You're building…something.

The whiteboards are covered with multicolored, indecipherable flowcharts, there are 16 empty coffee cups on your table, and both flat-panel monitors are covered with code. Your plant is dead. Again. It is in this moment that you discover the one thing about the thing you are building, the one feature that, when your users see it, will help them fully understand what you have been building.

This is the Reveal.

The Reveal is the other half of the Holy Shit. You, the developer, create the big idea—the Reveal—and when the idea is discovered by your users, when they recognize the magnitude, they literally say, "*Holy Shit.*"

A Reveal is a contradiction, and it's this contradiction that gives the Holy Shit legs. The contradiction lies in the Reveal's deceptive simplicity. It's the construction of a very simple idea from previously incoherent complexity. This is how it slips so easily into the mind of the consumer. It's a single word or image that completely sums up that which was until only recently described by a book, an application, or an entire college degree. The amount of unspoken information contained in a good Reveal is staggering, and that is why, when we see it, we say, "Holy Shit."

In a Reveal you have artfully and simply described the complicated, and while I know the taste of excitement when you discover the Reveal after that 16th cup of coffee, you haven't proven it yet. It needs testing, it needs definition...

It needs a demo.

Three Phases

As an engineer, you need to be able to construct and deliver a demo. You may not have a world-changing Holy Shit on your hands; you may just need to get feedback from a single executive or from your boss. But regardless of the magnitude, a demonstration of your idea is a unique meeting that has specific requirements and goals. Let's start with the ground rules:

A demo, like a magic trick, has three phases:

1. Setup. Context setting. What do you need to know before we begin?

2. Story. The arc. I'm going to take you somewhere now and I'm going to explain as we go.

3. Reveal. Voilà! See where we are now? Holy Shit, am I right?

A demo is not a presentation; it's a conversation.

The are a great many demos out there being held at this very moment, maybe even in your building, but these meetings are being run by sales guys who have an entirely different motivation: they want to make a sale. There will be a time and place where you do want to sell your idea, but that's not where you're going to start. The point of your demo is to have a conversation about the idea so that you can figure out how to make it better.

Regardless of your audience, your goal is the same.

Is it your boss who asked for a demo? His boss? The business? The VC? We'll talk about different means of preparing for different motivations in a moment, but this preparation all serves the same goal: you want information. The rule is: an idea only gets better with eyeballs. I know when I find a Reveal because I can barely breathe. *This is...hot shit and I need to tell... everyone.* The problem is that the Reveal isn't just the simple, compelling idea, it's the Setup and then it's the Story, which leads to the Reveal, and all three need refining.

Three Alphas

Let's build a demo. For the sake of this chapter, I'm assuming this is a one-hour demo where you're catering to a small group of strategic people. Where there is a single Alpha person whose opinion will carry the room, it is this Alpha person you care about. It is their opinion that is going to tell you whether you've got a Holy Shit.

I believe there are three Alphas that you care about.

Alpha Nothing: "I'm saying absolutely nothing."

Possibly the most frustrating of our three Alphas, this is a person who is going to spend the entire hour saying nothing. The entire time. Zippo. Here's what you do...

Alpha Nothing is going to force you to carry the entire hour, which means, yeah, this is a lot like a presentation. You need to prepare to fill the entire hour with your tap dancing, but the good news is that this work is reusable for all of the different Alpha personality types.

The core of your demo is your Reveal, and as an engineer, you're really going to be excited about getting to the Reveal. You know it's the shit, and your thought is that the sooner you get there, the more jumping up and down everyone is going to do. The problem with your enthusiasm is that it assumes and has forgotten all of the endless boring work it took to find your epiphany.

The Setup and the Story leading into your demo need to document key points of your journey to the Reveal. It's not the entire journey, it's a brief summary, but it allows your audience to see and critique how you discovered the Reveal. Let's talk briefly about each:

The Setup

Likely the smallest section of your demo, the Setup provides all the background information and special knowledge the room is going need to understand both your Story and the impact of your Reveal.

The Story

Now that the room understands the problem space, you need to describe the process you went through to get to the Reveal. What did you need to learn? How did you stumble around before you discovered the Reveal? Everyone likes to think the research in R&D is a bunch of bright people in lab coats with their hands on their chins nodding knowingly at a whiteboard. What you and I know is that research is what you do in between what you're doing, and that's a great story to tell.

Back to the problem at hand. Alpha Nothing is saying nothing, so you can go long on both Setup and Story. Perhaps too much of either is just the thing to break the icy stare of Alpha Nothing. Maybe not. Let's try something else.

I build each of the three parts of the demo around knowable, containable chunks of information. From a high level, there are three major chunks to start with—the Setup, Story, and Reveal—but there might be smaller chunks that you want to shape into digestible complete thoughts. The chunks serve two purposes: first, to allow you to structure your demo, but also to give you a place to pause during your demo and ask a simple question:

"Does what I just told you make sense?"

This check-in might seem pointless with Alpha Nothing in the room, who is just sitting there and nodding each time you ask, but this chunk-by-chunk check-in not only sets a comfortable information pace for your demo, it also sets the stage for you to get the information you came for in the first place.

You're thinking your Reveal is the point, it's your killer feature, and you might be right. But it's the entire story that needs constructive feedback, because the Setup, Story, and Reveal are intimately tied together. You just don't know when stopping to ask for feedback might allow your audience to make a simple comment that has immediate and lasting impact on your Reveal.

Given all the work you put into the demo for Alpha Nothing, you're going to feel a sense of sad emptiness when you finish and it's more of the same uninformative nothing. Still, there is some reason you've decided to pitch this unreadable schmo. Let's assume your instincts are good and this silent powerbroker is going to do something. In my experience, you're going to hear the feedback, but it's going to come via a backchannel. It's either an email from a random person in the meeting or a request for another demo where you're going to get the real feedback.

I always assume that a demo is going to be given more than once. Since I never know how many times I'm going to demo, or which Alphas I'm going to demo to, I always build my demo for Alpha Nothing because it gives me the most demo flexibility. This will make more sense as we explore the other two Alphas.

Alpha Game: "I'm game, but you drive."

After the frustrating silence of Alpha Nothing, Alpha Game is a delight. He actually wants to engage in a conversation, whether it's the Setup, Story, or the Reveal. Alpha Game is also going to stay on script. He's going to let you drive the demo and will respect the structure of the meeting, and when you get to the end of a knowable chunk, he'll constructively chime in.

Even with the collaborative nature of Alpha Game, you still want to structure this meeting around knowable chunks. Your goal with any demo is information acquisition and, as we learned with Alpha Nothing, information often likes to hide. Your demo isn't just the script; it's the tone and tempo of the meeting. At the end of the first knowable chunk, you stop and you ask, "Any questions? Thoughts?" Perhaps there's no feedback at the first pause, but after you've done it three times, everyone in the room knows that there will be ample opportunity to weigh in. However, getting them to talk is only solving half the problem.

"I don't get it."

What?

You're only halfway through your Story and a previously friendly Alpha Game says again, "I don't get it." It's the nightmare scenario. It's what you've been worrying about since this meeting was scheduled: "Am I full of shit?"

A deep breath.

Remember the rule: all ideas get better with eyeballs. The perspective you need to have isn't whether the feedback is right or wrong, it's what's the intent? What is he trying to say? What doesn't he get? Ask him. If you still don't understand his point, you keep asking questions. You need to ignore the fact that you're pissed that he's unintentionally invalidating your entire pitch. The question is, how is he doing it? "I don't get it" isn't a point, it's an opener. It's an attention grabber, which leads to a larger and hopefully strategic discussion.

The hope with Alpha Game is that he has a point—that you're dealing with a rational, informed, articulate person. Just as your Setup, Story, and Reveal are built around knowable chunks, so is your conversation with Alpha Game. Each observation and question is a chance for you to see your demo from a different perspective, and that's how you figure out whether you're close to a Holy Shit.

Remember, you not only have the entire picture in your head, you also have all of the experience that led to the construction of that picture. The confusion in the room about your demo often isn't a dismissal of your entire idea; it's where you mentally zigged when they expected you to zag, which is precisely the kind of information you're here to find out.

Managing the conversation, regardless of which Alpha, is an art, and you get better at it with practice. And you're going to need all the practice you can get to deal with the last Alpha.

Alpha Drive: "I'll drive."

You arrive 10 minutes early and go through the unavoidable 2.7 minutes of dongle projector confusion. You check your slides. You check your demo. Both are solid. You have two whole minutes to nervously chat with the team before the storm hits.

Alpha Drive.

You don't even get to start before she says, "Skip the slides. Show me the demo."

Wait, what?

Alpha Drive has an ego or Alpha Drive is in a hurry. I don't know what her deal is, but she's going to drive the whole damned thing and you're just going to go with the flow. Don't believe me? Think you're dealing with Alpha Game? OK, go ahead and try to convince her about the point of a well-structured presentation and how you're....

"That's not how I work. Show me the demo."

Told you.

You've prepared for this. You've built your presentation around this inevitable chaos. When she asks for the demo, you jump to the demo. When she gets confused because she skipped a key knowable chunk in your Story, you detect this, call an audible, and jump to that one slide: "Did you mean this?" When the hour is over, you will have likely done your entire demo...completely out of order.

Alpha Drive is an intense reminder that everyone processes in their own order and at their own pace. Just because your Setup and Story naturally lead to your Reveal in your head doesn't mean that this is how others are going to get there. Yes, Alpha Drive may eventually get to the Reveal and might say Holy Shit, but the journey will be entirely hers unless you take action.

Both of my favorite ways to reign in Alpha Drive involve time, and both techniques can be used effectively for any Alpha:

#1: A perfect silence

When you land a key knowable chunk and ask if there are any questions, wait 15 seconds before you proceed to the next chunk. 15 seconds in a meeting full of people is forever, but in the case of an out of control Alpha Drive, your silence can demonstrate who is actually driving the meeting.

#2: Demo tempo

Everyone wants to see the demo; they want to see what is real versus what is being talked about. By the time you get to the live demonstration, you can almost taste the Reveal, you're excited, and you blow right through it. Time and time again I've watched eager engineers furiously clicking and dragging and sliding their demo all over the screen. Their enthusiasm is obscuring the entire reason we gathered in the first place. My rule of thumb is that when I get to the live portion of the demo, I set my head at half speed. This mental slowdown combined with my inevitable adrenaline balances out to a sane and consumable demo tempo.

The one guarantee with the demo to Alpha Drive is that it will not go how you expect. You can pull every move out of your meeting management bag of tricks, but Alpha Drive will take you off-script and in an unusual direction.

The advice remains to remember your goal—information acquisition. Alpha Drive's annoying habit of taking you elsewhere is yet another opportunity to see your idea from a different perspective, and that's another way to learn about what you've built.

The Holy Shit Event Horizon

The perfect demo has nothing to do with you.

That's right.

Your final, often unachievable goal for your demo is your absence. The purest Holy Shit is one where a person sees your idea or your application, *sans* Setup and Story and, most importantly, *sans* you.

If you consistently figure out how to do this, please tell me how.

Meanwhile, the rest of us are balancing our creative bursts of energy along with a healthy dose of constructive feedback provided courtesy of a variety of Alpha personalities. Whether they're silent, helpful, or annoying, their position and their perspective will have impact on your thinking, and that's where the real art lies.

You'll know you have a good Reveal when Alpha Nothing says something. You'll know you're onto something when Alpha Game becomes Alpha Drive in a fit of excitement. All of this feedback and perspective is relevant, but the hardest part for which I have the least advice is when to decide to ignore it all and trust that you've really built...something.

YOUR NEXT GIG

Toward the end of *Being Geek*, you'll find yourself back at the beginning—considering your next career move. This section of the book describes scenarios both positive and negative that might influence your next gig.

Bad performance review? Time to become a manager? The company is collapsing? Just plain bored? The urgency created by each of these scenarios varies, but understanding how they actually play out is an essential part of planning your next play.

Whether the need for change is pressing or not, these chapters are worth your time because you've chosen to work in an industry that will always move faster than you. Change is a constant, and that means you constantly need to consider what is next.

CHAPTER 33

The Screw-Me Scenario

It had all the signs of a good meeting. And I hate meetings. We were:

- Talking about a product we loved
- In great shape from a feature, quality, and schedule standpoint
- A group that historically did not kick ass
- A group that was kicking ass

The slides looked great and the dry run was flawless, so why hadn't I slept in two nights?

I couldn't sleep because I couldn't see the Screw-Me.

You Might Be Lying

There are endless interesting variants of meetings, but the one I want to talk about is the executive cross-pollination communication clusterfuck. The point of this meeting is alignment. Big alignment. You've likely got several different groups who don't normally spend a lot of time together being forced to sit in the same room so the execs can compare stories, measure reality, and figure out who is lying.

Before I explain how to get your head around this meeting, I want to talk about intent behind this meeting. Intent starts with a question: "Why does this meeting exist?" If you're responsible for the presentation in this particular meeting, it exists because someone hates you.

It's not personal hate. It's professional hate, and it's exacerbated by a simple fact of organization: different groups speak different languages. Marketing speaks marketing, Legal speaks legal, and Engineering speaks engineering. There's a fundamental communication breakdown somewhere in the building, and someone is feeling wronged. They're feeling bullied and since they don't speak your dialect, they're complaining up rather than across.

Normally, we deal with these Tower of Babel situations with the direct application of middle management, program managers, and other folks we pay big bucks to sit in meetings and translate between organizations. However, translation has not worked in this case. Someone high up on the org chart is hearing two very different stories and wondering which is true. Story reconciliation is certainly on the top of your list of items to resolve in this meeting, but job #1 is to figure out who hates you.

A Rubber Stamp Affair

For these critical meetings, your goal is to make them a rubber stamp affair. In the week before the meeting, you will have personally vetted your slides with each of the meeting invitees. You will have heard their concerns and made the appropriate adjustments to your deck. When the cross-pollination meeting arrives, your goal is an utter lack of drama and the finishing pronouncement of, "Yeah, we should do that and you know how."

It never happens like this.

We're "busy" and we have "things to do," but mostly we're "looking forward to blindsiding you with a Screw-Me at the least convenient moment in front of your executive team."

It's a disappointing trait of human nature that folks who feel wronged like to exact their revenge by flaunting their knowledge and dishing out the Screw-Me at the worst possible time, but roll with it. You're already a step ahead just expecting to be screwed. Besides, your enemy is working more with emotion than content, and that will turn into their own personal Screw-Me Scenario at a later date. Right now, your job is data.

No Guilt, No Doubts, No Fear

Ideas get better with eyeballs, and before this meeting goes down, your job is to get as many eyeballs on your presentation as possible. You're not going to get everyone in the meeting, but that's not the point. The task is cross-pollination. Casting the information net as wide as possible and incessantly asking:

- Does this make sense?

- What is missing?

- How am I going to get screwed?

I've got the Russian Lit major* for vetting my strategy. Who do you have? I'm not talking about your boss or your coworker; I'm talking about the person who can objectively look at your presentation and start poking holes. These people are rare because it's another disappointing trait of human nature that we often think we're doing each other a favor by listening well but then tell each other what we want to hear.

You lose yourself in any significant project. You've long forgotten your strategic initial assumptions, but more importantly, you've forgotten what other people need because you're furiously worrying about the daily tactical fire drills. A fresh perspective is a chance to test your entire idea and find the Screw-Me. You need someone to poke holes. You need to find and fill the gaps, and as each gap is filled, you're going to build confidence around your pitch because, well, that's one less potential Screw-Me entry point.

You're not going to find them all. That's OK, because in the process of constantly refining your pitch, you're mentally refining yourself. You're preparing yourself by seeing each of the different perspectives in your deck. That improves the chances that you'll know what to do when someone starts dishing out the hate.

---

* *http://www.randsinrepose.com/archives/2006/09/06/russian_history.html*

Game On

The meeting's on. You're walking in with a head full of data, and my hope is that through your constant cross-pollination, you are legitimately the most informed person on this particular topic in the room. There's still work to do:

Size the room.

> Who is here? What groups do they represent? What do they want? Any unexpected visitors? Really? Why would they randomly show up? Who brought them? What possible Screw-Mes could they represent? *OK, let's get started.*

Carry the room.

> Start your deck. You've got it memorized, right? They can tell this is the 32nd time you've done it, right? Good. It's smooth. You've already defused two Screw-Mes by slide 12. Really well done there. *Amanda, you have a question?*

Manage the room.

> Questions aren't Screw-Mes. You can clarify and stay on track. You know that Amanda is going to ask about hard data, right? Don't let her take over the conversation. Say, "I've got your data in the appendix, but let me get through this first, OK?" Yeah, you just shut down a Senior VP. Nicely done. No way you can do that without serious confidence in your preparation. *Yes, Tim?*

Tim's got the Screw-Me, and you didn't see it coming. Total left field. Completely valid strategic observation and you don't have a clue how to answer. Shit.

You will recognize the Screw-Me by the complete silence that fills both the room and your head. That's the realization everyone is having that you're Screwed. First, let's not make it worse....

The Unforgivable Spin

Tim: "Rands, what about THIS?"

I'm a poker player and an experienced meeting surfer, so the room will not immediately know from the look on my face that This has Screwed me, but what I choose to do next will define my ongoing relationship with the room.

There are two options when you are cornered by This. Your animal brain, when cornered, will try to find a way out. You can taste this approach even before you begin. *I am going to spin. I am going to talk quickly and confidently about This, and I am going to hope that in my furious verbal scurrying they are going to believe I've got This handled.*

That's not what they're seeing or hearing.

This is not your staff meeting where a little verbal soft shoe is going to entertain and delight. These are the execs, and no matter how many meetings you've surfed, they see straight through spin, they know this dance, and the longer you sit there spinning, the longer you give your boss an opportunity to step in, try to make the diving save, and make you look like a blithering fool.

It takes a little practice to make the correct move when you feel the spin coming. You are going to do three things:

1. Acknowledge the Screw-Me.

2. Admit "I don't know."

3. Concretely explain the steps you're going to take to find out and give yourself a deadline.

You have completely defused Tim. See, Tim was pissed, which is why he waited until precisely the wrong moment to throw down the Screw-Me. He wanted to see you spin and make a fool of yourself in front of your management team, and what you did with the instant acknowledgment was crush emotion with structured sanity.

You can get lucky with spin sometimes. There are times when you spin so hard that you talk yourself into a Screw-Me solution that actually makes sense. But this is rare and unreliable, and in my experience, this frenetic verbal journey erodes confidence and wastes time.

The only question on everyone's mind during the cross-pollination clusterfuck is, "Do you know what you're talking about?" It's lame that Tim doesn't speak Engineer and waited until precisely the wrong moment to Screw you, but my hope is that through your incessant vetting of your slides, you can deliver the "I don't know" with confidence. Tim only knows what he's pissed about and you, through your preparation, can see the entire picture.

A Screw-Me Detection Policy

An aggressive Screw-Me detection policy is, I believe, essential to navigating groups of people. It's not just constantly knowing the potential worst-case scenario in any situation; it's that you are instinctively always looking for it. When I am looking at any situation, I'm always trying to figure out what sequence of events could occur that will screw me.

This strategy sounds a lot like paranoia, and yes, an unchecked Screw-Me detection policy can result in a conspiracy theory lifestyle where THEY are out to GET YOU.

Yes, only the paranoid survive, but paranoia is a lot of work. You can burn a lot of calories worrying about all possibilities, but this is not an approach I recommend. What I'm asking is that you look at specific key events strategically. Step back and look at the whole board. Ask, "What sequence of moves is going to benefit me? Can I see what is coming? And how could I get screwed?" Because teams that kick ass aren't just ones that deliver; it's that they deliver even when they're screwed.

CHAPTER 34

No Surprises

At the end of each fiscal year, companies take stock of their performance. How'd we do? Better or worse? This is a natural time to reflect upon individual performance. This is when your boss writes your review.

In my ideal management world, a review is simply a documentation of well-known facts about your performance over the year. It also contains constructive advice and insight regarding how your boss believes you can improve on that performance. My dream is that you already know all of this information because you've been getting year-round feedback from your boss.

I wish.

Whether your manager is consistently delivering this information or not, getting written feedback is completely different from receiving it verbally. The path to your brain via the written word is dramatically different than for the spoken word. Reading the highs and lows of the past year makes them permanent and makes them real.

And then there's the surprise.

Show Me the Money

Bad news. The surprise has nothing to do with money. We're not talking about compensation here. Yes, you did a splendid job this year, and I think they should be throwing raises, bonuses, and stock your way. But it's even better if it's clear why you think you did a splendid job. Can you articulate it? And you might know, but does your boss? Can he explain to you, in detail, how well you kicked ass?

I didn't think so.

See, your boss has you and a bunch of other yous who are all allegedly kicking ass, and all of that ass-kickery is tricky to monitor, especially over an entire year. It gets even worse when one of your team members is not kicking ass. Legitimately or not, that's actually where a lot of your boss's attention is going. You read that right: someone else's failure is distracting from your phenomenal year.

Let's fix that.

There are three strategies I'd like you to employ when it comes to your yearly review. They are:

1. Ignore the measures, and focus on the content.

2. Prepare for the fact that a review is a discussion and, sometimes, a negotiation.

3. Deconstruct the surprise.

Measures Versus Content

I've experienced a lot of different review formats at different companies, but let's boil it down to three buckets. A review describes:

1. What you did

2. How you did it

3. What you need to do next

This is a massive simplification of your review. Your review has all sorts of other corporate and division focus areas, but these impressive-sounding labels are still just lenses through which you understand how you did versus what was expected.

For each of the buckets, there are two classes of information: the content and the measure. I want to explain how you can save yourself a lot of sleepless nights ignoring the measures, but first, a definition.

Sprinkled across your review are measures. These are words like "Needs Improvement," "Satisfactory," or "Excellent." These words grab you because they're easy to understand. They are effectively your grades, and you've spent a lot of your formative years waiting for grades to show up.

If I told you that you got an A on a piece of work, you'd internally translate that letter into a pleasant "I did about as well as I could. Go me." Grades—measures—are efficient, and they do convey information, but they lack essential content. I'll explain via example.

When I arrived at University of California, Santa Cruz, in the 1990s, they had no grades. Hippies. At the end of the quarter, you received a written evaluation. For each student in the class, the professor or the teaching assistant would produce a written evaluation—a plain-English description of the type and quality of the work produced over the semester.

I don't know who came up with the idea of ditching grades, but my hope was that they wanted to ditch the measures. The intent of measures are not to derive useful information; they are designed to allow for comparison and, duh, measurement. Am I higher or lower than you? How many As? Are there more As than Bs? It's interesting data, and I'm sure if you took a classroom full of data and plotted it on a graph, you'd learn something. Look! A bell curve!

A measure doesn't help you in your career. Your performance review isn't about comparisons to others. It's about what you did and what you could do. What you're looking for is the content.

Tell me which is more useful:

"You did well."

or:

"You finished the work on schedule, the customer was happy with the results, but there were lingering quality issues with the code. Looking at the last two releases, you had 2x the numbers of bugs than in prior releases. Focus on...."

We get hung up on grades, on measures, because they are so gosh darned digestible. They give us the illusion that they show us where we fit, but they don't tell us what's next. At UCSC, the point of the gradeless report card was to create a vacuum where the professor would actually say something useful. You're not going to get rid of measures—they serve a distinct purpose—but when you're first reading your review, I want you to ignore those seductive one-word assessments of your entire year. Their simplicity, while comprehensible, is just going to obscure the complexity of your year.

Rather, look at the content behind the measures. Whatever your particular areas of focus are, does your boss do an effective job of explaining what you did, how you did, and what you could do better? It's a simple set of requirements, but your boss is going to mess it up, which is why you need to be clear that...

A Review Is a Conversation

The written word is intimidating. An assessment of a year is a big deal, so what are you going to do when you sit down with your boss and he hands you three poorly crafted paragraphs littered with the word "significant"?

No, you don't ask about the raise. You freak out about the paragraphs. THREE PARAGRAPHS? I'VE WRITTEN MORE IN EMAIL THIS MORNING THAN YOU JUST WASTED ON MY YEAR.

Calm yourself.

Think of this pathetic piece of paper as an opening offer—a poor offer. Your job is to transform this travesty into an accurate reflection of your year, and you're not doing this just out of a sense of self-righteousness; you're doing this to set the record straight.

This piece of paper is one of the only official documents of your career at this company. If you move, if your boss leaves, if there's a reorg, this is often the first document reviewed to understand the degree of your ass-kickery, and that means you want your boss to comprehend it.

"But Rands, I was just...so pissed. Three paragraphs? I spent my entire winter on the project. I was FURIOUS."

Again, your review will contain surprises, and they will rattle you, which is why you prepare with a self-review.

Whether your company asks for it or not, the moment the mail from HR alerts you to the review season, you start cobbling together your self-review. Same buckets as above. My move is to keep a yearlong log of significant work as a task in whatever task tracking system I'm currently ignoring. Even if you haven't been paying consistent attention, you'll be surprised by what you can dig up in a weekend of considering your year.

Take a look at your year. How'd you do? No, really, I'm not actually reading it, so you can have an honest opinion. Was it a great year or did you just think it was great? Yes, your boss's opinion about your year is key, he does sign the checks, but it's a key surprise-reducing technique to walk into the review with an opinion. This moment of personal honesty you're having with yourself is a big deal because that's the foundation you're going to stand on when the three pathetic paragraphs show up. Having a justifiable opinion regarding your year is a powerful, defensible position.

While it's important to send the self-review long before your boss writes his review, it's more important that you have this opinion, this well-defined opinion, when sitting down to read your boss's review. Does it document what you did? Everything? Does the description of what you did match your perception? No? Why? Don't tell me, tell your boss, and make sure he gets it because it's these types of historical perception mismatches that form an unhealthy basis for emerging misunderstanding and resentment.

The point of a review is the debate—to align your perceptions with those of the person who signs the checks—but even with all this structured healthy debate, there's still going to be a...

Surprise!

I don't know what the surprise is. It's your review. Some of the doozies over the years from mine include:

- The total absence of recognition for a multi-month, multi-team project that kicked ass.

- A reversal of opinion regarding a piece of work I'd done, usually toward the negative.

- Completely contradictory areas of improvement.

Unfortunately, the surprise is the point. A review not only forces the alignment discussion, it serves as a warning for the coming year: *what do I need to do differently to avoid being blindsided when the next review arrives?*

Fact is, you're never fully going to get your boss on-board with your year. There are opinions he has that aren't going to change, which means if you don't want another surprise next year, you have to change.

A review's value lies not only in the documentation of what was observed, but also what was not.

The Permanence of the Written

In many years of reviews, the only consistency I've noticed is that they're getting shorter. My unsubstantiated paranoia is that lawyers apply subtle corporate pressure to retain less descriptive documentation of what actually happened in the company. But perhaps it's just a growing professional laziness.

Whatever the reason, a brief review is just sad. If you're staring at three useless paragraphs, you have a couple of problems. You've got a company that allows crappy reviews, and you've got a boss who is unable or unwilling to articulate either the quantity or quality of the work you've done.

That's all sorts of screwed, but a complete breakdown occurs only when you don't react.

The first review I wrote was awful. It was three paragraphs derived from scanning status reports from the past six months. I sat in the room as she read the review, and she didn't have to say a thing for me to understand that I'd be spending the weekend actually writing the review. I got an accusing, furious glare. *You didn't even try.*

So I did.

CHAPTER 35

A Deliberate Career

I want to hear the story of how you got your first gig in high tech. Like me, you probably did all the things you were supposed to do: you went to the career center, searched the job boards, and attended the career fairs.

It was all vaguely confusing. Nothing was concrete. You threw your pathetic excuse for a resumé to dozens of randomly smiling people and wondered, "Am I ever going to get a job?"

And then it happened. A vacation in Italy. Some bizarre, unimaginable confluence of events that started with you being blind drunk and broke in Florence. You met this guy on the street who was clearly American, you hit it off, and long story short, this chance meeting on the other side of the planet resulted in you getting your first engineering gig at a fashionable start-up in Silicon Valley.

Your thought as you settled into your bright'n'shiny new gig was, "I've no control over what is happening to me. I just need to go with the flow, and I'm going to randomly meet someone who is going to randomly believe in me and then money will rain from the sky."

As an avid fan of instinct, a frequent receiver of random career blessings, and a professional identifier of random opportunity, I understand and have lived this perspective, but hope isn't going to define your career: you need a strategy.

Three Choices

When I write the word "strategy," I picture this thick book with a light-blue cover and black binding. The title is *My Career Strategy*, and below the title in block letters it says "TOP SECRET". This is not, however, what I mean by having a strategy. I'm talking about a half-hour exercise in thinking about your future.

The only thing I know about your future is that you don't know what's going to happen or when. Opportunity is going to show up at the least convenient time, and the moment it arrives, whether you're ready or not, you're going to have to make a decision in a moment. *Am I going to make a move?*

My thought: the more you know what you want, the better decision you'll make.

I see three big questions you can ask yourself to define a rough strategy for your career. These are questions about your next job, but combined, the answers to these questions will help you understand where you want to go, what you want to build, and how you want to build it throughout your career.

Question #1: Start-Up or Established?

Start-up

There is nothing quite like a start-up as an introduction to our industry. If you're looking for a fire hose full of information pointed straight at your face, I highly recommend the start-up. However, its ability to present you with information is only exceeded by its ability to change that information randomly.

Perhaps the biggest opportunity in the start-up is to build something radically new. That's why random venture capitalists are throwing money at this no-name group of fine people. They believe that they have a chance to build a thing that has never been built before, and, hopefully, figure out how to make a lot of money from that new thing. The existence of the start-up is a defiant cry that, "Yes, we can do something different," and that means you are guaranteed to see opportunities and gain experience early in your career that you're unlikely to see at an established company. It also means you'll experience an abundance of failure.

During the first Internet bubble, there was only one measure of success. Did you IPO? If you didn't, you were considered a failure. When the first bubble burst, we discovered there were all sorts of fascinating ways to fail, varying from buy-out to outright take-it-apart-and-fire-everyone failure.

Most start-ups are going to experience some definition of failure, but, well, failure is awesome. I mean it. There's no experience like the diving saves you'll perform in an attempt to save your job or your company. It'll be hell when it's happening, but when it's over, you're going to be the guy who attempted to pull off some amazing professional moves, and these aren't moves you'll be asked to perform at a larger company.

The single biggest asset to consider when thinking about joining a start-up is the experience you'll acquire. If you choose to dream about the millions of dollars you might end up with, I ask that you equally consider the experience of watching your team dismantled as your formerly high-flying company slowly runs out of cash and scrambles to restructure itself because three college drop-outs the next town over built your idea better, faster, and cheaper.

Whether your start-up fails or not, the guarantee I make is that you're going to end up with some amazing stories, and each of those stories will contain a lesson. Sure, these lessons are available at larger companies, but the velocity, intensity, and passion of the start-up will make these stories uniquely yours.

Established

If your average start-up is metaphorically sprinting, your average successful, established company is lumbering along at a comfortable trot. This company believes that it's running, but it's not. It ran at some point, became successful and large, and has gently slowed down thanks to its own weight.

This lumbering trot won't be obvious unless you've already experienced the pace of a start-up, and that might be part of the attraction. There's nothing quite like the calm deliberation of an established company after the frenetic chaos of a start-up, but it comes with a cost.

There's a constant threat in a start-up, and that's the threat of failure. You can ignore it when you're busily working three weekends straight, but it's always there: "We could fail." The larger company's success has hidden this threat under a guise of predictability, domesticity, and sheer momentum. You'll have fewer responsibilities because there are more of you. The projects will take longer because what's the hurry? You won't worry if your paycheck is going to clear, and you'll bitch when you have to work a few weekends. It sounds kind of sleepy, but there is still much to learn.

Any job, any company, represents a wealth of experience. The risk associated with acquiring that experience at an established company is far less than at a start-up because your larger company has hit its stride. They made it, and one would think they made it because they did something right. The questions are, what did they do right, are they still doing it right, and how is the rightness covering up things they're doing horribly?

The risk of the established company is that they've become used to their lumbering trot. It's become stable and familiar, and that familiarity defines the entire company's processes and culture. *This is how we do things*. This makes their days predictable and measurable. Again, if you've been suffering through endless days of risky unpredictability at your last gig, a large company might be the perfect next move.

Question #2: Industry and Brand

The next choice to make is what industry you want to explore. In my career, I've been a database guy, a browser guy, a web apps guy, an ecommerce guy, and an operating system guy. If you were to map current industry trends to this career, you'd notice that my career switches followed the bleeding edge. I was at Borland when Windows application development was beginning, and did the same move at Netscape around the emergence of the Internet. All of this varied experience had a point: cross-pollination.

It's great that you've figured out how to get Ruby to scale, and I'm certain you could continue to explore the frontiers of scalable Ruby, but in doing so, there's a point of diminishing returns regarding your career. It's comforting to know what you're talking about and to be recognized by those around you as an expert in whatever it is that you do, but when I stare at a resumé where the past five years have been spent in the same gig, I wonder, "Why hasn't he gotten bored?"

Granted, your geek instincts and your nerd attention deficiency disorder are likely to continually push you toward the new, so I'm not that worried about you moving on to tackling new technical problems. But while we're here, I want to talk briefly about brand.

The name, the reputation of a company, is a thing to consider. If you were to tell a complete stranger the name of the company you're considering, what's their reaction? Is it well known? Is it viewed as successful? Can they name a product this company produces? This is useful information because when you eventually leave this gig, it's that name that you'll be putting on your resumé, and it's that name that is going to be quickly digested by future employers.

All that said, brand and reputation are not the pivotal decisions in considering a new gig, especially when anonymous start-ups are in the mix. But if you're considering an unknown quantity in terms of company, try this: describe the opportunity you're considering. Can you? Something about web services? OK, what about web services? What excites you? What are you going to own? What are you going to build?

Question #3: Management or Development?

There are two career tracks in engineering: development and management. That's it. As you're probably already an engineer, this decision is easy to describe but hard to understand: do you want to be a manager?

Why would anyone want to be a manager?

Fact. There is more money to be had in management. This money is a result of more responsibility, and by responsibility, I mean frequent moments when everyone in the room is staring at you, expecting you to make a critical decision on the spot with incomplete information.

Fact. You'll code less, you'll work more, and at the end of the day, you won't be sure you did anything.

Fact. You'll meet lots more people and be expected to get along with them.

Fact. Much of what you've done to be a good engineer isn't going to apply to being a good manager.

The next two chapters will explore these facts further and go into more detail on the role of management. But the question remains: is this a direction you want to head as part of your next gig? This doesn't need to be an absolute decision. There are smaller steps you can take toward management. Technical Lead is usually the title for a gig that is a primer for management. Such roles usually have larger decision-making responsibilities without all the bothersome performance reviews, so you can get a feel for wearing a management hat without fully committing.

A Complete Opportunity Move

Here's a different version of the questions:

- Where do I want to go?
- What do I want to build?
- And how do I want to build it?

As you answer these questions, other smaller questions will pop up that matter specifically to you and that you should also explore. How many people do you want to work with? How much do you want to work? How much responsibility do you want? How much stress can you handle?

Ideally, you should be able to answer these questions independently before you search for your next gig, because the moment a new opportunity presents itself, you're not thinking about yourself; you're thinking about the potential new gig. You still need to able to see how this gig fits with your personal strategic direction, as well as answer one more question: what's the opportunity to grow?

A start-up is more likely to be in a state where it's hiring lots of people, aggressively attacking new problems, and having a sense of urgency. Still, you can find the same attributes in a large company in a specific group that has been tasked with the new and sexy. This hybrid might be the best of both words—the urgency of a start-up supported by the stability of an established company—but is it a fit for you? Does it represent an opportunity you've never seen?

At the end of this analysis is an unfortunate truth: you're not going to know what you're getting until you're there. The only guarantee is that it will be different than where you are now, and that means you're going to learn...something. Good. The more you know, the fewer the surprises.

CHAPTER 36

The Curse of the Silicon Valley

In 20 years of engineering life in the Silicon Valley, I have never heard an engineering manager tell me, "My degree in engineering management sure came in handy there." In fact, outside of company-sponsored management training, I've never heard of training specifically in engineering management. I'm certain it exists, but the fact that no coworker I've ever worked with has showered praise on an external engineering management class is intriguing.

Many of us spend years in college becoming computer scientists. So, where are the managers coming from? How are they getting trained?

The answers are both a blessing and a curse. Let's start with the good news.

Apprenticeship

You are in an industry where, for the most part, your managers used to be you.

That's right.

They have the same degrees you have. They have been through all the trials and tribulations of being an engineer. The names of the companies are different, and they probably know a few long-forgotten languages, but the core problems they faced are the same:

- The product is late.

- We have too many bugs.

- I believe Product Marketing is insane.

- No one is writing anything down.

- My manager is out of touch.

Really. Your current manager used to sit in *your chair* and think, "Who is this schmo and how in the world did he get this gig because I'm not sure he even knows what we do."

He does, because he did.

We'll talk in the next chapter about the process of becoming a manager, but we're going to start by acknowledging and appreciating that ours is an industry where we choose our engineering leadership typically from among our own ranks.

Whoa whoa whoa, Rands. I did not pick this guy, I was re-org'd under him—didn't have a hint of a choice.

First off, you choose by being there. Yes, there are quality of life issues if you quit right this minute, but you can quit whenever you like. Second, that's not the point. The blessing of the Silicon Valley is that our engineering leaders mostly came from the trenches. They fixed bugs and shipped product, and perhaps they did it well enough that someone thought they should help make decisions and communicate about how it gets done. Which leads us to the curse....

On Language

You do not work in an industry where some hotshot MBA fresh out of Harvard is going to pop out of nowhere and take over front-line engineering management. Why? Because any reasonably bright engineering team would eat the Ivy Leaguer alive:

Hey, Harvard, can you walk through this stack trace with me?

The benefit of an industry where our management was once us is that we have leaders who speak our language and understand our problems. This is also the beginning of the curse.

The story is this: a talented young graduate joins a start-up fresh out of college. His manager pairs him with a bright senior engineer, and over the course of two years our college grad learns software development both hands-on and by osmosis: be productive, be fantastically clever when necessary, speak truth to power, hit your dates, and don't ship crap.

Our engineer ships his product, many times. Mistakes are made, lessons are learned, and suddenly six years have passed, and our college grad has become a senior engineer. The lessons he's learned have become the lessons he teaches. He has a reputation for delivering quality...no matter what. He's dependable, he wants to grow, and he wants more responsibility. So someone decides to promote him to management.

First cross-functional meeting. Product management, sales, and tech support, and they're asking why the team can't do a certain feature, and our freshly minted manager suddenly realizes he's totally unable to describe the technical and performance implications of their request, so he lamely says, "Well, it's hard."

Cold stares of hate cross the table, and our manager wonders, "Do they hate me?"

They do.

Everyone Hates Engineering

Outside of engineering, no one really likes engineering. Here's why:

No one knows what we actually do to build the software, so they assume it's easy

In everyone else's head, it's really simple just to add that checkbox to that page and "just branch the code or something...use an If/Then statement or something."

Cute. And totally annoying.

What's being asked for there is the world's worst specification, but the real problem is that the person asking assumes they're describing all of the work involved. They believe that their understanding is somewhat related to the work involved in developing a product.

Worse, this misunderstanding goes both ways....

We take our work personally and believe no else does

We take our role as owner of the bits extremely seriously. We've been staring at these bits for months. We've stayed up until 3 a.m. making sure they are just right. We've successfully defended these bits against our well-intentioned QA department and they've shipped and, I'm sorry, what are you asking?

Um, it's not quite right. Could you move that field over here and that button up here because....

You know when this would've been good feedback? At 3 a.m. four months ago, after I'd given up five weekends to hit that insane date. That would have been a good time to ask me for a new feature.

Our bits are our world. We've heard of product marketing, technical support, and sales, but we erroneously and passionately believe the bits are the whole game. See...

Our relationship is with the bits

One of the defining characteristics of a career in computer science is that there is little initial fortune tied to successful face-to-face interaction with human beings. In fact, ours was initially a career where social ineptitude might be a benefit.

Go back to the list:

- Be productive: generate good bits.
- Be clever: generate lots of good bits.
- Speak truth to power: defend your good bits to those who know what they're talking about.
- Hit your dates: deliver your good bits when you say you will, but...
- Don't ship crap: make sure the bits are good.

A healthy ambivalence regarding human beings goes a long way toward achieving these goals. Not busying your mind with the endless complexities of human behavior saves you precious time to focus on the bits, and our career is based on the bits. Our incentives are bit-based. At the end of the year, when our manager is describing our performance, they're describing it in terms of our bit-based success.

Little of what we need to be successful engineers involves interaction with those outside of engineering, which leads us to the Curse.

The Curse

The curse of the Silicon Valley is: we're often placing our most valuable talent into a job they are utterly unequipped to handle and probably don't want.

Much of what we do as engineers on a day-to-day basis has enabled us to develop a lot of very technical and complex skills. Unfortunately, generally they aren't skills that are valuable when dealing with people—communication, translation, soft skill mentoring, empathy, etc. Pick a management challenge:

- Communicating with a hostile room
- Writing a performance review for someone who is failing
- Firing a friend.

Tell me what experience in your eight years of writing great code has prepared you for handling any of these situations? Sure, you've had meetings where folks were going toe to toe on a hard issue, but THOSE WERE ENGINEERS. You know how they think and how they speak, and after the meeting you can all just return to your cubes and get back to work. Try going a few rounds with angry on-site legal counsel, and tell me what that feels like and how they act the next time you have to deal with them.

Management is the art of gathering, organizing, and distributing information to the right people, and doing so means being able to quickly and effectively communicate with a wide variety of personalities—engineering and nonengineering alike. A productive, clever, and reliable engineer has had little incentive to figure out human beings. In fact, we've constructed a mythical mental place called the Zone where we achieve maximum productivity, and the rule of the Zone is: no one is welcome; I am working on the bits.

The managerial leap is painful. In engineering, the truth is a clear and measurable thing. Management is a job where the truth is blurred by endless political intrigue and personality warfare.

Geeks Gone Mainstream

The generation of geeks who are currently managing teams are the ones who were used to being viewed as antisocial freaks. The managerial arrival of Generation Y with a view of a world that has never been without the Internet disposes of the geek-related stigma. This is a generation that will soften former hard geek social edges.

Ours is an industry that is maturing. What was an obscure career choice two decades ago is now understood by a good portion of the planet because they stare all day at the tools we build. Those tools are in their pockets, and they are part of the daily conversation.

As our industry becomes less obscure, the pool of candidates we can draw from for future software engineering managers is growing larger. And the larger the mix, the more talent and personality cross-pollination will occur. That will make software engineering no different than any other industry, and bad management won't just be a function of our geek predilections.

CHAPTER 37

A Disclosure

My management career began with a misunderstanding.

"Rands, you're doing a great job on tools development, and I'd really like you to Lead the effort."

It sounded like your standard professional compliment. Atta boy! Go run with it! Problem was, I didn't hear the capital L.

Lead is what my manager had said. Not lead, but Lead. He asked poorly and without definition and specifics, but he did ask. He was subsequently baffled two months later when I said, "I don't think I can finish this by next month, I need more time."

Him: "Why don't you hire another engineer?"

Me: "Wait, I can do that?"

I see three possible situations whereby you might become a manager:

- You decide. "I believe I am going to be a better manager than engineer. I choose management."

- You evolve. This is what happened to me. Essentially, a series of small decisions and actions where, at the end, you end up being a manager.

- You have no choice. "You. Manage this team. Go."

Whether you get to choose or not, there are aspects of management that you need to understand.

Management Is a Total Career Restart

Now, if you're evolving into the career, this will be less obvious, but if management just landed in your lap, realize that while you're in the same game, it's a totally new game board and you're at square one. You will use the skills that made you a great engineer, but there's an entirely new set of skills you need to acquire and refine.

This sensation will appear at the end of the day when you ask, "What did I build today?" The answer will be a troubling, "Nothing." The days of fixing 10 bugs before noon are gone. You're no longer going to spend the bus ride home working on code; you're going to be thinking hard about how to say something important to someone who doesn't want to hear it. There will be drama. And there be those precious seconds when there is no one in your office wanting... something.

You Go to a Lot of Meetings

You already knew this, but Managers Go to Meetings. Meetings are the bane of my existence, and I consider it my personal goal to kill as many as possible, but I still go to a lot of meetings. As best I can tell, there are two useful types of meetings: alignment and creation. Briefly:

Alignment meetings sound like this

> "It's red. Are we all in agreement it's red? OK, swell. Wait, Phil thinks it's blue. Phil, here are the 18 compelling reasons it's red. Convinced? Done now?"

Creation meetings sound like this

> "We need more blue. How are we going to do that? Phil, you're our blue man. What should we do here?"

There are other meetings out there, but you will learn to avoid them. One being the therapy meeting. They sound like this: "Show of hands, who likes to talk about blue? Or red? I don't care. Let's explore our color feelings for the next 60 minutes."

In time you will learn which meetings to attend, but when you start, you will go to all of them because...

You Are a Communication Hub

One of your primary jobs as a manager is to be a communication hub, not only for all of those working for you, but for everyone who needs something from you. This means you are going to spend an inordinate amount of time sitting in random conference rooms and listening. Hard. Who are they? What do they need? Do I understand what they are saying? Should I say no now or let this fester?

Confusingly, as a manager, you often get credit just by showing up, sitting there, and nodding. As a career management strategy, the "nodding fly on the wall" approach isn't proactive or helpful. But there are critical times when all that is being asked of you is that you are the receiver of the rant. Simply by listening, by letting an idea be heard, you are helping.

However, you need to do more than listen. Whatever is being said in this meeting isn't just for you; parts of it are for your team, which means you need amazing skills of...

Abstraction and Filtering

During these endless demands for your time, you do need to communicate, but if you're relaying all the information that's being thrown at you during the day, all you'll do is relay. Your new job is one of abstraction, synthesis, and filtering. During that 30-minute status meeting, you need to develop the mental filter to listen for the three things you actually need to tell the team in your alignment meeting, but in a mere 3 minutes instead of 30.

Your thought is, "If there are only three things I need to know, why the hell are we spending 30 minutes in this meeting?" First, I relate to your frustration. Second, the three things you need to relay are different than the three things each of the other folks in this meeting needs to relay. Third, if you blow this, here's what's going to happen: more meetings.

See, your world has expanded, and now...

You Will Be a Multilingual Translator

Each group in the company has a different language they speak and a different set of needs. As a manager, you need to be able to speak all the corporate dialects of those you depend on. Think of the healthy tension between Engineering and QA. Remember that flame war that went on between you and the QA guy for a week in the bug database? Engineering and QA actually speak the same language but have different goals. As a manager, you will discover an entire company of languages and goals. For example:

- Sales cares about selling and doesn't much care how hard it is to build.

- Marketing is passionate about brand, content, and voice, and will argue endlessly for details you find to be irrelevant.

- Tech support talks to the customer ALL DAY, but still feels no one listens to what they say.

- Admins speak many of these languages and have more power than you think.

Everyone believes their job is essential, everyone believes everyone else's job is easy, and, confusingly, everyone is right.

These roles exist for a reason. The groups each bring something unique to the corporate organism. You can giggle and make fun of their bizarre acronyms as an individual, but as a manager you must speak their language, because once you do, you're going to better understand what they want.

Learning new languages is tricky, especially when you're just getting started. You're going to spend 90 days being totally confused, and it gets worse because there's...

Drama Everywhere

Your manager calls you into her office first thing on a Monday morning. It's clearly urgent. She sits you down and starts, "I'm, uh, making a change in the organization. Amanda is really excelling in tools development, so I've asked her to take over Jerry's management responsibilities. I think this will make everyone more successful."

Wondering what happened to Jerry? Feel like you're getting half the story? Wrong. You're getting 1/10th of the story. People are messy, and a huge part of the management gig is managing this messiness. Who knows what personal or professional issue Jerry has that is forcing this management change? It's really none of your business. However, it is your manager's business because the people are her job.

As an individual, you're seeing 10% of the organizational drama your manager is seeing. I know it's intriguing to get the full story, but again, it's often none of your business, and it's not your job. As a manager, you get front-row seats for all of the drama in all its messy glory. This is why you have a monthly 1:1 with Human Resources. Their job is to train you how to manage the drama. This is why you need to become a great...

Context Switcher

This is your morning. Six 30-minute 1:1s starting at 9 a.m. This day is unique in that in your fourth 1:1, your architect resigns. The guy who has been designing the heart of your application for 18 months has been poached by a start-up and had piles of money thrown at him, and it sounds like there's no way of saving him. Sounds grim. What's harder is that when your sky-is-falling 1:1 is done, you've got your next one with your QA Director who has no clue your architect resigned, and she urgently wants to talk bug database, and that's exactly what you need to do. You need to quietly and confidently forget that you're fucked and give this team member your full attention.

There will be a steady stream of curveballs headed in your managerial direction, each with its own unique velocity. One of your jobs is to not only deftly handle the pitch, however bizarre, but also shake it off and calmly expect an even stranger one.

There's a reason you'll see an inordinate amount of bizarre organizational crap as a manager. See, the individuals can handle—and should handle—the regular stuff. You want a team of people who aren't bringing you every little thing, but if you successfully build this team, your reward is that what ends up in your office is uniquely kooky.

As these freakish pitches whiz by, you will be judged in two very different ways. First, what did he do about the pitch? Are we going to see more of these? Second, how was his composure as that pitch whizzed by, missing his nose by an inch? Does it look like he handled it, or is he freaked out and ready to bolt?

Leadership is not just about effectively getting stuff done, but demonstrating through your composure that you aren't rattled by the freakish. Fortunately, one of the new tools you have to control the proliferation of freakishness is the ability to...

Say No

This is your second most powerful tool. Whether you're a manager, considering management, or just here for the Rands, I want you to pick the hardest problem on your plate. The one that is waking you up at 4 a.m. I want you to decide and to say out loud:

"No."

You're not going to do that thing. QA can't test it. Engineering won't finish it. If we attempt to do it, we will fail, and we don't fail, so the answer is "No."

You had this tool as an individual. You could say no, but you usually did so by cornering your manager and explaining, "Here is why No is the right move here," and then he'd say no.

As a manager, you are caretaker of No for you group. When it is time to do the right thing by stopping, it's your job to bust out the No. You defend your team against organizational insanity with No.

No does not come without consequences. Saying No because you can rather than because it's right slowly transforms you into a power-hungry jerk, but again, this is your new tool to do with as you see fit. Also, it's not all No; you can also...

Say Yes

Yes is how you begin building both people and things. It's not just a positive word; it's the word that provides the structure for moving forward. "Yes. Begin." "Yes, I know he's leaving. What are we going to do?" And, "Why yes, we should tackle the audacious."

There will be times when your Yes needs to be unencumbered by reality, where it needs to be the inspiration that demonstrates how you perceive the unknowable.

"Yes, I think you'd be a fine manager."

Trust So You Can Scale

As a new manager, whenever the sky falls, you'll become an engineer again. You're going to fall back on the familiar because those are the tools you know and trust, but it's time to trust someone else: your team.

If I could give you one word, a single, brief piece of management advice, the word would be "scale." Your job as a manager is to scale the skills that got you the gig in the first place. You used to be the guy who did the impossible when it came to fixing bugs. OK, now you're the guy whose entire team does the impossible bug fixing.

It's time to translate and to teach what you're good at to those you work with, and that starts by trusting them to do that which you previously only asked of yourself.

Defining and maintaining this trust creates a satisfying productivity feedback loop. By trusting your team, you get to scale, and scaling means you hopefully get to do more of what you love. The more you do, the more you build, the more experience you gather, the more lessons you learn. The more lessons you learn, the more you understand, and that means when more shows up, you'll have even greater opportunity to scale.

CHAPTER 38

Mind the Gap

"Everyone is replaceable."

The first time you'll hear this rationalization is when someone valuable regrettably leaves the group. The team is off because no one wanted this person to leave, so your manager gets everyone together and lays down the departed's reasoning: "He's been here five years, he's looking for new challenges, blah blah." The thing is, if any of this reasoning was the actual truth, there would be no reason to have this meeting, and your manager knows this. Which is why he finishes with, "Everyone's replaceable."

And he's right. Nature abhors a vacuum. When someone vital walks out the door, you learn all sorts of interesting things about the folks who remain.

The Gaps

In this chapter, I'm going to walk through an analysis of some individual regrettable departures of someone on your team. You don't want this person to leave, because they're adding something unique to the team, and when you learn they're leaving, you believe that something essential is permanently being lost.

There are certainly situations where the departure of a single key person can lead to the collapse of a team or a company, but in this chapter we assume the team is going to make it because although it's sad that a person you like is leaving, I believe you're underestimating everyone else.

As with any departure, there's a knee-jerk belief that this person's absence is going to result in immediate and irrevocable change. But the reality is that a group of people is a complex social organism, and change doesn't happen that fast. Yes, the departure will create a gap that you're going to worry about. I don't know what kind of gap, because I don't know who is leaving, so we'll look at the obvious from the perspective of your worst fear, and why you shouldn't worry, but how you should continue to pay attention.

Knowledge and Ability: "Alpha Knowledge"

The Irrational Fear: *He has knowledge about the product that no one else does. He is the only one who knows how to debug the hard problems. He is the only one who has the entire system in his head. He's the guy we call when the problem is really, really hard, and without him we won't be able to solve really hard problems anymore.*

Don't Worry: This is clearly your Alpha when it comes to the knowledge of your team. The blessing and the curse of Alpha Knowledge isn't just that they know everything; it's that everyone else knows that they know. This is informationally convenient for the group because whenever someone has a hard question, they know exactly who to ask.

While the absence of this person is alarming, what you'll quickly discover is that all the answers to those questions everyone was asking Alpha Knowledge actually stuck in the heads of those folks. In fact, they were often asking their question as a means of confirmation rather than as a process of discovery. See, after the third time they ask, they know the answer. They know how it works, but Alpha Knowledge's presence meant they questioned themselves: "Well, I think I know, but I'd best confirm with Alpha before proceeding."

My assumption is that the majority of the knowledge you believe is in Alpha's head has already cross-pollinated to other team members. Alpha's departure will give others the incentive to trust what they already know.

But Pay Attention: While it's likely that formerly quiet team members will step in to fill the knowledge gap, there *is* knowledge and ability walking out the door. But it's not the broad knowledge you're concerned about—it's the little undocumented knowledge. Why is it that variable has that particular name? What is the story behind the naming scheme for the servers? What is this cryptic note in the code that reads, *"Two more of these and we're screwed"*?

You can ask this person to document the state of the world as much as you like, but they're going to forget something small and something essential to the inner workings of the product. You're going to discover this omission months after they're gone, and worse, when they've totally forgotten about their prior professional life. *"Two more of what things? I've no idea what you're talking about."*

What you need to pay attention to when Alpha Knowledge leaves is the team's ability to handle the unexpected. It's not the day-to-day operations of the team that will be impacted by the absence of Alpha. It's when shit hits the fan that you're really going to miss him because it's his undocumented improvisational skills that are gone and are not coming back.

Again, there is essential information walking out the door, but most of the time the group can live without that information. Teams work around the absence because they don't have a choice, and once they've worked around it once, they've learned what is missing, and they've updated the way that works.

Power and Influence: "Maestro"

The Fear: *She's looking out for us. She's shielding us from the bullshit. She's protecting our culture. We have additional opportunity because she is here. Decisions are being made in our favor because she's sitting at the table fighting for us.*

The Reality: We're going to call her Maestro because she's conducting the business of the group. She's likely a senior manager, director, or VP, and now she's gone. Like Alpha Knowledge, the vacuum created by her absence will send those interested in her job into a frenzy. Who is going to inherit her crown? Who deserves it? What are they going to do to get it? All of these questions are interesting, but the reality is that you need to understand why she left. You're sad she's leaving, but is everyone?

Leaders define the culture that surrounds them. The reality about this culture is two-fold. First, when Maestro leaves, she's permanently taking part of that culture with her. And second, the culture above and around her is going to seep in. Whether or not this now intruding culture is a fit with your team is the real question. Was Maestro protecting her team from this culture? If so, why? And, most importantly, is any of the reason for her departure a result of conflict with this external culture?

Leaders optimize reality to their favor, and the more powerful and influential they are, the more they can define a comfortable reality for themselves and their team. The more this reality conflicts with the rest of the company, the more your team will need to adapt when Maestro leaves the building with her personal reality distortion field, and that's where you need to pay attention.

But Pay Attention: What you're going to learn in the first month after an influential leader has left the group is how much her view of the goals of your group differ from the goals set by the company. Ideally, your former leader did a fine job of translating corporate vision into regionally relevant goals. Ideally, her daily direction for the group was aligned with the direction of external groups and those of whoever steps in to fill her spot.

But maybe it wasn't.

There's shielding the team from politics and nonessential crap that they don't need to know so they can focus on getting work done, but there's also shielding to an unnecessary degree. This is why, when an influential leader has left the building, I pay attention to blank stares.

There are inevitable organizational investigation meetings that occur when a person in a position of power leaves. There are questions for the remaining team, and when those questions are directed to me, I'm looking to see how my answers are being received. Nodding is the universal sign that those sitting with you are on the same page. Nodding means they understand. A blank stare means there's a disconnect, and when the blank stares are coming from the people your former boss interacted with, I begin to wonder what she was telling them and what she wasn't.

Whether Maestro was shielding you from crap, was creating her own reality, or was a perfect fit with the culture external to the group, a cultural gap will be created by her absence. New leaders will bring their own culture with them, and that means the team will need to adapt.

Network and Communication: "The Insider"

The Fear: *He knows everything. He's incredibly well connected, and that means we were always ahead of the game. He was the person I always went to when I wanted to know what was going down. He eliminated surprises.*

The Reality: The Insider is the person on the team who thrives on knowing what is going on in the company. He's known for it. In staff meetings, all eyes turn to him when juicy data needs confirmation:

Boss: "And it looks like they're three months late."

<all eyes turn to the Insider>

Insider: <nods>

Boss: "So, they're screwed."

The role of the Insider isn't just gossip; he's the person on the team who is, as I talked about in a prior chapter, the keeper of the truth. Insiders are genetically compelled to know what is going on everywhere, and they hopefully use the skill as a means of keeping the folks around them equipped with the latest, greatest information, wherein lies the reality.

While the Insider is the perceived keeper of the truth, information moves in a group of people in more ways than you can imagine—especially the juicy stuff. You don't need to fear suddenly not being in the know; information will travel as a function of its interestingness. The Insider's absence will put a kink in your one-stop information shopping, but his absence won't leave you permanently in the dark.

But Pay Attention: Your former Insider had two roles—collector of information and conveyor of information—and it's the latter where you want to pay attention. Part of the Insider's makeup isn't just that they know what to ask whom, but also knowing who needed to know what.

What I'm looking for in the Insider's absence is who is now lost? Who was dependent on the Insider for knowing what was going on in the group and in the company? What essential and nonobvious communication flow has stopped with the Insider's absence? This sudden dearth of communication is likely happening in a place you don't expect. It's not a meeting the Insider no longer attends, it's that random hallway check-in he's no longer performing, and it means that someone is silently adrift. This isn't mission-critical information they're now missing; it's the comfortable information of the now.

You'd think that with the menagerie of meetings managers insist on holding that communication in a group of people would be well structured and predictable. It's not. For every useful piece of information that happens in a staff meeting, there's an equal amount of information traveling in hallways, emails, and random cube conversations. With the Insider gone, communication has stopped flowing...somewhere, and the consequences of this information standstill can vary from simple confusion to organizational chaos.

A Matter of Perspective

Again, a group of people is a complex organism, and your perspective of the organism is limited to what you can see from where you're sitting. Your perspective of this person who is leaving is just one perspective. Just as everyone's perspective about this person is different, so is his or her opinion about this fine person's departure.

The number one thing to pay attention to in this departure is the unexpected, because there is some key relationship that no longer exists. There is someone who is utterly destroyed by this person's absence, and there are likely people who are delighted and just waiting to make their move. It's these unexpected social tertiary side effects that may affect your day to day, and you need to be looking for them. You need to know who these people are and you need to understand their opinions because the organizational landscape has changed.

The vacuum created by this departure not only creates organizational confusion, but also opportunity. The jockeying to fill whatever position of power starts the moment the hint of the rumor starts wandering the hallways, and you need to figure out where you fit in this now rapidly changing landscape. Did you always want to be Alpha Knowledge? Now would be a good time to try to fill those shoes. Do you know someone who would be a great Insider? Have you told them this?

Finally, remember that change, especially the departure of key personnel, freaks people out. They're not thinking that everyone is replaceable; they're quietly wondering, "What do those people know that I don't? I'm happy here, so why aren't they? Who's next?"

The biggest risk with a key departure is that it's an indication of a larger movement. The biggest risk is that it's a sign that the sky has begun falling.

CHAPTER 39

The Exodus

It's a day like any other. The regular flow of morning mails from the highly caffeinated. Two morning meetings with nothing unusual. The usual lunch followed by your staff meeting where...Andy shows up late. Andy is never ever late for anything. *Odd...well, whatever.*

Staff finishes, still nothing notable, except Andy says nothing the entire time, which is also odd. You're now officially wondering what is up with Andy, so you grab him and pull him to the closest office.

You: "Dude, what's up?"

Andy: "I'm leaving."

In a fraction of an instant, you are able to do all the political and social math regarding Andy's departure. You can see the complete set of unchangeable reasons he's leaving, you can predict who is going to follow, and you know that there isn't a damn thing you can do about it.

This is the Moment, and in that moment, you can see how it's all going to come crumbling down.

This Sucks

At some point of your career, hopefully through no fault of your own, an organization will start collapsing around you. It's a horrific experience that I hope you can avoid, but one you nonetheless need to understand.

Sorry about the collapse. That sucks. Everything that follows is a dispassionate and judgment-free review of the awful things that are going to occur, but before I start I'd like to point out the singular upside to this collapse: you're going to learn to see it coming.

Having been through three of these organizational disasters, you'd think I would have learned my lesson. Well, I have. I've learned that often there is no preventing organizational fuckups of this magnitude, and sometimes the best you can do is either get the hell out or find a comfortable place to hide.

Second, nothing in this chapter is going to help you prevent this cataclysm. In fact, this chapter assumes your disaster is in progress, guaranteed to be as bad as possible, and you're in it for the whole thing. Again, sorry.

Two Threads

To understand how this exodus begins, you need to understand how information moves around your company. There are always two ongoing types of conversations in the building. One is tactical, and one is strategic. Each of these conversations or threads drives a specific part of your company and, consequently, drives a specific part of your organizational collapse.

Let's talk about the tactical first.

Tactical

This is the daily conversation of the company. It includes the thoughts and opinions of everyone on the team. Content varies wildly by team and by group, but these are the public topics associated with the work that the team produces. We all care about our local scenery and whatever might eventually affect that scenery.

When everything is normal in the group, the tactical thread is kind of boring, but as we'll see, it changes when the sky is falling.

Strategic

The easiest way to start thinking about the strategic conversation is, "This is what managers are talking about all day," and when I say managers, I mean from your boss all the way up to the CEO. The strategic conversation is the constantly evolving plan of action for the company. How are we doing? What's next? What's not working? How can we do better? Who is screwing up?

If you're reading that paragraph and filling with inner rage about the secrecy of managers and not being included in this conversation, I want to remind you that the fucking sky is falling and you need to chill out so you can figure out what to do next. Your being included in these strategic conversations very well might have prevented this worst-case scenario; your knowing might have given you insight that may have changed your course of action. But the collapse is happening, and all we're doing here is understanding how it might play out.

Whatever the underlying reasons are for this organizational collapse, they will first travel the strategic thread, as this is where early detection and triage will occur. These participants in the strategic thread are usually those who comprise the first wave of folks walking out the door. If you're viewing the tactical thread as content provided by a bunch of docile sheep waiting to see when the next wolf will show up, you're a manager and you're judging. Remind yourself of the world where your daily work was blissfully ignorant of the strategic shenanigans of the management caste.

The First Wave

The first wave of departures consists of folks privy to the strategic conversational thread. They've heard what's coming, and they've done the political and social math, so they're out. A few things to pay attention to here.

Where does this exodus begin?

Without a single conversation, you can infer a lot simply from the starting location of the exodus. If sales is bleeding people, one might assume something is wrong in sales, and if sales are bad, well, everything's bad. A mass departure from engineering says the same thing: something is wrong in engineering, which means something is wrong with the product, which means you may not have anything to sell.

Why are they leaving?

Now is a good time to figure out why. There's going to be a well-crafted message traveling the hallways that explains these departures, but the message has been created to spin whatever it is that this wave of departures is fleeing. You need the truth.

If you want to understand why a bright strategic person is gone, you need to get them behind a door in a safe place where you can ask: "OK, WTF?" This is how you're going to get the real story.

Why are they letting them go?

In any exodus, there's a lynchpin departure in the first wave. This is the person perceived in the group or organization as absolutely essential to the business. *If they leave, we're dead.*

And they're leaving.

The troubling part of the lynchpin departure is that everyone knows this person is essential. Worse, everyone who's in on the strategic conversation knows this *and* they know the reasons why this person wants to leave *and* this person is still leaving.

If this person is essential, that means everything has been done to retain them and they're still merrily getting the hell out of the building. Whether you've successfully uncovered the root cause of the exodus or not, the lynchpin departure is a good leading indicator of what's about to happen: the second wave.

The Second Wave

If the first wave is the departure of strategic resources, the second wave is tactical, and for each person in this wave it starts with the Moment.

While randomness is part of doing business on planet Earth, most folks spend a lot of time insulating themselves from this randomness. They go to school to learn what randomness might occur so they can try to predict it, they get married to reduce randomness of the heart, and they get a job so their day is full of predictable things to do.

Injections of randomness freak people out. They see these events as assaults on the foundation they've built against the randomness, and in this attack there are two typical responses: fight or flight. This is the Moment. It's the instant recognition that your world has been forever changed by the uncontrollable random, and there's likely not a damned thing you can do about it, so you either decide to dig in or make a run for it.

Now, the first wave is already in progress, so why am I talking about the Moment relative to the second wave? The Moment occurs for everyone in the first wave, too, but the Moment has much more potential for organizational damage in the second wave.

It's the tactical conversation thread that drives the second wave, and once the exodus has begun, the tactical thread mutates from the daily dish to the formidable grapevine. See, in an absence of actual information, people make shit up (think back to Chapter 15). The scary potential of the second wave is that the legitimate strategic reasons behind the first wave transform into crazy conspiracy theories based on people's core discomfort with a random world.

The one thing to pay attention to in your role as observer of this hypothetical disaster is: "What is being done to inform the second wave?" Management has two approaches.

Approach #1: Wait it out

Remember, we're in the middle of the first wave and the beginning of the second wave. The time to prevent this disaster has passed, and now we're into damage control. The question is, when do they start? I'm presupposing your management team has already screwed up by not reacting during the first wave because I'm assuming a worst-case scenario. It's the second wave now—are they still waiting?

Management sees acknowledgment of the disaster as a disaster in itself. They believe that if the world knows this disaster was allowed to occur there would be significant downstream impact, which is ironic because the downstream impact is already happening and they're making it worse by ignoring it.

Sigh.

Approach #2: Stem the tide

Hopefully, at some point, a conversation will begin. Someone is going to stand up in front of the room and project a list of bullet items that are directly targeted at explaining this disaster. This will be a well-shaped message geared to answer one question: "What are we doing to stop this random shit from happening?"

The good news is that management has decided to do something. Given the incredibly bizarre theories that are traveling the tactical channel, any message is better than the destructive silence.

The specific managerial repairs that need to be made are a function of the disaster, and I don't know what disaster that is, but if you do know the true nature of the disaster, my questions are: Do they actually talk about it? Are they doing something to stem the tide, or are these crafted messages just different versions of waiting it out?

Never underestimate the ability of a management team to interpret reality to their benefit. Managers at all levels are incentivized to observe and report on a world that supports a business's view of progress. These reports vary from subtle adjustments to the truth to outright lies.

As an aside and in defense of managers who are doing their best, this optimization for the self is natural human behavior. It's not that you believe that the world revolves around you; it's just from where you're sitting, it seems like it might. The problem with this self-optimization relative to management is that they have the unique responsibility to optimize both for themselves and for you, and there are situations where those separate goals are in conflict. Think of it like this. Your manager is going to have their world-altering Moment just like you, and the question is: are they going to look out for their interests or yours?

The second wave is when things just get weird. Half-true stories are being told in the hallways, and personalities have altered as people are shoved out of their comfort zones. The normal workday is full of drama and intrigue, and that's the other problem with the second wave: its existence is a reason to leave.

Whether they're doing something about it or not, management's hope is a quick end to the second wave because they're under the false impression that the completion of the second wave is the end of the exodus.

Again, wrong.

The Third Wave

In this hypothetical disaster, you're still here. You needed front row seats so you could fully understand the mechanics of the exodus, and you've got one more wave.

The third wave is the devious wave.

The first wave is gone, the second is gone or about to be gone, and one morning you have a brief glimpse of normality. No one walks into your office with their Moment on their face. No one has resigned in a couple of days. It almost feels normal.

And you want it to be normal. All of this wave bullshit has been exhausting, and during all of these waves, productivity is shot along with morale, so when a day has just a glimmer of normality, you mentally leap on it: *hey, do I actually get to work today?*

Not so fast.

What's happened during the first two waves is that a pile of people has been cast to the wind. Maybe they landed inside of the company, maybe they landed elsewhere. One of the things they took with them is an intimate knowledge of the inner workings of your group. This means that every talented person who hasn't left in the first two waves is going to be recruited by these annoying, happy former coworkers who dangle just one thing: *you know where I am there's no disaster, right?*

The folks who have survived the multiple wave exoduses are tired, demoralized, and adrift, so the moment a familiar face shows up with good news about a bright future, they are susceptible. If they're talented and situationally aware, I've no idea what they're still doing on the sinking ship, but they're still there...for now.

The third wave isn't of the same magnitude as the first two waves. It's aftershocks, but anyone who has been through a natural disaster knows it's the aftershocks that drive you crazy. The third wave wears on the folks who have weathered the storm; the third wave might be the reason they choose to leave.

Which Wave?

This wave model I've described is inevitable. Horrible news leads to leading departures. Leading departures lead to larger departures. All those departures lead to even more departures. It's how groups of people react when their formerly safe home becomes professionally treacherous.

I'm sorry to have hypothetically kept you in the building for this entire event, but knowing how it's going to play out gives you context so you can figure out your move. Are you the first one out? Or are you going to wait for your friends to throw you a lifesaver?

Here's the good news: you've just been through hell. You've just acquired years of professional experience watching the intricacies of your organization slowly collapse around you. You've made three new lifelong friends with now former coworkers who took you aside before they left and said, "The best part of working on this project was working with you." And unless this disaster kills your company, this rapid restructuring of your group will result in opportunities you would have never seen.

Surviving the collapse of an organization is like surfing big waves. You only know the wave is big when it gets close, surfing it scares the hell out of you, screwing up during the ride results in an additional beatdown, but when you're done, you're better equipped to handle the next wave.

CHAPTER 40

Bad News About Your Bright Future

You…are kicking ass.

A wealth of experience makes decisions appear to be easy. Experience gives you confidence, and you use that confidence to deliver your experienced decisions with moxie. Those watching you think, boy, he's got it figured out. The rub is this: confidence is a delicious answer to uncertainty, but confidence is a feeling, a perception. What you're really banking on is your experience and your history of hard knocks, which have given you a useful and valuable perspective on which to base your decisions.

And experience has a half-life.

Confidence working well with experience creates success, and when you're successful everyone says, "Way to go!" and you believe those compliments and turn them into additional confidence that turns into more success and then more confidence, and the cycle repeats.

Again, you are kicking ass.

Success. Fame. These are a type of experience, but they aren't what got you the compliment in the first place. It's that you did something significant; you worked and did something significant. Not that you said you did something with confidence.

Like any industry, high tech is full of folks who are confusing success and fame with experience. They're thinking that showing up at conferences, giving interviews, and writing books about things they did in the past is experience. It's not. It's storytelling, and while it might be valuable storytelling, these people are slowly becoming echoes of who they were and moving further from the work they did that matters. They're confusing compliments for experience.

You may not be one of these people, but it doesn't mean that you're not exhibiting the same behavior. My question is: each day, are you struggling to build something new or just easily repeating the success of your past? Success feels good, but you're not actually doing anything.

Building stuff every day exercises all the muscles necessary to remaining vital. Experience fades and becomes irrelevant without a constant flow of the new.

I'm happy you are kicking ass. It's ass that needs kicking, and you are doing it well. I believe the success-based environment can be deliciously deceiving. I think that much of what created that environment was blood, sweat, and tears, and who wants more tears? Look deeply at your favorite success story and you're going to find a bit of misery. It's a great motivator, but who wants to do that again?

You do.

What's Next

This book began with a mantra:

We seek *definition* to understand

the *system* so that we can discern

the *rules* so that we

know what to do next so that

we *win*.

Each person on the planet has a small set of rules they silently repeat to themselves when they find themselves at a crossroads, and it's these core beliefs that structure their thinking and give them impetus to choose.

No trait is more important to the geek than their structure. The specific type of structural obsession varies from geek to geek. Some are fixated by the constraints of time, others carefully observe and enforce rules, but for each geek, I believe the quest is: "Learn enough about my world to predict what's next."

Surprises disrupt structure, which means when the unexpected occurs, the nerd or the geek panics. *Wait, I had definition, I understood the system that dictated the rules...WTF?*

There were two goals for this book:

1. Improve your improvisation skills of the moment.

2. Define your career strategy.

You'll notice that "Learn enough about my world to predict what's next" is not included as a goal for this book, because whether you've been wildly successful or not you'll never know what's going to happen next, and embracing that idea is a strategic career advantage.

More bad news: not only can you not predict what's going to happen, I'm pretty sure you're not even fully appreciating what's going on right now.

Biased by the Now

The traditional reason to leave a gig is because something has gone wrong or is no longer to your liking. The degree of wrongness varies from simply boredom to complex hatred, but whatever the story is, it's clear it's time to make a change. If this is the case, go back to Chapter 2 and get started. Here at the end, I want to talk about non-obvious reasons to make a change and some of the ways your brain is deceiving you. I want to explain why you'd leave your job when everything's swell and you believe you're kicking ass. I want you to think about why you'd leave a job you love.

You are biased by the now. I would go so far as to suggest that you are incapable of imagining what your professional life would be like if you were no longer doing it.

It's not that you're not bright or aware of your surroundings; it's that there's too much data. There are the intricate personalities of the people you work with that compose an entire unique culture of the team, the organization, and the company. There's the politics that change the professional mood of the building every day. There's everything you're living and breathing right now, and while I believe you could explain to me over a beer what it's like to work at the company, it would be a description of the moment. You would carefully and descriptively explain to me what it was like to work there for the past two weeks, but it would not be a complete description, because there's far too much data to organize and describe.

You have an opinion and impressions about your gig, but these are based on your brain gathering together all the data it sees as important and carefully fitting that data into your view of the world so that it makes sense, so that it fits in the system. After that, the data is thrown away because it's too much data. It's not that you shouldn't trust your opinion about your gig, but I am suggesting that just because you think you've got it figured out and are happy doesn't mean you're growing.

I'll ask the same questions I asked in Chapter 3:

- Have you failed recently?

- Is there someone within throwing distance who challenges you daily?

- Can you tell me the story of something significant you learned in the last week?

The intent behind these questions is disruption: when has something occurred that you did not predict? It is these disruptive and decidedly non-geek-friendly moments that engage your brain in interesting ways, and I'm of the opinion that your brain's reasonable and healthy quest for happiness isn't always aligned with your professional growth, because your brain does not seek conflict.

An Uncomfortable Ending

You should be uncomfortable with this chapter. I'm uncomfortable writing it. I am suggesting:

- Just because you're kicking ass doesn't mean you're successful.

- Misery is productive.

- Conflict is learning.

My hope is that at the end of this book you're better equipped to deal with misery, change, and conflict. Perhaps you understand your boss better and maybe the reorganization will make more sense. Your professional improvisation skills may have improved by reading the stories of how I've navigated Werewolves and Leapers. Finally, and hopefully, you have a better idea of where you want to head in your career because having that structure can help when your career is not going according to plan.

Knowing all of this helps, but misery, change, and conflict are going to show up randomly, and sometimes I think you should create them in a professionally healthy sense. Without reason, with no big plan, just a leap in a strange direction for no other reason than to see what it teaches you.

You're in a hurry.

Hurry

Most interesting ideas come to me between 8 a.m. and 10 a.m. This is sacred time. The day is young, I am rested, and the coffee is fresh. I spend most of this time in the car driving to work. The music is providing a creative, catalyzing ambiance to structure my thinking. I create two or three start-ups during the average drive to work.

And then I get to work and I google my ideas. "How about a service that adds threading to Twitter?"

It's called Twonvo. Crap.

"Wait, wait, wait, what we need is people feeds. An RSS-type thing that shows me the relevant events for the people I care about."

Friendfeed. Right. Goddammit.

You're in a hurry.

Do the math. We are all staring at the same set of data. Yes, there is a lot of data and there is a very low probability that you're able to surf it all, but here's the rub: there's a lot of us. In fact, there's a shit-load of us, and when you combine all of us with the equally huge amount of data, you understand that when I arrive at work and google my great ideas, I'm no longer surprised when my precisely designed drive-to-work business model is already in play.

You're in a Hurry

The epiphany I want to talk about is this: what are you waiting for? Seriously. I know you've got a mortgage and 1.5 kids, but during your sacred time when you discover that bright idea, and subsequently discover that no established competitor exists…why aren't you making the leap?

I know what you're waiting for.

See, you've been doing the same comfortable thing I've been doing for 20 years. You're obeying the structure of the organization where there are charts that describe who owns what and who owns whom. I am intimately familiar with the mindset that reads:

"We will complete our work by following the rules of mediocrity."

Do just enough. Don't rock the boat. Make yourself indispensable without being noticeable.

And it works. There is absolutely no way to argue that following the rules doesn't result in a comfortable life, but…

You're in a hurry.

Maybe you're waiting for validation. You're waiting for that someone you respect to say, "Yes, you bright person, you should do that thing." It was your parents when you were a kid, and then it was your first boss, but now it simply needs to be you.

What you need to understand about these people who support you is that they're not here to slow you down; they're here to get the hell out of your way so you can be brilliant. You need to discover the moment when you actually know better than everyone around you—when you make the first move without asking permission.

Try it. You don't need to quit your job and go build the next Twitter. Try it with something small. A thing where you'd normally preflight it with your boss, bounce the idea around the hallway a bit, and then move forward. Skip the preflight. Skip the hallway, and move on your idea.

Don't worry if someone else is already working on your idea. I'm certain they are, but they are decidedly not you, and it's the you that makes your idea unique.

Whether you're successful or not, it's a terrific way to get in a lot of trouble. There's a long list of established rules and regulations that you violate with your creative impertinence, but it feels great, right?

Trusting your gut and charging forward. It can be addictive.

It's not your only operating procedure. There are teams to communicate with and strategic corporate alignment that needs to be maintained, but then there's you, on the subway to work, drinking a Starbucks when inspiration strikes, and rather than just soaking in that brief moment of illumination, I want you to do something about it because...

You're in a hurry.

The Rules of Back Alley Bridge

Back Alley is a simple version of bridge with some strong similarities to Spades and Hearts. A quick search of the Web reveals a version of Back Alley Bridge was popular during the Vietnam War. I learned this version during my college career at University of California, Santa Cruz.

A full game is a relatively long experience, running roughly 1 to 2 hours, depending on speed of play. Don't play drunk; it's not fun.

Preparing for Back Alley Bridge

You will need:

- 1 deck of 52 standard playing cards (including jokers).

- The 2 jokers need to be marked to make them distinguishable from each other. I recommend using a felt-tip pen to mark 1 joker with the word "BIG" and mark 1 with the word "LITTLE" (see "Rules of Play").

- 1 pad of paper and writing utensil used to keep score.

- 4 players (2 teams).

Rules of Play

1. PLAYERS AND CARDS DEAL

   a. The players form 2 teams. Players on the same team sit facing each other.

   b. The game is played clockwise.

   c. The trump in Back Alley is always SPADES.

   d. The BIG joker used in Back Alley is the highest trump card. The LITTLE joker is the second-highest trump card.

   e. The cards in each suit rank from highest to lowest:

      1. A K Q J 10 9 8 7 6 5 4 3 2.

      2. For the trump, or Spades, the BIG and LITTLE jokers would come before the ace.

2. DEAL

   a. Initial dealer is determined at random.

   b. The dealer shuffles and deals out all cards so that each player has 13 cards. This will leave 2 cards left over.

   c. Turn to deal rotates clockwise.

   d. Each subsequent hand is dealt with 1 less card (i.e., 13, 12, 11, etc.). 2 hands are dealt with a single card, followed by dealing with 1 more card (i.e., 2, 3, 4, etc.) for a total of 26 hands. (Variation: deal every OTHER hand, i.e., 13, 11, 9, etc. This allows the game to be completed in roughly 1 hour.)

3. BIDDING

   a. Starting with the player to the left of the dealer, each player bids as to how many tricks they can take, and each team's bids are totaled. If the player does not bid any tricks, they "pass."

   For example: Player 1 bids 5, Player 2 bids 2, Player 3 bids 3, and Player 4 bids 2. That totals 12 out of a possible 13 tricks.

b. There are 2 special bids in Back Alley called BOARD and BOSTON.

1. If a player bids BOARD, they are saying that their team will take EVERY SINGLE trick in the hand (see: SCORING).

2. If a player bids BOSTON, they are saying that their team will take the FIRST 6 tricks in the hand (see: SCORING).

3. Unlike the BOARD bid, a player may not declare BOSTON when there are 6 or fewer tricks being played

4. Players may double, triple, or quadruple any of these bids.

5. This occurs very often when there are only a few cards in the hand. For example, Player 1 bids "BOARD," Player 2 passes, Player 3 bids "DOUBLE BOARD," Player 4 passes (see: SCORING). In this case, DOUBLE BOARD would be the highest bid and would lead.

6. A player may not bid a double, triple, or quadruple bid unless the appropriate single, double, or triple has already been bid. Example:

The first bid cannot be DOUBLE BOSTON.

4. REDEAL

a. There are 2 situations where a hand can be redealt:

1. If ALL players pass during the bidding process,

or

2. If, at 7 or more cards, a player's hand contains no aces, spades, or face cards.

5. THE PLAY

a. Highest bidder leads with anything they want, except trump, unless:

b. If the team has bid either BOARD or BOSTON, they may lead with the trump.

c. Each player MUST follow suit if possible. If they can't, they can trump and thereby normally take the trick. Or they can throw another card (usually low) of another suit because that way they cannot take the trick.

d. Once trump is broken, anyone can lead with a trump or other suit.

e. The BIG joker is the most powerful card (i.e., the HIGHEST SPADE). When the BIG is lead, both players on the other team must follow with their largest trump card while the partner may lead any spade (if they have one). The LITTLE joker is second-highest trump card (i.e., below the BIG joker but above the ACE) and has no other special characteristics.

f. In the following play, the person that took the prior trick leads the next trick.

6. SCORING

a. Team scoring is 5 points per trick bid and taken, with 1 additional point for any tricks taken over the bid. −5 points per trick bid if the team does not take the number of tricks they bid, which is referred to as being "SET." Examples:

  1. Bid 5 and get 5: the team receives 25 points. (5 tricks bid × 5 points.)

  2. Bid 7 and get 8, the team receives 36 points. (7 tricks bid × 5 points + 1 point for the extra trick.)

  3. Bid 4 and get 2, the team receives −20 points. (4 tricks × −5 points)

  4. Bid 4 and get none, the team receives −20 points. (4 tricks × −5 points.)

b. If a team bids BOARD, the points per trick are adjusted to 10 points per trick. −10 points per total tricks if the team does not achieve the number of tricks they bid. If a board is doubled, tripled, or quadrupled, the points are multiplied accordingly.

  1. Bid BOARD on a 2-card hand and get both tricks. Team receives 20 points. (2 total tricks × 10 points.)

2. Bid BOARD on a 3-card hand and get 2 tricks. Team receives –30 points. (3 total tricks × –10 points.)

3. Bid DOUBLE BOARD on 3-card hand and get all tricks. Team receives 60 points. (3 total tricks × 10 points × DOUBLE.)

c. If a team bids BOSTON, a flat bonus of 100 points is awarded to the team that successfully takes the first 6 tricks, plus 1 point per extra trick. A flat bonus of –100 points is awarded to the team that declares, but fails to take, the first 6 tricks.

1. Bid BOSTON on a 10-card hand and get the first 6 cards plus 1 additional trick. Team receives 101 points. (BOSTON + 1 extra trick.)

2. Bid BOSTON on a 7-card hand and get only get 3 tricks. Team receives –100 points.

3. Bid DOUBLE BOSTON (this does not happen very often and usually only as a last-ditch effort on the final hand) and get only 4 tricks. Team receives –200 points. (–100 points × DOUBLE.)

d. At the end of 26 hands, the team with the highest score wins.

Index

Numbers

1:1 meetings, 64, 109

A

abstraction, as management skill, 273
achievement in game play, 116, 118
alignment meetings, 68, 272
Alpha Knowledge team members, 280
Alphas, the three types of, 235–242
anger
  going ALL CAPS, 151
  motivation for new gig, 18
animations in slides, 220
answering questions during interviews, 33–35
apprenticeship in engineering management, 265

B

BAB (Back Alley Bridge), 129–132, 305–309
bad news, reactions to
  despair, 105
  Distiller, 103
  Dr. No, 101
  Handler, 104
  meeting gaps, 161
  My Bad, 104
  Raging Bull, 102
  Still Water, 102
  team members leaving the company, 280
  We're Doomed, 105
base salary, 48, 52
benefits, in the compensation calculation, 47

bickering, 127–132
bits, features, and truth exercise, 225–232
bits, owning, 268
bonuses, sign-on, 49, 52
bookstores, and quiet time, 204
bosses. *See also* managers
  assessment of, 64–71
  experience of, appreciating, 74–80
  understanding their motivations, 8
brand, as career choice consideration, 260
bright'n'shiny complex, 175
bubble, first Internet, 259
Buttons of interviewers, how to find, 37–44

C

calories, burning, 203
card games (BAB), 129–132, 305–309
career development
  management, moving into, 272–278
  strategy for, 257–264
  three aspects of, 9–16
career intangibles and networking, 133–137
career maintenance exercises, 47
careers
  blueprint for, 6
  defining moments of, 45
  hiring for, 145
  vs. gigs, 7
Cave, the, 167
CEOs
  asking for the impossible, 93–98
  interviewing with, 43

changing jobs. *See* job changing
chaos, and the deep breath, 107
circle of comfort for team mem-
    bers, 227
cliques vs. culture, 151
coasting, 12, 296–299
collapse of the organization,
    288–294
communication skills
    during phone screens, 27–30
    managers, types of, 66
    with your nerd, 169
communications within companies
    crossing boundaries, 69
    during times of crisis, 108–112
    group, within the Pond, 156
    management as hub of, 273
    partial information, 76–78
    random hallway chats, 183
    remote workers, 157, 160
    tactical vs. strategic, 288
    trash talking in BAB, 130–132
    varying agendas for, 122–125
companies, start-up vs. estab-
    lished, 258–260
compensation, 46, 47
compromise, in salary negotia-
    tion, 51
computers, nerds and, 166
confidence
    and giving presentations,
        210–214
    and the interview process, 35
    vs. experience, 295
conflict, as learning, 299
content vs. measures in the yearly
    review, 252–254
Contradiction List, 20–21
control issues, nerds and, 167
conversation, reviews as, 254
cookie jar metaphor, 69
coping mechanisms for bad news,
    100–106
corporate culture. *See* culture,
    work
corporate directories, uses for, 58
corporate surprise, reactions to,
    100–106
counteroffers in salary negotia-
    tions, 51

coworkers
    relationships, developing, 130
    toxic personalities, 148–153
    understanding their motiva-
        tions, 8
creation meetings, 272
creativity. *See also* strategic real-
    izations
    the Crisis and the Creative as-
        sessment, 190–193
    trusting your gut, 302
Crisis and the Creative assess-
    ment, 189–193
crisis situations
    collapse of the organization,
        288–294
    Crisis and the Creative assess-
        ment, 190–193
    management transformations
        during, 87–91
    meetings and deep breaths,
        107–112
    reactions to, 99–106
cross-pollination clusterfuck meet-
    ings, 245–250
culture, work
    chart, 57–61
    remote workers' participation
        in, 160
    understanding, 57–61
    vs. cliques, 151
    when leaders leave the com-
        pany, 281
curse of Silicon Valley, 269

D

damage control management op-
    tions, 291
decision-making
    authority for, 229
    when to ask for help, 75–80
delivery
    career philosophy of, 13–15
    remote workers and, 162
demos, presenting, 234–242
departures from the company,
    279–285, 289–294
despair, 105

detail orientation, as remote
    worker skill, 158
development vs. management, in
    career strategy, 261
disasters. *See also* crisis situations
    collapse of the organization,
        288–294
    meetings, and breathing
        deeply, 107–112
    toxic personalities as, 153
discovery process of games, 114
disruption, positive effect of, 298
Distiller, 103
doof managers, description of,
    78–80
drama, dealing with in manage-
    ment, 274
Dreamweaver, 200
Dr. No, 101
Dropbox, 199

E

editing presentations, 219–221
email and remote workers, 157
Enemy, 90
engagement at work, 19
engineers
    bits, features, and truth exer-
        cise, 225
    constructing a demo, 234
    management, where they
        come from, 265–270
established companies vs. start-
    ups, 258–260
Evening Scrub of the to-do list,
    177–179, 185
excuses, 82–85
exodus from the company,
    288–294
experience
    acquiring, at established com-
        panies, 260
    value of, 74
    vs. confidence, 295

F

failure
    avoiding, when working
        remote, 157

start-ups vs. established com-
    panies, 259
    vs. saying no, 14
fame vs. experience, 296
features/quality/time triangle,
    224–232
fight or flight reactions, 100, 291
filtering, as management skill, 273
final offers in salary negotiations,
    53
fretting about presentations, 214
friction detection, 161
fuckups. *See* crisis situations

G

games
    BAB (Back Alley Bridge),
        129–132, 305–309
    nerds and, 168
    process of consumption,
        114–117
    rules of, 117
    Werewolf, 121–126
    whiteboard, 119
gaps in the team, 279–285
geeks
    bad news, reactions to, 105
    games as systems, 114–119
    geeks as managers, 270
    worldview of, 4, 114, 166–
        172, 297
gigs, changing. *See* job changing
grades vs. content, as useful infor-
    mation, 253
growth
    career philosophy of, 12, 15
    growing your team, 142

H

Handler, 104
hate, professional, 246
hatred of engineering, 267
healthy tension on teams, 229
help, asking for, 75–80
High, the, 168, 172
hiring, 139–146
Holy Shit, the, 233–242
HR departments, realities of, 25
humor and the nerd, 168

I

ignorance, admission of, 34
Illuminator, 89
impossible requests from CEOs, 93–98
improvisation
  during presentations, 213
  structured, 186
inactivity, necessity of, 204–207
inbox strategies, 81
industry, career choice considerations, 260
information
  during times of crisis, 108–112
  flow of communication, 284
  game of, in companies, 83
  management's role with, 269
  movement of, and org charts, 75
  nerds' appetite for, 169
  tactical vs. strategic, 288
  truth, locating, 226
  when Insiders leave the company, 283
  working in the Pond vs. remote, 156
Insider team members, 283
inspiration, 302
Internet bubble, first, 259
Interrogator, 88
interviewers, types of, 39–44
interviews
  answering questions, 33–35
  the Button, getting interviewers to talk, 37–44
  the Nerves, handling, 31–35
  vs. phone screens, 26
I Quit response to bad news, 105
itches for change, types of, 17–23

J

job changing
  building a career strategy, 258–264
  engineer to manager, 174–179
  growth and, 46
  itch for change, 17–24
  nonobvious reasons for, 297
  recruitment, 144

Jobs, Steve, 216
judgment, as source of the Nerves, 31

K

keyboard support, 199
Keynote software, 217
knowledge
  Alpha Knowledge team members, 280
  as fundamental unit of growth, 15
knowledge workers, 74

L

language
  in company groups, 274
  industry, 266
lawyers, calls from, 17
leadership
  as composure under stress, 276
  evolution of roles, 123
  Maestro team members, 281
  role of, 228
listening
  detecting company culture, 59
  management responsibility for, 273
lists
  taste of the day, 175–179
  Trickle List, 181–187
"Look What We Built" meetings, 111
lying, as skill, 124
lynchpin departure, 290

M

management
  art of, 178
  asking for the impossible, 93–98
  assessment of, 64–71
  career growth and, 12
  damage control options, 291
  professional distance in relationships, 128
  promotions, yours, 59

responsibilities and realities, 272–278
switching gigs to, 174–179
technical direction and, 10
vs. development, in career strategy, 261
work in Crisis, 191
managers. *See also* bosses
doofs, 78
managing up, 75–80
micromanagers, 11, 90
organic vs. mechanic, 65
program managers, 223, 226
responses to fuckups, 87–91
status reports and communication, 67
when to bring issues to, 76–78
where they are coming from, 265–270
measures vs. content in the yearly review, 252–254
mechanic managers, 65
meetings
alignment and creation, 272
cross-functional, 223
cross-pollination clusterfuck, 245–250
during times of crisis, 109–112
1:1 and staff, 64–66
presenting a demo, 234–242
scenarios of, in game play, 125
technical and alignment, 68
mentors, bosses as, 65
micromanagers, 11, 90
misery, value of, 299
money as a reward, 118
Morning Scrub of the to-do list, 175–177, 184
motivations for changing gigs, 22
My Bad, 104

N

negotiation process
salary, what to expect, 46–53
yearly reviews as, 254
Nerd Attention Deficiency Disorder (NADD), 169
nerd handbook, 165–172
nerds. *See also* geeks
adrenaline rushes for, 168
appetite for information, 169
communicating with your nerd, 169
computers and, 166
control issues, 167
food, relationship to, 171
projects and, 171
puzzles and, 168
sense of humor, 168
shyness in, 172
toys and, 168
traveling with, 171
TV watching, 169
understanding, 166–172
nerves, how to handle
during interviews, 31
giving presentations, 210–214
networking, 133–137
newness vs. progress, 22
No, as powerful tool, 276
nothing, consideration of, 204–207

O

one-on-one meetings, 64, 109
open-ended questions during interviews, 32
operations questions for meetings, 110
optimization in game play, 115
organic managers, 65
organizational boundaries, 69
org charts
and company culture, 58, 70
understanding of, 75

P

Parking Lot for new ideas, 176
people dynamics, 122–125
people, messiness of, 4, 170, 275
people networking, 133–137
performance, presentations as, 210–214
performance reviews, yearly, 251–256

personalities
  of interviewers, 39–44
  remote workers, productive,
    157–159
  toxic, 148–153
phone screening calls
  adversarial interactions, 29
  background research prior to,
    26
  next steps, 30
  questions during, 27
poker face, 124
Pond workers vs. remote workers,
  155–162
presentations
  audience participation in, 213,
    221
  demos, 234
  how not to throw up when giv-
    ing, 209–214
  practicing, 210, 218, 219
  vetting of, 247
  vs. speeches, 215–222
prioritization
  Crisis and the Creative assess-
    ment, 190–193
  of tasks, 174–179, 182–187
Prioritizer, 88
problems. *See* crisis situations
problem solving questions, during
  interviews, 32
productivity systems, 174–179,
  181–187
program managers, 223, 226
progress vs. newness, 22
projects and nerds, 171
promotions, 59
public speaking, 209–214,
  215–222
puzzles, nerds and, 168

Q

quality/features/time triangle,
  224–232
questions
  career strategy, what to ask
    yourself, 262
  check in questions, during a
    demo, 236

company culture, how to un-
    derstand, 58
  excelling at, during phone
    screens, 26, 28
  Interrogator response to fuck-
    ups, 88
  interviewers, getting them to
    talk, 37–44
  managing, during presenta-
    tions, 248
  Screw-Me questions, 249
  types of, during interviews, 32
quiet time, necessity of, 203–207

R

Raging Bull, 102
Randomizer, 89
randomness, fight or flight re-
    sponse to, 290–292
recruiters
  cold calls from, 17
  hiring process, 142
  phone screening process with,
    25–30
  salary negotiations and, 51
relationships
  bits vs. human beings, 268
  changes when team members
    leave, 285
  toxic coworkers, 148–153
  Your People, 134–137
reliability, as remote working skill,
  158
remote, working, 155–162
repetition in game play, 115
repetitive motion, removing, 199
reputation
  company, and career moves,
    261
  hits to, 83
  low priority work and, 20
  maintenance of, 14
requisitions for hiring (reqs),
  140–142
research, prior to phone screens,
  26
resignation of team members,
  279–285
respect for management, 95

response to fuckups
   Enemy, 90
   Illuminator, 89
   Interrogator, 88
   Prioritizer, 88
   Randomizer, 89
responsibility for issues, 77–79
resumés, during phone screens, 27
Reveal, the, 233–242
revenge, and the Screw-Me scenario, 246
reviews, yearly, 251–256
Rolodex and work relationships, 21
routine meetings, importance of, 112
rules of games
   Back Alley Bridge (BAB), 306–309
   discovery of, 114, 168
   optimization of, 115
   universal rules of, 117
   Werewolf, 125

S

salary negotiations process
   counteroffers, 51–53
   final offers, 53
   negotiating roles, 50
   pre-game, 46
   self-evaluation, 47
   the swag, 48–50
scale, and teamwork, 74, 277
Screw-Me scenario, 246–250
self-direction, as remote worker skill, 158
self-review, 255
Setup and Story in the demo, 236
silence
   of the Alpha Nothing, 235–237
   pauses during presentations, 240
   punctuation as, 214
   wait it out damage control tactic, 291
Silicon Valley, 203, 265, 266, 269
skills needed in groups of people, 122–125
slides for presentations, 210, 217–222

social insecurity, 135
softball questions during phone screens, 27
software tools and productivity, 197–202
speeches vs. presentations, 215–222
spotlight, deflecting, 124
staff meetings
   assessment of, 65
   topics to cover, during crisis times, 109–111
start-ups
   ideas for, 301
   vs. established companies, 258–260
status reports, 67
Still Water, 102
stock
   in the compensation calculation, 48
   in the negotiation process, 50, 52
Story and Setup in the demo, 236
strangers, integrating with, 124
strategic information, 289
strategic realizations
   the Crisis and the Creative assessment, 190–193
   trickle lists, 182–187
strategy
   career development, 258–264
   considerations for meetings, 110
structured improvisation, 186
structured vs. unstructured interviews, 38
success vs. experience, 295
surprises
   reactions to, 99–106
   yearly review surprises, 255
synthesis, as management skill, 273
system thinkers, geeks as, 4, 114, 167

T

tactical information, 288
tactics considerations for meetings, 110

task tracking systems, 174–179, 182–187
teamwork
    damage to, and toxic coworkers, 149–153
    effective, roles for, 228–231
    people leaving the team, 279–285
Technical Lead position, 262
technical meetings, 68
tension, healthy, 229
TextMate, 198, 200
therapy meetings, 272
throwing up during public speaking, 209–214
time management. *See* task tracking systems
time/quality/features triangle, 224–232
titles, company, 49, 225
to-do lists
    Evening Scrub, 177–179
    Morning Scrub, 175–177, 184
    structured improvisation, 186
    Trickle Lists, 182–184
tools
    presentation software, 217
    productivity and, 197–202
toxic coworkers, 148–153
toys, nerds and, 168. *See also* games
translator, management as, 274
trash talking, the art of, 130–132
triangle of time/quality/features, 224–232
trickle down, 75
Trickle Lists, 182–187
trust, building, 127–132
trusting the team, 277
truth telling, 225–232

U

understanding your nerd, 166–172
unpredictable events, preparing for, 5. *See also* crisis situations
unstructured vs. structured interviews, 38

V

values, corporate, 58–61
verbal warfare, 127–132
version control, 199
vetting your presentation, 247
videoconferencing, 161

W

waves of departure during company exodus, 289–294
We're Doomed, 105
Werewolf party game, 121–126
whiteboard management game, 113, 119
winning, in game play, 115–117
working remote, 155–162
work satisfaction, signs to notice, 17–24
World of Warcraft game, 114, 117
written records, permanence of, 254, 256

Y

yearly reviews, 251–256
Your People, discovering, 133–137

Z

Zone, the, 269

About the Author

Michael Lopp is a Silicon Valley–based engineering manager. When he's not worrying about staying relevant, he writes about pens, bridges, people, and werewolves at the popular weblog, Rands in Repose. Michael wrote a book called *Managing Humans*, which explains that while you might be rewarded for what you produce, you will only be successful because of your people.

Colophon

The cover font is Trade Gothic Bold Condensed No. 20. The text font is Sabon; the heading font is Myriad. The cover image is copyright Mark Weiss/Corbis.